D0875549

THE BOOK OF ESTHER:
MOTIFS, THEMES AND STRUCTURE

SOCIETY
OF BIBLICAL
LITERATURE

DISSERTATION SERIES

edited by
Howard C. Kee
and
Douglas A. Knight

Number 44

THE BOOK OF ESTHER: MOTIFS, THEMES AND
STRUCTURE
by
Sandra Beth Berg

Sandra Beth Berg

THE BOOK OF ESTHER: MOTIFS, THEMES AND STRUCTURE

Scholars Press

1979

LIBRARY
McCORMICK THEOLOGICAL SEMINARY
1100 EAST 55th STREET
CHICAGO, ILLINOIS 60615

BS
1375.2
.B47
1979

Distributed by
Scholars Press
PO Box 5207
Missoula, Montana 59806

THE BOOK OF ESTHER: MOTIFS, THEMES AND STRUCTURE

Sandra Beth Berg
University of Northern Iowa
Cedar Falls, Iowa 50613

Ph. D., 1977   Adviser:
Vanderbilt University   James L. Crenshaw

Copyright © 1979
Society of Biblical Literature

Library of Congress Cataloging in Publication Data

Berg, Sandra Beth.
  The book of Esther.

  (Dissertation series ; 44 ISSN 0145-2770)
  Originally presented as the author's thesis, Vanderbilt
University, 1977.
  Bibliography: p.
  Includes indexes.
  1. Bible. O.T. Esther—Criticism, interpretation, etc.
I. Title. II. Series: Society of Biblical Literature.
Dissertation series ; 44.
BS1375.2.B47   1978   222'.9'06   78-32035
ISBN 0-89130-279-4 pbk.

Printed in the United States of America

1   2   3   4   5   6

Edwards Brothers, Inc.
Ann Arbor, Michigan 48104

To Max H. Berg

TABLE OF CONTENTS

		Page
ACKNOWLEDGMENTS		ix
LIST OF ABBREVIATIONS		xi

CHAPTER

I.	INTRODUCTION	1
	A. Historical Credibility	1
	B. Religious Credibility	11
	C. A "Literary" Approach to Esther	14
II.	DOMINANT MOTIFS: BANQUETS	31
	A. משתה	31
	B. Non-banquet Uses of משתה	35
	C. Fasts	37
	D. Purim	39
III.	DOMINANT MOTIFS: KINGSHIP AND OBEDIENCE/DISOBEDIENCE	59
	A. The Motif of Kingship	59
	B. The Motif of Obedience/Disobedience	72
IV.	THEMES AND STRUCTURE	95
	A. Themes	96
	1. The Theme of Power	96
	2. The Theme of Loyalty to the Jewish Community	98
	3. The Themes of Inviolability and Reversal	103
	B. Structure of the Book of Esther	106

V.   THE BOOK OF ESTHER AND THE STORY
     OF JOSEPH   123

     A.   Comparison of the Joseph and
          Esther Stories   124
          1.   Linguistic Correspondence   124
          2.   Similarities in Setting and
               Events   126
          3.   Literary Genre   128
               a.   Common Motif   129
               b.   Common Structure   133

     B.   Other Studies of the Joseph Story   136
          1.   Date of the Joseph Story   136
          2.   Narrative Style of the Joseph
               Story   138
          3.   Motifs of the Joseph Story   139
          4.   Summary   141

     C.   Comparison of the Joseph Story and
          the Book of Esther with Other Post-
          exilic Narratives   143
          1.   Daniel 2-6   143
          2.   The Book of Ruth   146
          3.   The Book of Jonah   148
          4.   The Book of Judith   149
          5.   Summary   151

VI. DATE, "THEOLOGY" AND
     CONCLUDING REMARKS   167

     A.   Date   169

     B.   "Theology"   173

     C.   Concluding Remarks   184

WORKS CITED   195

INDEX OF AUTHORS   209

INDEX OF PASSAGES   213

     A.   Canonical and Apocryphal Literature   213

     B.   Other   218

ACKNOWLEDGMENTS

This dissertation was submitted to Vanderbilt University in December of 1977. At that time, I was intensely aware of my debt to several individuals who guided this project throughout its various stages. I again take pleasure in expressing my gratitude to them.

I remain greatly and gratefully indebted to James L. Crenshaw and Walter Harrelson, under whose guidance the dissertation was written. I also am grateful to Lou H. Silberman, Douglas A. Knight and Paul W. Meyer. My study of the Book of Esther would be considerably poorer without their advice.

The publication of the dissertation was facilitated by the efforts of Thomas H. Thompson, Head of the Department of Philosophy and Religion at the University of Northern Iowa. To my typist, Ms. Ethelyn Snyder, I extend a special note of thanks for her remarkable patience with my scribal hand.

Finally, I wish to thank my father, Max H. Berg, for his unfaltering confidence in the merits of this study. For years, my father has complained that I always give him "such a *ganze megillah*." I dedicate this study to him in the hope that this time he is correct.

LIST OF ABBREVIATIONS

AB	Anchor Bible
Ag.Ap.	Josephus, *Against Apion*
Ant.	Josephus, *Jewish Antiquities*
Art.	Plutarch, *The Lives: Artaxerxes*
ASTI	*Annual of the Swedish Theological Institute*
ATD	Das Alte Testament Deutsch
AusBR	*Australian Biblical Review*
BA	*Biblical Archaeologist*
BBS	Bruce Vawter (ed.), Backgrounds to the Bible Series
BDB	F. Brown, S. R. Driver and C. A. Briggs, *Hebrew and English Lexicon of the Old Testament*
Bib	*Biblica*
BibLeb	*Bibel und Leben*
BibS(N)	Biblische Studien (Neukirchen)
BKAT	Biblischer Kommentar: Altes Testament
BR	*Biblical Research*
BTS	*Bible et terre sainte*
BZ	*Biblische Zeitschrift*
CBC	P. R. Ackroyd, A. R. C. Leaney and J. W. Packer (eds.), Cambridge Bible Commentary
CBQ	*Catholic Biblical Quarterly*
CBQMS	Catholic Biblical Quarterly -- Monograph Series
CCAR Journal	*Journal of the Central Conference of American Rabbis*
CRINT 1,2	S. Safrai and M. Stern (eds.), Compendia rerum iudaicarum ad Novum Testamentum, vols. 1 or 2
Est.Rab.	*Esther Rabbah*
ExpTim	*Expository Times*
FBBS	Facet Books, Biblical Series
Gen.R.	*Genesis Rabbah*
HAT	Handbuch zum Alten Testament
Hist.	Herodotus, *The Histories*
HSM	Harvard Semitic Monographs
HTR	*Harvard Theological Review*
HUCA	*Hebrew Union College Annual*
IB	*Interpreter's Bible*

ICC	International Critical Commentary
JAL	Morton S. Enslin (ed.), Jewish Apocryphal Literature
JBL	*Journal of Biblical Literature*
JEA	*Journal of Egyptian Archaeology*
JNES	*Journal of Near Eastern Studies*
JPSV	*Jewish Publication Society Version*
JQR	*Jewish Quarterly Review*
JR	*Journal of Religion*
JRAS	*Journal of the Royal Asiatic Society*
JSOT	*Journal for the Study of the Old Testament*
JSS	*Journal of Semitic Studies*
JTS	*Journal of Theological Studies*
J.W.	Josephus, *The Jewish Wars*
KAT	E. Sellin (ed.), Kommentar zum Alten Testament
KJV	*King James Version*
LB	*Linguistica Biblica*
LCL	Loeb Classical Library
LXX	Septuagint
Meg.	*Megilla*
MT	Masoretic Text
NEB	*New English Bible*
NovTSup	Novum Testamentum, Supplements
OTL	Old Testament Library
PCB	M. Black and H. H. Rowley (eds.), *Peake's Commentary on the Bible*
Pers.	Aeschylus, *The Persians*
Pirq.R.El.	*Pirqe Rabbi Eliezer*
RB	*Revue biblique*
RHA	*Revue hittite et asiatique*
RSV	*Revised Standard Version*
RTP	*Revue de théologie et de philosophie*
Sanh.	*Sanhedrin*
SBF	*Studium biblicum franciscanum*
SBM	Stuttgarter biblische Monographien
SEÅ	*Svensk exegetisk årsbok*
SPB	Studia postbiblica
TAPA	*Transactions of the American Philological Association*

TDOT	J. Botterweck and H. Ringgren (eds.), *Theological Dictionary of the Old Testament*, revised edition
TEH	Theologische Existenz Heute
Tg.Esth I,II	*First or Second Targum of Esther*
TZ	*Theologische Zeitschrift*
VT	*Vetus Testamentum*
VTSup	Vetus Testamentum, Supplements
WHJP[1]	Abraham Schalit, Eliyahu Feldman and Alexander Peli (eds.), World History of the Jewish People, First Series
WZKM	*Wiener Zeitschrift für die Kunde des Morgenlandes*
ZAW	*Zeitschrift für die alttestamentliche Wissenschaft*

CHAPTER I

INTRODUCTION

A. *Historical Credibility*

"All depends upon fate, even the Scriptures."[1] Jacob
Hoschander begins his commentary on the Book of Esther by
reference to this cabbalistic maxim. To Hoschander, this maxim
applies to the "ill fate" which the Book of Esther has experienced among its modern interpreters. These words, however,
describe Esther in a further sense, for they accurately characterize the content of the story. The narrative tells of the
dramatic rescue of the Jewish people from threatened destruction, and without any discernible assistance from Yahweh. The
narrated events seem to stand outside Yahweh's control of
history and to result from "fate."

Given the skepticism of our modern world, we might expect
the Book of Esther to be valued as one of the few credible
stories of the Hebrew Bible. It is surprising that the opposite has proven true. Hoschander's citation of this cabbalistic maxim is quite appropriate, for contemporary biblical
scholarship doubts both the historical and religious credibility of Esther.[2]

Opposition to the Book of Esther is not a modern phenomenon.[3] It is a well-known fact, for example, that Esther is the
only book of the Hebrew Bible not represented among the Dead
Sea scrolls.[4] The value of the book was disputed by the
Talmudic sages who questioned whether the Book of Esther "de-
filed the hands."[5]

Among more recent critics of the nineteenth and twentieth
centuries,[6] the greatest opposition to Esther stems from doubts
concerning its historicity.[7] As early as 1773, J. S. Semler
questioned the accuracy of the account,[8] and his scholarly
successors have expressed similar doubts.

This concern with historical questions seems natural given
the character of the account.[9] The story, as we have received
it,[10] purports to be an accurate and reliable report of events

1

which took place at the court of King Ahasuerus and their subsequent effect upon the Jewish communities of the Persian empire. The historiographical nature of the book is underlined
by its opening and concluding passages. The narrator begins
his work in a manner typical of biblical histories[11] and concludes with a challenge to verify his account with information
contained in the "chronicles of the kings of Media and Persia"
(cf. Esth 10:2).

The author's familiarity with both general and specific
features of Persian life during the Achaemenian period also
lends credence to his story. The setting of the tale in Susa
is not improbable,[12] and the story's intimate knowledge of
Persian court-etiquette and public administration strengthens
impressions of its accuracy.[13] In addition the story deals
with persons whose existence is known from other sources, notably Ahasuerus[14] and Mordecai.[15] The number of Persian words in
Esther[16] and its numerous Aramaisms[17] suggest the story's composition during a period not far removed from the events it
describes.

At first glance, these factors recommend that Esther be
understood as a more or less reliable account. On the other
hand, information gathered from sources contemporaneous with
the narrated events contradict the story.[18] Scholars who uphold the historicity of the tale often are forced to a reiden-
tification of its central figures and a resetting of the events
into new historical contexts.[19] Most recent studies of Esther
accept its familiarity with a Persian setting as authentic, yet
at the same time they deny the historicity of the account. The
narrator's familiarity with Persian matters is attributed to
his inheritance of traditions which preserved the memory of an
actual persecution during Achaemenian times.[20] These same traditions, however, were expanded with fictional and legendary
elaborations, which the author of Esther himself enlarged. The
present text of the book contains an historical kernel, but one
which is overlaid with novelistic elaborations.[21]

The Book of Esther frequently is characterized as an "historical novel,"[22] and this description implies that an historical incident gave rise to a fictional account.[23] Such a description, however, presents difficulties since we know of no
situation or event from another source which clearly suits the

3

narrated events. The difficulty may rest with the inadequacies of our sources and with our imprecise knowledge of the Jewish diaspora during the Persian period. Nevertheless, we possess no information concerning the historical situation posited in Esther apart from the story itself. Views that the book represents the novelistic expansion of an historical event thus rest upon a circular argument.

Our incomplete knowledge of the Persian period, and the recognition that Esther contains novelistic, perhaps legendary, features,[24] have stimulated interest in the literary characteristics of the tale.[25] Renewed interest in the narrative style and composition of Esther has shifted recent research away from the identification of specific persons and events toward a different type of historical interest, viz., the factors which gave rise to the book.

A frequent response to this problem views as crucial the relationship of the narrated events to Purim.[26] The general argument maintains that an independent festival of extra-Israelite origin was adopted and popularized by non-Palestinian Jews during the exilic and post-exilic periods.[27] Purim became so popular that the need arose to authenticate its celebration. Following the model by which other festivals were incorporated into Israelite traditions, Purim was associated with events which explained its origin, legitimized, and even regularized its observance.

Various criticisms are leveled against this approach, and we may summarize them here:

1) The story focuses primarily upon the court intrigues surrounding the conflict between Mordecai and Haman, and upon Esther's rescue of the Jews. Purim is not central to the narrative.

2) If the story was intended to explain and legitimate Purim, the narrator devotes a surprisingly small effort toward his task. The festival is mentioned specifically only in Esth 9:28-32, and alluded to only in Esth 3:7 and 9:24. These passages themselves may reflect secondary additions to the text.[28]

3) No extra-Israelite festival suggests itself as a suitable model for Purim or explains the particular mode of its observance. Nor can any one festival account for

Esther's literary features and plot developments.[29]

4) Purim did not arise out of a social vacuum but itself received some historical or cultural impetus. It seems odd that no specific recollection of Purim's origin was preserved and that a new explanation--and particularly one which is so tangentially connected to the festal celebration--was required.

The last point suggests that if Purim does not explain the story of Esther and Mordecai, neither does the story adequately account for Purim. At present, the question of Purim's origins and observance remains moot since our best information comes from the Book of Esther. The most that can be claimed about their relationship is that they were associated early in their respective histories.[30] In effect, we are left with the proverbial problem of the chicken and the egg: we know that they go together, but we cannot decide which came first.

If Purim is not an original part of the story, a question arises as to how and why they are joined. Posing this question differently, we may ask whether the narrator responsible for the present form of Esther[31] considered Purim as integral to his account. If so, how does Purim function in *his* story? We shall return to these questions in the following chapters.

The impasse reached in the investigation of Purim's relationship to the Esther-Mordecai story has encouraged discussion of the book's literary features.[32] A new line of inquiry was initiated by Henri Cazelles,[33] who argued that Esther represents a conflation of two independent texts. Cazelles notes a certain duplication in the events described in the book. For example, he points to the occurrence of two banquets in chapter one, two lists of the king's servants (1:10, 14),[34] two references to the assembling of the women (2:8, 19), Esther's two banquets for Ahasuerus and Haman (5:5; 7:1), Haman's two consultations with his wife and friends (5:14; 6:13), Esther's two unsummoned appearances before the king (5:2; 8:3) and the twofold account of the death of Haman's sons (9:6-10, 13-14). On the basis of this duplication of events, Cazelles suggests the presence in Esther of two originally independent texts. The first text is "liturgical" and centers upon Esther, upon the relationship between Jews and gentiles in the provinces, and upon the festival of Purim. Cazelles sees the festival itself arising in connection with the observance of the Persian New Year,[35] giving the text its liturgical focus. This liturgical text was combined with an "historical" account which centered upon the court intrigues of Mordecai's conflict with Haman and the persecution of the Jews in Susa.[36] The combination of these independent traditions resulted in the story essentially preserved in the MT.

Hans Bardtke offers a different analysis of Esther's composition.[37] Bardtke theorizes that the narrator had at his disposal a collection of various stories of heroes, heroines and persecutions.[38] He combined the originally separate tales of (1) Vashti, (2) Mordecai, with its court intrigues, and (3) Esther, who became a favorite of the king, into one account.[39] In both the Mordecai and Esther stories, the protagonists succeed in averting a persecution of their people, perhaps indicating one reason for their conflation into a single account.[40]

The provocative theses of Cazelles and Bardtke explain certain literary features of Esther. In addition, these theses suggest that the connection of Purim to the stories of Mordecai and Esther was neither arbitrary nor incidental. Rather, the traditions at the narrator's disposal already associated a festal celebration with the Jews' success over their foes. We no longer can recover the specific origins of Purim nor the precise manner in which it came to be associated with the story of Esther.[41] For the author of the scroll, as for us, the juxtaposition of this particular story with this particular festival was part of the received traditions.[42]

The cogent arguments of Cazelles and Bardtke, unfortunately, are not without problems. We must wonder if the various "seams" in the narrative of Esther are as visible as these two scholars maintain. In their present form, the allegedly separate traditions of the narrative are interwoven with great skill. For example, the story of Vashti provides a suitable and credible explanation of how Esther became queen. It further sets the story at the court of Ahasuerus, paving the way for the conflict which develops between Mordecai and Haman. Yet the conflict with Haman is not restricted to Mordecai. It is, in fact, Queen Esther who succeeds in overcoming Haman and averting the destruction of the Jews. Esther's success is partially grounded in her overwhelming beauty, which favorably

disposes Ahasuerus to do her bidding. Her beauty, in turn, is
made clear by the Vashti story. In short, each of these once
separate traditions now is integral to the account. The individual stories prove difficult to separate or to reconstruct,
rendering Cazelles' and Bardtke's theses questionable.

A new approach to Esther's literary and historical problems appeared with the publication of Gillis Gerleman's short
monograph,[43] later expanded and developed into a major commentary on Esther.[44] In both studies, Gerleman argues that the
Book of Esther was patterned after the story of the exodus.[45]
Gerleman finds in Esther all of the essential features of Exodus 1-12, including the setting at a foreign court, the mortal
danger to the Jews, the acts of deliverance and revenge, the
triumph of the Jews over their foes, and the establishment of a
festival.[46] The influence of the exodus story extends to even
minute details of the narrative. For example, both Moses and
Esther were adopted (cf. Exod 2:9; Esth 2:7) and kept their
origins a secret (cf. Exod 2:6-10; Esth 2:10, 20). The exodus
narratives portray Aaron as Moses' spokesman (Exod 4:15-16)
just as Esther speaks for Mordecai and executes his will (Esth
2:20; 4:8; 9:20-23).[47] The villain in the Book of Esther is a
descendant of the Amalekites,[48] the arch-foe of ancient Israel
since the time of the exodus (cf. Exod 17:8-16). Esther, like
Moses before her, was forced to appear repeatedly before the
monarch to intercede for her people (cf. Exod 7:14-12:28; Esth
5:2; 7:2; 8:3). Even the destruction of the enemies in Esth
9:1-6 parallels the destruction of the Egyptians in the exodus
account.

Gerleman suggests that the Book of Esther represents an
"Entsakralisierung" and "Enttheologisierung" of a central,
heilsgeschichtliche tradition,[49] adapted to suit the concerns
of a diaspora community.[50] Gerleman cites additional similarities between the two narratives which strengthen his comparison, but his argument does not withstand close scrutiny.[51]
Whereas it can be argued that the general outlines of the
stories are similar,[52] the minute details of the narratives do
not correspond in the manner indicated by Gerleman. For example, the attitudes of the protagonists to the foreign monarch
differ radically in the two stories. Moses does not work
through the Egyptian administration, but against it. In the

exodus story, salvation represents a freeing of ancient Israel
from Egypt and Egyptian influences. Yet the Book of Esther
gives no indication of the Jews' desire to leave Susa. Esther
is Ahasuerus' queen and Mordecai saves the king's life--facts
which the narrator does not condemn. To the contrary, he suggests that the Jews are saved by Esther's and Mordecai's working through the structures of Persian administrative policy.

Nor are the parallels between Moses/Mordecai and Aaron/
Esther so clear-cut. Gerleman argues for a correspondence on
the grounds that the figures in the latter pair act as spokes-
persons for those in the former. Yet a parallel is drawn between Moses and Esther as individuals who intercede with the
monarch for their co-religionists and who ultimately are re-
ponsible for the freeing of the people. We remain unsure
whether Esther was intended to parallel the figure of Aaron or
of Moses; or whether the narrator intended a double portrayal
of Esther, drawing parallels to both figures.

Both Moses and Esther are adopted, yet the roles of their
adoptive parents differ greatly. The Egyptian princess plays
no part in the story of the deliverance of the Israelites.
Mordecai, on the other hand, is not an insignificant figure in
the rescuing of the Jews. The distinction in the roles of the
adoptive parents points to different functions for this
motif.[53]

A similar difference in function appears in Moses' and
Esther's secrecy concerning their origins. In the Book of
Esther, the queen's silence is central to the plot of the
story. It is difficult to imagine Ahasuerus' authorization of
Haman's edict against the Jews, or his response to Esther's
words in Esth 7:5-7, if he knew his wife's identity. By contrast, Moses' secrecy regarding his ethnic identity is far less
significant to the exodus story.

The problem confronting the people of Israel in each story
also differs. In the exodus narratives, the primary concern is
with the freeing of the people from their bondage to Egyptian
masters. Only indirectly, through the edict against the lives
of male children (Exod 1:16), did ancient Israel face the threat
of death. In Esther, however, the existence of the entire
people is at stake. The difference in the problems confronting
the people of Israel in each story also explains the

differences between the festivals of Passover and Purim. Both
are commemorative, but the former recalls the freeing of the
people from their bondage to foreign masters. The latter commemorates the saving of the Jews from certain death, but holds
no suggestion of freedom from foreign influences. If Purim
were patterned after Passover, we would expect greater similarity in their festal observance.

In the final analysis, Gerleman's intriguing thesis remains unconvincing. While there may exist some influence of
the exodus story upon the Book of Esther, that influence is
neither controlling nor pervasive.

Werner Dommershausen recently suggested a different type
of analysis of Esther.[54] Dommershausen systematically investi-
gates the function of various stylistic elements within the
story,[55] linking his stylistic analysis to the method of form
criticism.

Dommershausen outlines four steps in his approach to
Esther.[56] He begins by defining the individual literary units
of the narrative on the basis of their stylistic function. He
then examines the syntactical and linguistic forms of each individual unit, noting where they depart from the usual manner
of expression in Esther. Dommershausen's third step is somewhat more complex. By using a "co-ordinating intuition," he
argues that one is able to recognize how the different stylistic features of the individual units complement each other,
giving a unified sense to the narrative. Finally, he classi-
fies each of the literary units according to their stylistic
features and literary *Gattungen*. Here, the key stylistic and
narrative techniques of the narrator are shown to coincide with
the narrative climaxes of theme and content. Dommershausen
applies this method to each literary unit of Esther and demonstrates the presence of different *Gattungen*, distinguishable by
both their style and content.

Dommershausen's concentration upon the individual literary
units of the Book of Esther focuses upon its narrative features
in a manner which distinguishes his approach from those of his
predecessors. The success of his analysis is attested to by
his identification of, and explanation for, narrative techniques previously unnoted by scholars. Dommershausen is able
to point to the presence of several parallel and chiastic

structures, and to stylistic techniques such as alliteration and assonance, hyperbole and metonymy, and the use of key words which direct the audience's attention to certain features of content. For example, crucial turns of plot are marked by references to drinking. The significance of Esther's speech to Ahasuerus in Esth 7:5-6 is underscored by its symmetrical structure. A comparison between the decrees of Haman and Mordecai is encouraged by their similarity of wording. Yet the two decrees differ in intent--a fact highlighted by contrasting responses to them (cf. 3:15b; 8:15-17). This contrast, in turn, underscores the dramatic reversal in the narrated events.

Dommershausen's remarkable analysis contributes greatly to our understanding of the story's style and rhetorical devices, and indicates why the narrator told his story in a particular way. Yet his attention to individual stylistic units proves not only the strength of Dommershausen's approach, but also its weakness. The significance of each individual unit is not always apparent when the narrative is considered as a whole. That is, the significance of each unit is modified by its function in the narrative, and by its relationship to other units. Dommershausen fails to account for these modifications in significance and function. Nor is the classification of individual units into their various *Gattungen* always helpful since, in this case, the whole does not equal the sum of the parts. Dommershausen, in fact, abandons his own distinction of individual *Gattungen* by classifying the book as a "Fest-Lesung."[57]

It is difficult to demonstrate that the various stylistic features discerned by Dommershausen result from the narrator's conscious intentions. There is no room in Dommershausen's analysis for any random elements such as changes in the text during its history of transmission. He attaches undue significance to word order and grammatical constructions whose presence may be due to Aramaic influences upon post-exilic Hebrew.[58] Dommershausen is to be credited for illustrating the significant relationship of narrative style to content and thematic concerns, but his atomistic analysis of Esther fails to demonstrate how style functions in the story as a whole.

Our discussion thus far suggests some of the ways in which scholars have sought to resolve the numerous historical questions posed by the Book of Esther. Two historical questions

not yet mentioned concern Esther's provenance and date. Speculations about provenance and date often prove central to evaluations of Esther's historical credibility--in fact, they sometimes play too great a role. The omission of these questions
thus is striking, but not unintentional. To the contrary, one
aim of this study is to consider the Book of Esther on its own
terms, without imposing upon the narrative any particular
understanding of the cultural milieu which gave it rise. This
approach to the Book of Esther is not unjustified, since it is
the presence of the book within the Sacred Scriptures which
legitimates our interest in such matters.

Nonetheless, the Book of Esther did not arise in a cultural vacuum, and it is not possible to ignore these questions.
This dissertation therefore utilizes the results of recent
studies and accepts the working hypothesis that Esther represents a product of the Eastern diaspora.[59] The setting of the
story in Susa, when considered along with the absence of any
interest in Palestine or its cultic institutions, strongly
favors this view. In addition, Esther's court setting and
court-related problems would be of less interest to Palestinian
Jews than to their diaspora counterparts who lived in close
proximity to the foreign rulers.

The narrator's familiarity with the general topography of
Susa may point to this city as the specific point of origin for
Esther. Again, the narrative setting suggests that close proximity to a center of court life provides the most plausible
locale for its composition. Susa constituted such a place during both the Persian and early hellenistic periods.[60]

The probable date of composition is less clear. Obviously, the present form of the narrative cannot antedate its Persian period setting. The narrator's familiarity with this setting suggests a time not far removed from the narrated events.
On the other hand, the Book of Esther hardly presents the accurate picture of Achaemenian Susa which it claims. It is implausible that the narrator would hope to convince his audience
of the reliability of his account when the audience knew that
such "historical" events did not take place. Presumably, he
could have presented a more convincing story had he chosen a
less precise historical setting. The Persian setting of the
narrative thus may represent only a literary device. For the

present, this study assumes only that the Book of Esther arose
sometime during the broad span of the post-exilic period. Further discussion of date is deferred to Chapter VI, where the
results of the following analysis of Esther may be brought to
bear upon this question.

The problem of date raises further questions concerning
the narrator's historiographical concerns. The Book of Esther
claims a precise historical setting and purports to recount
certain events which occurred at Ahasuerus' court. Do these
features, too, suggest only a literary device, lending an air
of verisimilitude to an otherwise palpably fictitious tale? Is
the role of the "historical" in the story, like that apparently
of Purim, incidental to the author's purpose in telling his
tale? At present, these questions remain unresolved.

B. Religious Credibility

Recent Esther research has focused largely upon historical
questions. Because of the story's lack of historical credibility, scholars often have sought solutions to historical
problems by analyzing Esther's literary features. Recent commentators, however, have not limited their interest in the
scroll to historical and literary questions. As suggested
above, opposition to the story on religious grounds marks the
history of Esther research and may date back to the period of
the Qumran community.[61] Doubts about the theological worth of
the narrative are not surprising since the scroll never refers
directly to the deity, nor even indirectly through the suggestion that prayer is a viable response to peril.[62] It displays
no concern for dietary laws nor for injunctions against inter-
marriage, matters of some concern in other post-exilic documents.

Religious opposition to Esther arose for a variety of
reasons. Martin Luther objected to the book because of its
"pagan impropriety" and because it "Judaized" too much.[63] More
recent commentators point to the story's jingoistic fervor and
antagonism toward gentiles.[64] L. E. Browne finds that "gentile
and Jew alike are represented in the story as actuated by the
basest motives of pride, greed and cruelty. If the book fills
any useful place in the Bible it is as a picture of unredeemed

humanity."[65] Other scholars similarly are moved to open dismay
at the inclusion of Esther in the canon. Robert Pfeiffer
writes, "Such a secular book hardly deserves a place in the
canon of Sacred Scriptures . . . ,"[66] and Samuel Sandmel adds,
"I should not be grieved if the Book of Esther were somehow
dropped out of Scripture."[67]

Scholars thus question the religious value of the story,[68]
as well as its historical veracity. Fortunately, not all students of the book are so negative in their judgments. Several
scholars have sought to account for Esther's "secularism" and
"offensive" features through ingenious arguments. For example,
one explanation given for the secularistic tone of the narrative is that its author was a religious cynic. According to
this view, the narrator no longer believed in the power of divine intervention in human affairs. He "appears to have made
no demands on God and have expected that God would make none of
him."[69]

Others locate the religious significance of the tale in
the same place where they find an explanation for its historical verisimilitude, viz., in Esther's function as a festal legend. These commentators hold that the narrator refrained from
any overt expression of his own theological beliefs because of
the secular character of the festival.

> From the earliest days Purim was a time of noisy merry-
> making, even to the point of the excess recommended in
> the Talmud, "Drink wine until you are no longer able to
> distinguish between 'Blessed be Mordecai' and 'Cursed
> by Haman'" (Megillah 7b) . . . . It seems plausible
> that because of the danger of blasphemy in connection
> with a festival when considerable license was allowed,
> the author deliberately avoided religious references
> which in any way would lead to the profaning of the
> sanctities of Judaism.[70]

A completely different explanation for Esther's secularism
is offered by Wilhelm Vischer.[71] Vischer argues that the Book
of Esther is concerned with "die Judenfrage" as a political and
cultural problem. The conflict between Mordecai and Haman
points to the central problem of the "Sein oder Nichtsein" of
the Jewish people.[72]

Other commentators see this problem of the continued existence of the Jewish people to be central to the story.[73] The
Book of Esther may be viewed as a record of the communal response of one segment of Yahweh's chosen people to a perilous

moment in its history.[74]   It is the survival of this people
which holds the theological significance of the tale.[75]

Shemaryahu Talmon recently offered a different solution
to the "secularism" of the Book of Esther.[76]   Talmon argues
that Esther is a "historicized wisdom tale" which enacts
standard wisdom motifs.[77]   According to Talmon, the wisdom
influence upon the narrator's thought explains his lack of
emphasis upon such aspects of Jewish piety as the dietary
laws, covenant and prayer.   The wisdom influence also accounts for the absence of divine intervention in the narrated
events.   In this respect, Esther is not unlike other wisdom
writing.[78]

Other explanations of Esther's religious significance
have been advanced in recent years.[79]   Robert Gordis finds the
value of the story in its suggestion that God operates in human
affairs through human agents, both worthy and unworthy.[80]   He
holds that:

> . . . the miracle of God's deliverance of His people,
> narrated in the Book of Esther, need not take the form
> of interference with the normal processes of nature or
> of history, but the lesson is clear--the Guardian of
> Israel will not let His people perish.[81]

A similar view is taken by Michael Fox who argues that
Esther is built upon an implicit but clear theology.[82]   According to Fox, God's activity lies beneath the surface of human
events but may be discerned in the pattern assumed by those
events.   Arndt Meinhold, on the other hand, argues that the
Book of Esther is modeled after the Joseph story, and he sees a
connection between their theologies.[83]

In a recent study, Bruce W. Jones objects to views that
the Book of Esther delights in cruelty and a chauvinistic na-
tionalism.[84]   He maintains that such understandings of the book
are misguided and ignore the humorous nature of the account.[85]
Jones sees the scroll's purpose in the reconciliation of Jewish
audiences to their minority status among gentiles whose attitudes toward Jews varied unpredictably from honor to persecution.[86]   It was the ability of the Jews to maintain their sense
of humor in the face of adversity that enabled them to survive
the perilous moments of their history.[87]   Jones finds nothing
in the Book of Esther which would offend the religious sensi-
bilities of a perceptive reader.   Rather, he suggests that the

14

very elements which some find objectionable illustrate how the
Jews could successfully overcome the vicissitudes of diaspora
life.

Recent Esther research, then, points to a concern for the
story's religious significance. Various attempts to account
for the secularistic and/or offensive nature of the story have
been offered. Some of these will be analyzed in detail in the
following chapters. At present, however, we may ask if charac-
terizations of Esther as a secular document are proper. Would
an ancient Jew have understood history to stand outside the
control of Yahweh? If not, we then must ask why the Book of
Esther gives this impression.

The history of Esther research emphasizes two particular
concerns, viz., the historicity of the account and its religious significance. These two problems are not unrelated. For
some scholars, the recognition that the account given in Esther
is not historically reliable renders the book even more religiously reprehensible. For other commentators, however, it is
precisely the fictional nature of the account that provides
clues to the story's "theology," or at least explains the absence of a theology in Esther.

This relationship between historical and religious questions becomes most apparent when we attempt to discern the narrator's purpose in explaining the origin of Purim. Recent
scholarship indicates that the institution and legitimation of
Purim may not constitute the sole aim of the narrative. What
then is the nature of the relationship between the festival and
the Esther-Mordecai story? Is the celebration of Purim integral to the story preserved in the MT? Or, is Purim secondary
to the present account, creating obvious "seams" in the narrative?

C. A "Literary" Approach to
Esther

Few scholars accept the Book of Esther as a reliable, historical account. At most, the story is viewed as an "historical novel" which recalls an actual event. This characterization of the narrative is proper in another sense, for in its
present form, the Book of Esther provides the "historical"

grounds for the celebration of Purim. Nevertheless, Purim has
a provenance outside the Esther-Mordecai story, to which it has
been joined.[88] The present "author"[89] possibly joined the
story and festival, or he himself could have inherited traditions in which the two were juxtaposed. In either case, the
limited amount of narrative description devoted to Purim[90] suggests that the narrator intended, quite simply, to tell an interesting story. His success is partially attested to by the
canonization of the book into the Jewish Scriptures, and by the
number of commentaries and expositions it has elicited.[91]

The narrator, then, had at least two reasons for telling
his tale. Had he any additional purposes as well? There exists an obvious danger in assuming that one knows an author's
intentions when they are not explicitly stated. Great caution
and restraint are required in any attempt to delineate the purposes which Esther's author had in telling his story. The
approach to the Book of Esther taken here seeks to exercise
such restraint by its concentration upon the narrator's method
of presentation as the locus of his message.

The nature of the account in Esther is less "historical"
than "history-like."[92] Our primary clues to the narrator's
purposes in telling his story rest with the narrative itself.
That is, we possess little external evidence to assist us in
determining the factors which motivated the narrator to tell
his story in a particular manner. We can depend only upon the
style and narrative techniques through which the storyteller
chose to present his "argument." The intentions of the author
thus are to be located in his story's plot, and in the words
and actions of the *dramatis personae*.

This dissertation follows the lead of Werner Dommershausen
in concentrating attention upon the narrative and stylistic
features of Esther as the primary locus for our understanding
of the text. The approach taken here, however, differs somewhat from that followed by Dommershausen. As suggested above,
the weakness of Dommershausen's analysis rests with his emphasis upon the individual stylistic units. The significance of
each individual unit, modified by its function in the narrative
as a whole, is not always apparent. Nor is it always possible
to demonstrate that the various stylistic features which
Dommershausen discerns result from the narrator's conscious

intentions.

While some attention is given to the individual stylistic elements which comprise the Book of Esther, this study focuses upon those narrative features which pervade the story. It is hoped that by limiting this analysis to those literary features which govern the account, it will be possible to avoid the shortcomings of Dommershausen's approach while retaining the strengths of his method.

This study of the Book of Esther will depart from previous investigations in a further respect. Since Gunkel's study of the book, attempts to determine its proper literary *Gattung* have met with varying degrees of success.[93] The discovery of various *Gattungen* in Esther contributes greatly to the current understanding that Esther is more history-like than historical. Dommershausen's study of Esther, however, illustrates that the discovery of various *Gattungen* within the narrative does not itself recommend the *Gattung* of the book as a whole.

Recent attempts to classify the Book of Esther within a *Gattung* of *Diasporanovelle* may not be misguided. But as the discussion of Chapter V indicates, the existence of such a *Gattung*, and the criteria for including Esther within it, are yet to be demonstrated. I thus refrain from any attempt to suggest Esther's genre or from allowing any preconceived notions of its *Gattung* to influence my interpretation of the tale.

The primary aim of this dissertation is to analyze the literary and stylistic features of the Book of Esther. Prior to an indication of the specific approach taken here, it is necessary to indicate the terminology which is employed. Throughout this study, the term "motif" is used to indicate a situation, element or idea which recurs in the Book of Esther in such a manner that the repetition contributes to the unity of the narrative. A governing motif in Esther is not portrayed in isolation but is bound to a specific context or situation to which the narrator draws attention. The term "motif" thus points to situations, elements or ideas which pervade the story, potently recalling or anticipating their earlier and later occurrences. As Chapters II and III demonstrate, the narrator employs an adumbrative style, and motifs recur at key points in the plot and structure of the story.[94]

In addition to these motifs, the author employs "auxiliary motifs." These motifs also recur throughout the story, but are more limited in their use. For example, it is suggested in the following chapter that the storyteller uses an auxilary motif of fasting to highlight and contrast with the dominant motif of feasting.

"Motif" thus is used in this dissertation in a broad sense. Occasionally, reference also is made to "formulaic motifs," implying a much narrower understanding of the term.[95] Formulaic motifs refer to situations, elements or ideas which imply specific contexts or type-scenes.[96] Such motifs may be found in other literary works or folkloristic contexts, perhaps representing stock phrases or scenes which the narrator used to expand the plot of his story.

These formulaic motifs often contain the *märchenhaft* elements which underlie suggestions as to Esther's various *Gattungen*. One such formulaic motif is suggested by the story of Vashti in Esther 1. This story resembles those found in "A Thousand and One Nights."[97] One may also compare the story of Vashti to an incident recounted by Herodotus concerning the beauty of Candaules' wife (cf. *Hist.* 1.8-13). Similarly, the "beauty contest" of Esth 2:8-14 is vaguely reminiscent of Herodotus' report of a custom of the Eneti in Illyria (cf. *Hist.* 1.196). There, once each year, women of a marriageable age were gathered so that interested males might choose wives.[98] These examples point to the presence of stock-scenes through which Esther's author expanded his own account.[99]

Finally, the term "theme" is not used interchangeably with the word "motif." Rather, its use is reserved for the message or idea which the author conveyed by his use of the story's motifs. This understanding does not necessitate the view that the Book of Esther was didactically intended, although I suspect that the story suggests a particular view of diaspora Jewish life. Rather, the "themes" of the Book of Esther refer to the central, dominant ideas which underlie the narrator's use of motifs, and to which those motifs point.

The preceding discussion of terminology employed in this study already suggests the nature of its approach to the Book of Esther. An analysis of the plot and characterization of the story reveals certain narrative motifs which recur throughout

Esther. By examining these motifs, it may be possible to recover something of the narrator's own understanding of his
story and gain insight into his motives in telling his story in
a particular way.

Such an approach, however, leads to a danger. One may
mistakenly identify the writer's own presuppositions as his
conclusions. By posing the wrong questions to the text, we may
conclude that the author sought to further some point or belief
which, in actuality, was one of his assumptions.

Again, I have sought to minimize this danger by limiting
my study to those motifs which demonstrably pervade the story.
I have assumed that the recurrence of these motifs at key
points in the plot suggests features to which the storyteller
attached importance and to which he wished to draw attention.
Even in those cases where these motifs point to something
assumed by the narrator or his audience, we may presume that
they are stressed for a reason. Our task, then, is to discern
the reasons behind the recurrence of, and emphasis upon, these
elements.

Central to this study is an examination of the prevalent
motifs through which the narrator developed his story. The inclusion of only these motifs does not exclude the presence of
others in the tale. Rather, the limitation of my study to
those motifs which govern Esther safeguards against assigning
to the narrator emphases which he did not consciously intend.
The interdependence of these motifs may indicate that my own
reading of Esther is not entirely subjective.

Subsequent chapters of the dissertation explore the implications of the narrator's use of motifs for our understanding
of Esther. The author's choice of motifs and their use in
Esther provide clues to the story's themes. Taken together,
the motifs and themes suggest how Esther's narrator understood
his own story and presumably intended it to be understood by
others.

The central motifs of the Book of Esther suggest the narrator's themes and his purposes in presenting his story as he
did. An analysis of these motifs thus provides a starting
point for our attempts to understand the method and message of
the book.

NOTES

[1] Jacob Hoschander, *The Book of Esther in the Light of History* (Philadelphia: Dropsie College, 1923) 1.

[2] In 1923, Hoschander, ibid., rendered a similar verdict regarding the fate of the book.

[3] Carey A. Moore, *Esther* (AB 7B; Garden City, N.Y.: Doubleday, 1971) xxi-xxiv, summarizes the opposition to the book in various Jewish and Christian circles.

[4] Moore, ibid., xxi-xxii, suggests that the Qumran community rejected the Book of Esther for theological reasons and that its omission from the Dead Sea Scrolls is no archaeological accident.

[5] In *b. Meg.* 7a, Judah reports in the name of Samuel that Esther does not "defile the hands." A similar opinion is attributed to Levi ben Samuel and Huna ben Ḥiyyah in *b. Sanh.* 100a.

[6] The best survey of pre-twentieth century evaluations of Esther is found in Lewis Paton, *The Book of Esther* (ICC; Edinburgh: T. & T. Clark, 1908) 1-120, especially 97-100. Also see the summaries of the history of Esther research given by Hans Bardtke, *Das Buch Esther* (KAT 17/5; Gütersloh: Gütersloher Verlagshaus Gerd Mohn, 1963) 255-265; Gillis Gerleman, *Esther* (BKAT 21; Neukirchen-Vluyn: Neukirchener Verlag, 1970-1973) 1-7.

[7] Moore, *Esther*, xxxv.

[8] See the discussion, Paton, *The Book of Esther*, 112.

[9] My intention here is not to review the entire history of research on the Book of Esther. Such a task would extend beyond the scope and interests of this study. Rather, I wish only to indicate some of the problems presented by the scroll which have occupied past researchers and which will be addressed in the following chapters.

[10] A shift in the meaning and function of any tradition could occur at various stages of its development. My concern here, however, is with the stage of certain traditions as they are preserved in the MT of the Book of Esther. Unless otherwise noted, any references to the Book of Esther are restricted to the MT.

[11] See Paton, *The Book of Esther*, 64; Moore, *Esther*, 3 (on Esth 1:1); Helmer Ringgren, *Das Buch Esther* (ATD 16; Göttingen: Vandenhoeck & Ruprecht, 1967) 113.

[12] Susa was the ancient capital of the Elamite empire and became a royal capital and spring residence of the Achaemenian kings by the time of Darius I. See A. T. Olmstead, *The History*

of the Persian Empire (Chicago: University of Chicago, 1948) 168; André Barucq, "*Esther* et la cour de Suse," *BTS* 39 (1961) 3-5. Extensive renovations of the palace structures were undertaken by Xerxes, presumably the "Ahasuerus" of our account. For a comparison of the view of Xerxes given by the Book of Esther and other ancient sources, see Moore, *Esther*, xxv-xli.

[13]Paton, *The Book of Esther*, 65, and Moore, *Esther*, xli, list some of the characteristics of Persian government suggested by the Book of Esther which seem historically valid. The accuracy of the story, from an archaeological perspective, is defended by Barucq, "*Esther* et la cour de Suse." See also W. F. Albright, "The Lachish Cosmetic Burner and Esther 2:12," *A Light Unto My Path* ([Festschrift Jacob M. Myers], ed. H. N. Bream, R. D. Heim and C. A. Moore; Philadelphia: Temple University, 1974) 25-32; Carey A. Moore, "Archaeology and the Book of Esther," *BA* 38 (1975) 69-79; A. Leo Oppenheim, "On Royal Gardens in Mesopotamia," *JNES* 24 (1965) 328-333.

The excavations of M. A. Dieulafoy, and more recently of Roman Ghirshman, indicate that the distinction made between "city" and "acropolis" in references to Susa reflects sound historical information. See Dieulafoy's study, *L'acropole de Suse* (4 vols; Paris: Hachette, 1890); and that of Ghirshman, *Persia, from the Origins to the Time of Alexander the Great* (The Arts of Mankind; ed. André Malraux and Georges Salles; London: Thames & Hudson, 1964). Also see below, Chapter II, n. 10.

[14]Hoschander, *The Book of Esther in the Light of History*, 42-80, identifies "Ahasuerus" with Artaxerxes II Mnemon. Most commentators, however, identify him with Xerxes I. The reader again is referred to the various commentaries on Esther, and especially to Paton, *The Book of Esther*, 51-54.

[15]The name "Mordecai" appears to be genuine, and the word *mrdk* appears in an Aramaic letter of the fifth century B.C.E. See G. R. Driver, *Aramaic Documents of the Fifth Century B.C.* (Oxford: Clarendon, 1954) 20, n. 2. Variant forms of the name also appear in the treasury tablets found at Persepolis. See G. G. Cameron, *The Persepolis Treasury Tablets* (Chicago: University of Chicago, 1948) 84. Perhaps of greatest significance is the mention of a *Mardukâ* who was an accountant from Susa during the last years of Darius or the initial years of Xerxes. See the discussion of Arthur Ungnad, "Keilinschriftliche Beiträge zum Buch Ezra und Esther," *ZAW* 58 (1940-1941) 240-244. Ungnad is correct to point out that the existence of two high officials from Susa with a similar name during this period is improbable. Also see the discussion of Siegfried H. Horn, "Mordecai: A Historical Problem," *BR* 9 (1964) 274-292.

[16]See the list in Paton, *The Book of Esther*, 66-71; J. D. Davis, "Persian Words and the Date of Old Testament Documents," *Old Testament and Semitic Studies* ([Festschrift William Rainey Harper], 2 vols.; ed. Robert Francis Harper, Francis Brown and George Foot Moore; Chicago: University of Chicago, 1908) 2.271-284; Henry S. Gehman, "Notes on the Persian Words in the Book of Esther," *JBL* 43 (1924) 321-328.

[17]On the story's Aramaisms, see Charles C. Torrey, "The Older Book of Esther," *HTR* 37 (1944) 33-40; more recently, Frank Zimmermann, *Biblical Books Translated from the Aramaic* (New York: KTAV, 1975) 69-91.

[18]See the discussions of Paton, *The Book of Esther*," 71-77; Bernhard W. Anderson, "The Book of Esther," *IB* 3 (New York/Nashville: Abingdon, 1954) 826-827; Moore, *Esther*, xlv-xlvi.

[19]I distinguish here between scholars who find an historical event to underlie a predominantly fictitious account and those who uphold the basic historicity of the Book of Esther. The latter group includes Jacob Hoschander, *The Book of Esther;* Siegfried H. Horn, "Mordecai: A Historical Problem"; Johannes Schildenberger, *Das Buch Esther,*Die Heilige Schrift des Alten Testaments; Bonn: Peter Hanstein, 1941). A more moderate position seems indicated for André Barucq, "*Esther* et la cour de Suse"; A. E. Morris, "The Purpose of the Book of Esther," *ExpTim* 42 (1930-1931) 124-128; Isidore Lévy, "La répudiation de Vashti," *International Congress of Orientalists, 21st, 1948* (Paris: Imprimerie Nationale, 1949) 114-115; B. Schneider, "Esther Revised According to the Maccabees," *SBF* 13 (1962-1963) 190-218.

[20]The Elephantine Papyri indicate that Egyptian Jews encountered some hostility from their non-Jewish compatriots in the fifth century B.C.E. See the discussion of Bezalel Porten, *Archives from Elephantine* (Berkeley/Los Angeles: University of California, 1968), especially chap. 9, "Conflict and Resolution."

[21]Aage Bentzen, *Introduction to the Old Testament* (2 vols.; Copenhagen: G. F. C. Gad, 1952) 2.192; Yehezkel Kaufmann, תולדות האמונה הישראלית ([The Religion of Israel], 8 secs.; Jerusalem: Bialik Institute and Dvir, 1956) 8.440-443; Otto Eissfeldt, *The Old Testament: An Introduction* (New York: Harper & Row, 1965) 509-510; Georg Fohrer, *Introduction to the Old Testament* (New York/Nashville: Abingdon, 1968) 253; Bardtke, *Das Buch Esther*, 248-252; Moore, *Esther*, lii-liii; Arndt Meinhold, "Die Diasporanovelle--eine alttestamentliche Gattung" (Dr.theol. dissertation, Ernst-Moritz-Arndt Universität, Greifswald, 1969) *passim*; idem, "Die Gattung der Josephsgeschichte und des Estherbuches: Diasporanovelle I, II," *ZAW* 87 (1975) 306-324, *ZAW* 88 (1976) 79-83. I am grateful to Dr. Meinhold who, despite great difficulty, was able to provide me with a copy of his dissertation.

[22]Eissfeldt, *The Old Testament*, 507, n. 3. Ernst Würthwein, *Die Fünf Megilloth* (HAT, 18; Tübingen: J. C. B. Mohr, 1969) 167, disagrees with this characterization of the scroll.

[23]J. M. Myers, *The World of the Restoration*, (BBS; Englewood Cliffs, N.J.: Prentice-Hall, 1968) 92, notes that "the emphasis has fallen too much on the noun rather than the adjective." This opinion is shared by Moore, *Esther*, liii.

[24]Emmanuel Cosquin, "Le Prologue-cadre des Mille et une Nuits. Les legendes perses et le livre d'Esther," *RB* 6 (1909) 7-49, 161-197, sees a resemblance between Esth 1:1-2:14 and

22

harem tales such as those found in "A Thousand and One Nights."
Others find novelistic features in Esther which recall other
biblical narratives. See Gerleman's discussion in *Esther* and
Chapter V below. Mention also might be made of Robert H.
Pfeiffer, *Introduction to the Old Testament* (New York: Harper
& Bros., 1941) 745-746. Pfeiffer thinks the author of Esther
contrived the story and the festival, neither of which pos-
sesses any basis in history.

[25]As in so many other areas of biblical scholarship,
Hermann Gunkel's study may be cited as the first major work to
investigate the non-historical, "legendary" features of the
scroll; see *Esther* (Religionsgeschichtliche Volksbücher für die
deutsche christliche Gegenwart II/19-20; Tübingen: J. C. B.
Mohr, 1916). Interest in the language and syntax of Esther is
represented best by the investigations of Hans Striedl, "Unter-
suchung zur Syntax und Stilistik des hebräischen Buches
Esther," *ZAW* 55 (1937) 73-108; Ruth Stiehl, "Das Buch Esther,"
WZKM 53 (1956) 4-22; and Franz Altheim and Ruth Stiehl,
"Esther, Judith und Daniel," *Die aramäische Sprache unter den
Achaemeniden* (Frankfurt am Main: V. Kostermann, 1963) 195-213.

[26]Some discussion of the festival of Purim, as it functions in the narrative, is presented below. An investigation
into the origin and provenance of the festival itself is beyond
the scope of this dissertation. The reader consequently is referred to the studies of Paul Haupt, *Purim* (Leipzig and Baltimore: J. C. Hinrichs and Johns Hopkins, 1906) 21-22; Julius
Lewy, "Old Assyrian puru'um and pūrum," *RHA* 36 (1938) 117-124;
Augustin Bea, "De origine vocis פור," *Bib* 21 (1940) 198-199;
Victor Christian, "Zur Herkunft des Purim-Festes," *Alttestamentliche Studien* ([Festschrift Friedrich Nötscher], ed. Hubert
Junker and Johannes Botterweck; Bonn: Peter Hanstein, 1950)
33-37; Theodor Herzl Gaster, *Purim and Hanukkah in Custom and
Tradition* (New York: Henry Schuman, 1950); idem, *Myth, Legend
and Custom in the Old Testament*, (2 vols.; New York: Harper
& Row, 1969) 2.829-837; Helmer Ringgren, "Esther and Purim,"
SEÅ 20 (1955) 5-24; Saul P. Besser, "Esther and Purim--Chance
and Play," *CCAR Journal* 16 (1969) 36-42.

[27]For example, Gunkel, *Esther*, suggests that Purim imi-
tates a Persian festival occasioned by the murder of the Magi;
cf. Herodotus, *Hist.* 3.68-79. J. Lewy, "The Feast of the 14th
Day of Adar," *HUCA* 14 (1939) 127-151, equates Purim with the
Persian New Year. He argues that the narrative recalls a con-
flict between the devotees of Marduk and those of Mithra and
Anahita. A similar connection between the Book of Esther and
extra-Israelite New Year's observances are suggested by Gaster,
Purim and Hanukkah in Custom and Tradition, 35; idem, *Myth,
Legend and Custom in the Old Testament* 2.829-837; Ringgren,
"Esther and Purim," 24.
Perhaps the most ingenious theses regarding the origins of
the story and festival are those of H. Zimmern, "Zur Frage nach
dem Ursprunge des Purimfestes," *ZAW* 11 (1891) 157-169; and
Peter Jensen, "Elamitsche Eigennamen. Ein Beitrag zur Erklärung der elamitischen Inschriften," *WZKM* 6 (1892) 47-70, 209-
226. The Book of Esther supposedly recalls a myth where the
Elamite gods Human (Haman) and Mashti (Vashti) are overcome by
the Babylonian deities Marduk (Mordecai) and Ishtar (Esther).

This explanation is provocative but not convincing. In
the Book of Esther, we do not find Haman and Vashti associated
in a joint battle against Mordecai and Esther. Moreover, "Mordecai" is a genuine name, if not an historical person; see n.
12 above. The name "Esther" may derive from the Persian,
"star," not from "Ishtar"; see Moore, *Esther*, li, n. 80.

[28]See below, Chapter II.

[29]The exhaustive studies of Gaster and Ringgren, cited in
n. 26 above, provide the best evidence for this assertion.
Also see the discussion in Chapter II below.

[30]Either Purim represents a secondary accretion to the
narrative, or vice versa.

[31]As indicated above, this study is concerned with the MT
of Esther. It nevertheless is more appropriate to refer to the
present forms of the narrative, particularly in light of the
great divergencies between the MT and the LXX. On the Greek
translation of Esther, see Torrey, *The Older Book of Esther*;
Carey A. Moore, "The Greek Text of Esther" (Ph.D. dissertation,
Johns Hopkins University, Baltimore, 1965); idem, "A Greek Witness to a Different Hebrew Text of Esther," *ZAW* 79 (1967) 351-
358; Herbert J. Cook, "The A Text of the Greek Version of the
Book of Esther," *ZAW* 81 (1969) 369-376; Hans Bardtke, "Zusätze
zu Esther," *Historische und legendarische Erzählungen* (Jüdische
Schriften aus hellenistisch-römischer Zeit 1; ed. Werner Georg
Kümmel; Gütersloh: Gütersloher Verlagshaus Gerd Mohn, 1973)
15-62.

[32]Analyses of Esther which concentrate upon its literary
features are not new in the history of research. This will be
indicated more fully in the chapters which follow. Recent
years nevertheless have witnessed a resurgence of interest in
the narrator's literary skill, and several scholars believe
that his narrative techniques hold clues to the story's underlying purposes.

[33]Henri Cazelles, "Note sur la composition du rouleau
d'Esther," *Lex tua Veritas* ([Festschrift Hubert Junker], ed.
Heinrich Gross and Franz Mussner; Trier: Paulinus-Verlag,
1961) 17-30. See also the review of Cazelles by Hans Bardtke,
"Neuere Arbeiten zum Estherbuch," *Vooraziatische-egyptische
Genootschap: Ex Oriente Lux, Jaarbericht* 19 (Leiden: E. J.
Brill, 1967) 519-549.

[34]Ibid., 26. Cazelles follows the lead of Jacques
Duchesne-Guillemin, "Les noms des eunuques d'Assuérus," *Muséon*
66 (1953) 105-108, who suggests that the second list reverses
the order of the first.

[35]More specifically, Cazelles suggests an association between the festivals of Purim and Sakaia.

[36]The existence of independent traditions centering upon Mordecai is supported by the reference to "Mordecai's Day" in 2 Macc 15:36.

[37]Bardtke, *Das Buch Esther*, 248-252.

[38]Bardtke thinks that the "chronicles of the kings of Media and Persia" (Esth 10:2) might be a reference to this collection of tales. If Bardtke is correct, these "chronicles" explain the narrator's challenge to his audience to verify his account.

[39]Moore, *Esther*, lii, adds that in addition to this collection of tales suggested by Bardtke, the narrator also had other collections of tales available to him. These undoubtedly include stories preserved in the canonical literature; see Chapters III and V below.

[40]Bardtke accounts for the attachment of Purim to the present form of Esther as part of the traditions inherited by the narrator. He suggests that the origins of the festival are no longer available to us but probably represent a Babylonian-Mesopotamian development.

[41]In discussing Bardtke's thesis, Moore, *Esther*, li-lii, seems to indicate that Purim is to be associated with the story of Mordecai. Again, the reference to "Mordecai's Day" in 2 Macc 15:36 supports this view.

[42]Bardtke, *Das Buch Esther*, 248.

[43]Gillis Gerleman, *Studien zu Esther*, (BibS[N] 18 Neukirchen-Vluyn: Neukirchener Verlag des Erziehungsvereins GmbH, 1966).

[44]Gerleman, *Esther*; see n. 6 above.

[45]The belief that the Book of Esther was modeled after earlier traditions is not new. L. A. Rosenthal saw literary and stylistic affinities with the Joseph story, a view reaffirmed in recent years by Moshe Gan. See Rosenthal's "Die Josephsgeschichte mit den Büchern Ester und Daniel verglichen," *ZAW* 15 (1895) 278-284; idem, "Nochmals der Vergleich Ester, Joseph-Daniel," *ZAW* 17 (1897) 125-128; also P. Riessler, "Zu Rosenthals Aufsatz, Bd. XV, S. 278ff.," *ZAW* 16 (1896) 182. Gan's views are found in מגילת אסתר באספקלריית קורות יוסף במצרים" [The Book of Esther in Light of the Story of Joseph in Egypt] *Tarbiz* 31 (1961-1962) 144-149. On the other hand, W. McKane, "A Note on Esther IX and I Samuel XV," *JTS* 12 (1961) 260-261, finds affinities between Esther and Saulide traditions. Each of these arguments is considered below in detail.

[46]Gerleman, *Esther*, 11. Gerleman's thesis has not proven influential in recent studies of Esther. The greatest support for his views has come with his suggestion of parallels between the festivals of Passover and Purim. See, e.g., Robert Martin-Achard, *Essai biblique sur les fêtes d'Israël* (Geneva: Labor et Fides, 1974) 149-150; M. E. Andrews, "Esther, Exodus and Peoples," *AusBR* 23 (1975) 27-28. Independent support for

Gerleman's views may be found in J. van Goudoever, *Biblical Calendars* (Leiden: E. J. Brill, 1961) 81-83.

[47]David Daube, *The Exodus Pattern in the Bible* (London: Faber & Faber, 1963) 59, suggests a parallel between Moses and Mordecai. Daube thinks that the reference to Mordecai's "greatness" in Esth 9:4 is an attempt to endow him with a "Mosaic trait." See, however, the remarks of Bardtke, "Neuere Arbeiten zum Estherbuch," 528, on this parallel. The correspondence Gerleman finds between Aaron/Esther and Moses/Mordecai is discussed below.

[48]See the discussion of Chapter III.

[49]Gerleman, *Esther*, 23.

[50]I shall argue for a similar conclusion, albeit on different grounds, in Chapter VI.

[51]See the reviews of Gerleman's *Esther* by Xavier Jacques, *Bib* 47 (1966) 461-463; and Carey A. Moore, *JBL* 94 (1975) 293-296.

[52]For example, the settings at the foreign court, the threat confronting the Jews, the presence of two protagonists in each story, and the establishment of a festival to commemorate the Jews' triumph over their foes.

[53]Mordecai's adoption of Esther serves several functions in the narrative. These are suggested in the chapters below.

[54]Werner Dommershausen, *Die Estherrolle* (SBM, 6; Stuttgart: Katholiches Bibelwerk, 1968).

[55]Dommershausen acknowledges his debt to Hans Striedl, "Untersuchung zur Syntax und Stilistik des hebräischen Buches Esther," in developing his method of analysis. Forty years ago, Striedl undertook a syntactical-stylistic investigation of Esther. Dommershausen's study represents the first major work to continue Striedl's line of inquiry. See also the stylistic analysis of D. Schötz, "Das hebräische Buch Esther," *BZ* 21 (1933) 255-276.

[56]Dommershausen, *Die Estherrolle*, 15-16.

[57]Ibid., 156.

[58]For example, several arguments are based upon the word order of clauses whose subjects or objects precede the verb. Such sequences are not uncommon in Esther and characterize its late biblical style. Dommershausen assumes that word order which departs from that of classical Hebrew must be due to the narrator's conscious intentions. He does not consider that the sequence of verbs, subjects and objects in the Hebrew known to our narrator and his audience perhaps was not identical to that of pre-exilic Palestine.

[59]As the following notes indicate, I rely heavily upon the studies of W. Lee Humphreys, "The Motif of the Wise Courtier in

the Old Testament" (Th.D. dissertation, Union Theological Seminary, New York, 1970); idem, "A Life-style for Diaspora: A Study of the Tales of Esther and Daniel," *JBL* 92 (1973) 211-223; and Meinhold, "Die Gattung der Josephsgeschichte und des Estherbuches: Diasporanovelle I, II."

[60]Susa was a royal capital during the Achaemenian period. As such, it seems a likely candidate for the story's place of composition. It is less clear that Susa provided proximity to the foreign rulers during the hellenistic period. As the only *polis* east of the Tigris River during the early hellenistic period, however, Susa retained some of its former prestige and status. Further comments regarding this possibility are found in Chapter VI.

[61]See above, n. 3.

[62]The significance of the phrase אחר מקום in Esth 4:14 is discussed below. Several researchers consider it an allusion to God.

[63]Martin Luther, *Tischreden* (D. Martin Luther's Werke, Weimar edition: 6 vols.; Weimar: Hermann Böhlaus, 1914) 3(no. 3391a).302.

[64]For example, Robert Pfeiffer, *Introduction to the Old Testament* (New York: Harper & Bros., 1941) 747; Bernhard Anderson, "The Place of the Book of Esther in the Christian Bible," *JR* 30 (1950) 32; L. E. Browne, "Esther," *PCB* (London: Thomas Nelson & Sons, 1962) 383.

[65]Browne, "Esther," 381.

[66]Pfeiffer, *Introduction to the Old Testament*, 747. Eissfeldt similarly remarks, "Christianity . . . has neither occasion nor justification for holding on to it [Esther]" (*The Old Testament*, 511-512).

[67]Samuel Sandmel, *The Enjoyment of Scripture* (New York: Oxford University, 1972) 44.

[68]Objections to Esther on religious grounds are not limited to the nature of the story. They also extend to the character of Purim. For example, Max Brod, "Eine Königin Esther," writes, ". . . solange sie dieses Fest feiern, kann der Messias nicht in die Welt kommen." Brod is quoted in Schalom Ben-Chorin, *Kritik des Estherbuches* (Jerusalem: "Heatid," Salingré & Co., 1938) 4. Ben-Chorin himself, 5, proposes that Purim be eliminated from the festal calendar and Esther removed from the canon.

[69]Pfeiffer, *Introduction to the Old Testament*, 743.

[70]Anderson, "The Book of Esther," 829-830. Moore, *Esther*, xxxiii, criticizes this view since it accounts only for the absence of God's name in the Book of Esther. This view does not explain the similar absence of references to law, covenant, dietary regulations, prayer, angels or afterlife.

[71] Wilhelm Vischer, *Esther* (TEH 48; Munich: C. Kaiser, 1937).

[72] Ibid., 15. Vischer's thesis is sharply criticized by Gerleman, *Esther*, 42.

[73] For example, Wesley J. Fuerst, *The Books of Ruth, Esther, Ecclesiastes, the Song of Songs, Lamentations* (CBC; Cambridge: Cambridge University, 1975) 38.

[74] Anderson, "The Book of Esther," 830.

[75] The survival of the Jews in the Book of Esther perhaps expresses one understanding of the concept of election. This possibility is examined in Chapter VI.

[76] Shemaryahu Talmon, "'Wisdom' in the Book of Esther," *VT* 13 (1963) 419-455. Talmon's thesis is criticized by Bardtke, "Neuere Arbeiten zum Estherbuch," 541-545, and by J. L. Crenshaw, "Method in Determining Wisdom Influence upon 'Historical Literature,'" *JBL* 88 (1969) 129-142. See also N. A. van Uchelen, "A Chokmatic Theme in the Book of Esther," *Verkenningen in een Stroomgebied* ([Festschrift M. A. Beek], Amsterdam: [publisher not given], 1974) 132-140.

[77] Dommershausen, *Die Estherrolle*, considers the wisdom character of Esther to be "veiled." Humphreys, "The Motif of the Wise Courtier in the Old Testament," finds the presence of a motif of the wise courtier in Esther. Humphreys' thesis is discussed more fully below.

[78] Talmon is not the first commentator to discern a connection between the Book of Esther and wisdom literature. Almost half a century ago, A. E. Morris suggested a similarity of thought between the Books of Esther and Qoheleth ("The Purpose of the Book of Esther"). Even earlier, *b. Meg.* 10b applied the words of the Preacher to Mordecai and Esther.

[79] Gerleman, for example, sees Esther as the "Enttheologiesierung" of the exodus narratives; see above.

[80] Robert Gordis, *Megillat Esther* (New York: The Rabbinical Assembly, 1972).

[81] Ibid., 12.

[82] Michael Fox, "The Structure of the Book of Esther," forthcoming in a Festschrift to I. L. Seeligmann. See below, Chapter IV, n. 35.

[83] Meinhold, "Die Gattung der Josephsgeschichte und des Estherbuches: Diasporanovelle, I, II."

[84] Bruce W. Jones, "Two Misconceptions about the Book of Esther," *CBQ* 39 (1977) 171-181. My sincere thanks to Prof. Jones for an off-print of his study and for his generous and helpful suggestions during the course of my research.

[85]Humorous elements in the Book of Esther were detected earlier by T. H. Gaster, "Esther 1:22," *JBL* 69 (1950) 381. My own suspicion is that Gaster and Jones are correct to detect humor in the scroll. Unfortunately, it is not always easy to discern where the narrator *intended* humor. Jones finds humor in the repetition and hyperbole of the story. I argue below, however, that these rhetorical devices serve other functions.

I do not wish to deny the possibility of the narrator's humorous intentions; rather, I point out only that what appears to us as humorous may not have been so intended. For example, Esth 5:14 reports that Haman constructed a gallows of 50 cubits, upon which to hang Mordecai. The exorbitant height of the gallows undoubtedly delighted ancient audiences and perhaps was intended to be amusing. On the other hand, the height of the gallows also could allude to Mordecai's importance and status in the narrator's eyes--an insignificant figure would not require a gallows of such impressive stature. Haman, then, unknowingly honors Mordecai with such a gallows. This honor gains an ironic significance by its location in the narrative, i.e., just prior to Haman's open honoring of Mordecai in Esther 6.

Similarly, Esth 2:12 details the year-long beauty rituals of the queen candidates. Is this description of harem life intended humorously? Are we to chuckle as we imagine the women immersed in perfumed oils for a full year? Or, are we to think of how much more attractive these already-beautiful women must appear after a year's devotion to their looks?

[86]Jones, "Two Misconceptions about the Book of Esther," 171.

[87]Ibid., 181.

[88]The probability of this view and the function of Purim in the narrative are considered in the next chapter.

[89]I would not deny the possibility of a lengthy history of transmission for the story or for its constituent traditions. The Book of Esther nevertheless displays a careful structure and a consistent literary style. These features are most easily explained by the assumption that the present form of the story comes from a single hand. The narrator may have composed his tale orally or in writing, although the text contains some features which are best explained by oral transmission. The use of such terms as "author" or "writer" distinguishes the narrator of this story from a teller of tales who created publicly and extemporaneously before an audience. On the latter, see Robert C. Culley, *Studies in the Structure of Hebrew Narrative* (Society of Biblical Literature Semeia Supplements 3; Missoula, Mont.: Scholars Press, 1976).

[90]We may summarize the evidence by noting that Purim's observance is confined to Esth 9:20-32. This passage displays stylistic and linguistic differences from the rest of the narrative. The limited role played by the casting of lots, from which the name of the festival purportedly derives, also suggests the artificiality of the connection between the story and festival. See Chapter II.

[91]A commonly held view is that the Book of Esther attained "canonical" status because of the popularity of Purim. But canonization was less a selective decision than a declarative act which acknowledged the inherent authority of a document. With respect to the story itself, the Talmudic discussion over the status of Esther suggests that some ancient rabbis were opposed to it. But the fact that such a discussion was recorded indicates that the story was popular in some circles. The additions of the LXX, the existence of two Targumim, and of numerous midrashim on Esther, testify to the story's popularity. Maimonides' verdict that the Torah and Esther would remain when the Messiah came points to the book's popularity among some medieval Jews. In addition, certain textual traditions locate the story immediately after the Pentateuch, perhaps suggesting its significance.

[92]This characterization perhaps extends to the entire narrative corpus of the Hebrew Bible. Various narratives possess certain features which belong to history and thus seem history-like. Certain segments of these narratives indeed may constitute dependable historical sources; but the degree of reliability varies between narratives and between segments within each narrative. Only in conjunction with evidence from external sources do the biblical narratives permit a reconstruction of any particular historical period. Unfortunately, we presently lack the type of external evidence necessary to reconstruct the historical event which several scholars believe gave rise to the Book of Esther.
On the relationship between "historical" and "history-like" in biblical narratives, see Hans Frei, *The Eclipse of Biblical Narrative* (New Haven: Yale University, 1974), especially chapter 1. Extremely helpful is the discussion of James Barr, "Story and History in Biblical Theology," *JR* 56 (1976) 5-7; also, Johannes Schildenberger, *Literarische Arten der Geschichtsschreibung im Alten Testament* (Schweizerische Katholische Bibelbewegung, Neue Folge, 5; Einsiedeln/Zurich/Cologne: Benziger Verlag, 1964) 17-19.

[93]See the discussion of G. Johannes Botterweck, "Die Gattung des Buches Esther im Spektrum neuerer Publikationen," *BibLeb* 5 (1964) 274-292.

[94]The terminology employed here is intended to be descriptive rather than prescriptive. The terminology which I suggest grows out of my own reading of the Book of Esther and may be limited in its application. A similar understanding of the term "motif," however, is suggested by Sylvia Barnet, Morton Berman and William Burto, *A Dictionary of Literary Terms* (Boston/Toronto: Little, Brown & Co., 1960) 57.

[95]I use the term "formulaic motifs" to distinguish between my use of the term "motif" in a broad sense and a narrower usage which also is common. What I call "formulaic motifs," for example, are labeled simply "motifs" by Donald Redford, *A Study of the Biblical Story of Joseph* (VTSup 20; Leiden: E. J. Brill, 1970).
Unfortunately, scholars have demonstrated little consistency in their use of such terms as "motif," "theme" or "formula." Robert C. Culley, *Oral Formulaic Language in the*

Biblical Psalms (Toronto: University of Toronto, 1967), indicates the variety of scholarly uses of these terms. Since the
terminology of other scholars is not totally applicable to
Esther's narrative style, I offer my own.

[96]That is, the "formulaic" aspects of these motifs are not
limited to specific types of word choice or phrasing. The
motif may be "formulaic" in the situation or context which it
either describes or presupposes. A common biblical motif which
I would call "formulaic" is that of the younger brother who
supersedes the older. Here, the formulaic aspect is less that
of linguistic components than of situation or context; in this
case, Yahweh's choice of the younger brother who therefore
proves much more successful than his sibling.

[97]Cosquin, "Le Prologue-cadre des Mille et une Nuits. Les
legendes perses et le Livre d'Esther."

[98]Judges 21:16-23 reports that certain Benjaminites chose
wives from among the Shiloh women who had gathered to observe
an annual festival. Is this report another variation of the
formulaic motif recorded in Esther?

[99]Certain other narrative features, e.g., Esther's adoption and introduction to court, despite her lowly origins, re-
semble legends about Semiramis. See the discussion of Ben
Edwin Perry, *The Ancient Romances* (Berkeley/Los Angeles: University of California, 1967) 356-357, n. 10.
   In some respects, the plot of Esther could be described as
an expansion of a formulaic motif of the beautiful Jewess who
wins the favor of the foreign ruler and prevents the destruction of her people. We find a similar story outline in the
Book of Judith. The similarities of these two narratives are
discussed in Chapter V.

CHAPTER II

DOMINANT MOTIFS: BANQUETS

According to Bernhard W. Anderson, the governing purpose
of the Book of Esther

> . . . is to explain and justify the celebration of
> a festival for which there is no basis in the Law,
> by appealing to "history" to furnish the reason for
> its origin and institution. Esther is a festal leg-
> end which attempts both to explain the origin of
> Purim and to authorize its continued celebration.[1]

Most scholars would agree with Anderson's estimation, and
with good reason. The narrated events directly lead to, and
explain, their festal commemoration in Purim. The festival
provides an important, if not primary, reason for the Esther-
Mordecai story.

The importance of the festival to the narrative account
cannot be denied. This impression is strengthened by the fact
that feasting, which especially characterizes Purim,[2] recurs
throughout the narrative. The Purim banquets, in fact, are
only the last of several feasts mentioned in Esther.[3] Banquets
provide the settings for several significant plot developments.
As such, they form an important motif in Esther, and one with
which we may begin our investigation.

A. משתה

The term משתה ("feast") is used almost exclusively to indicate the concepts of eating and drinking on special occasions. The term occurs 20 times in the Book of Esther, appearing only 24 times elsewhere in the Hebrew Bible. The frequency
of משתה itself suggests its importance in Esther.

The story begins with descriptions of two feasts prepared
by King Ahasuerus for his subjects. The monarch's first banquet includes "all his princes and servants," whom the author
identifies more specifically through the asyndetic, apposition-
al phrase, חיל פרס ומדי הפרתמים ושרי המדינות לפניו ("the administration of Persia and Media, the nobles and the governors of

31

the provinces in his service"). By contrast, the second banquet is reserved for הנמצאים בשושן הבירה למגדול ועד־קטן ("those
who resided in the acropolis of Susa, high and low alike").
The use of a merismus here indicates that everyone[4] in the
acropolis of Susa[5] was invited to the second banquet.

The all-inclusive nature[6] of the guest list to this second
banquet is reinforced by reference to a third feast. Esther
1:9 reports that Vashti hosted a banquet for the women, simultaneous to the king's banquet for Susa residents.[7] The terse
notice of Esth 1:9 assures the audience that the women were
included in the festivities. At the same time, it provides the
necessary backdrop to subsequent plot developments.

In some ways, the conclusion of Esther parallels its beginning:[8] just as the story begins with the description of a
feast, it ends with a portrayal of Purim and its festal banquet. The balance between the beginning and conclusion of
Esther becomes more apparent when we consider Purim's dates.
Most Jews in the empire celebrate Purim on Adar 14; but the
Jews of Susa observe the festival on Adar 15.[9] Purim, then,
consists of a one-day celebration marked by the festal meal.
The festal observance nevertheless entails two separate ban-
quets--the festal meal of Adar 14 and that of "Shushan Purim"
on Adar 15.[10] The Adar 14 feast, like the king's first banquet, includes residents of the various provinces. The king's
second banquet and the feast of "Shushan Purim," however, are
restricted to Susa residents.[11]

The initial and concluding pairs of banquets bear striking
similarities; yet they also suggest obvious differences. For
example, Ahasuerus' two banquets were not recurring events. By
contrast, Purim was to be observed each year and in every gen-
eration, even by future converts to Judaism (cf. Esth 9:27).
In addition, the king's banquets both were held in Susa, while
the Jews observed Purim in every province of the empire (cf.
9:27-28). The two banquet pairs thus contrast as well as correspond, and do not permit a direct parallel. They nevertheless provide a certain balance to the story.

In addition to these banquets, we find a third pair, viz.,
the feasts given by Esther for Ahasuerus and Haman. Do
Esther's meals continue the correspondence between banquet
pairs?

In Esth 1:1, the audience is introduced to Ahasuerus as
the monarch who rules over the 127 provinces of the empire,
from India to Ethiopia. Our initial encounter with the king
suggests an immediate association with the provinces. The following verse reinforces this association and gives the general
setting of the tale by reference to Ahasuerus' occupation of
the imperial throne. Again, we think of Ahasuerus in terms of
his rule over the provinces.

By contrast, we associate Haman, from his introduction in
3:1 to his death in 7:10, almost exclusively with the Susa
court. Only four occasions exist when Haman functions outside
of the court, and even these are court related. We thus find
mention of Haman in his home environment in 5:9-14, 6:12-14 and
7:9. On the first two occasions, Haman returns home in anger
after his confrontations with Mordecai. There he seeks advice
as to how he should respond to Mordecai's impertinences. Even
at home, Haman's concern is with court matters. In 7:9, Haman
is to be hanged on the gallows near his home, which he constructed for Mordecai. Again, the reference to Haman's home
reflects his life at court.[12]

At first glance, we find the continued differentiation between banquet guests suggested by the other pairs of feasts.
In the highly restricted guest list of Esther's banquets, Ahasuerus represents guests from the provinces while Haman represents those from Susa. This correspondence, however, seemingly
collapses when we note that *both* Ahasuerus and Haman are invited to Esther's banquets. The parallel is retained, however, by the precise language which the narrator employs.

In Esth 5:4, the queen invites the king and Haman to a
feast prepared "for him" (אשר־עשיתי לו). The referent of לו
("for him") in this phrase is ambiguous--perhaps intentionally
so, since the audience remains unsure at this point whether
Esther's invitation involves some scheme to save her people.
This ambiguity is resolved by the following verse which suggests that Haman was not informed of this banquet--an odd set
of circumstances if Haman was the guest of honor. The לו of
5:4 must refer to Ahasuerus, an understanding confirmed by
Haman's words to Zeresh in 5:12. Esther's first banquet, like
those of the other pairs, was designed for a guest from the
provinces.

34

If this understanding is correct, Esther's initial banquet
presents an ironic contrast to the banquet of Esth 2:18, where
משתה last occurred prior to Esther 5. There, the king prepared
a banquet for his officers and his servants in honor of Esther's coronation. Now, ironically, Esther's feast honors the
king, with the monarch's principal officer and servant as a
guest.

In contrast to her first banquet, Esther's second feast is
prepared "for them" (cf. 5:8). Both Ahasuerus and Haman are
guests of honor at this meal. This banquet, however, ironically proves to have been prepared in "honor" of Haman, whom
Esther exposes to the king as her adversary. Esther's second
banquet clearly is held with a specific Susa guest in mind.

The ironical contrasts between the story's feasts are not
limited to comparisons with Esther's banquets. Rather, irony
pervades the motif of banquets. For example, some suggest that
Ahasuerus' feasts were coronation banquets.[13] If this indeed
was the author's understanding, then the enthronement feast of
Ahasuerus proves to be the disenthronement banquet of his
queen. The banquet mentioned in Esth 1:9 provides the narrator
with an opportunity to eliminate the reigning queen.[14] The
term משתה next occurs in Esth 2:18. This משתה, like the preceding, is a queen's banquet; but in this instance, one for the
king's officials and servants in honor of the new queen. The
guest list for this feast is reminiscent of the king's banquet
in Esth 1:3-4, and Esther's coronation banquet suggests a parallel to the king's initial (coronation?) banquet. Simultaneously, it contrasts with Vashti's disenthronement feast, i.e.,
the king's second banquet.

The ironical contrasts between various banquets point to a
further correspondence between the pairs that mark the beginning, middle and conclusion of Esther. This correspondence is
found in the disempowering of influential personages. Esther's
second feast provides the occasion when Haman is stripped of
his power (cf. 7:1-10), just as Vashti was deposed as a result
of Ahasuerus' second banquet. On both occasions, the narrator
employs a similar term to indicate the abatement of Ahasuerus'
anger,[15] reinforcing our juxtaposition of these meals.

The feasts of Purim portray both the empowerment and the
disempowerment of individuals. Purim commemorates the reversal

of the expected fate of the Jews and the radical transformation
of a powerless people into one which inspires fear. This new-
found power is achieved at the expense of the "enemies" of the
Jews. Mordecai has authority to issue royal decrees and serves
as Haman's successor. The festal legislation itself results
directly from Mordecai's occupation of Haman's former post.
Purim thus marks the empowerment of the Jews and the disempowerment of their enemies. It further parallels Esther's second feast, the occasion of Haman's demise. The specific mention of the death of Haman's progeny on both Adar 14 and 15
(cf. Esth 9:7-10,14) enhances the continuity between these
feasts.

The banquets of Ahasuerus and those of Esther display a
further similarity: they are sponsored by royalty. If the
correspondence of these banquet pairs to the Purim feasts
holds, we might expect similar sponsorship of the Purim meals.
If one accepts Esth 9:29-32 as original,[16] Esther's participation in the institution of Purim suggests a continuation of
the parallel. Even if one denies the integrity of these
verses, there is evidence that the narrator portrays Mordecai
as a quasi-royal figure.[17]

If this understanding is correct, Esther's author constructed a tale whose beginning, middle and conclusion center
upon the motif of feasting.[18] In addition, each of these banquet pairs recalls the others, simultaneously paralleling and
contrasting with them.

B. Non-banquet Uses of שׁתה

There exist four additional uses of the root שׁתה in Esther. When contrasted with the motif of banquets, the non-
banquet uses of this root display certain ironies.

The first non-banquet use of שׁתה appears in 1:8 as the
hapax, וְהַשְּׁתִיָּה. Gerleman thinks this word is synonymous with
מִשְׁתֶּה.[19] He explains its peculiar form as the narrator's attempt to parallel the form of הַשְׁקוֹת in the preceding verse.
More probable, however, is the author's desire to establish a
verbal link with the following verse and a play on the queen's
name: וְהַשְּׁתִיָּה ... וַשְׁתִּי הַמַּלְכָּה.[20] This word play suggests a connection between Vashti and the "drinking" which highlights the

king's banquet--a link which subsequent events clearly establish.[21]

Esther 1:8 describes the "drinking" as being כדת אין
אנס.[22] Many commentators find this phrase problematic, since
"according to the law" contradicts "without compulsion."[23]
Gordis, however, is probably correct to translate, "drinking
was according to the principle of 'no compulsion' . . . ."[24]
His translation, however, does not preserve the nuance of דת.
This term occurs 19 times in Esther and always with reference
to a royal decree.[25] The sense here, particularly as it is
clarified by the words which follow, כי־כן יסד המלך ("for the
king had ordered"), indicates that the monarch issued special
commands to govern this special event. The author suggests an
ironical situation when even the nonregulation of drinking is
governed by royal decree.[26]

The brief flashback of Esth 1:8[27] indicates the law governing drinking is the king's command על כל־רב ביתו, "upon each
of his stewards." But the choice of words here is significant.
This concise phrase anticipates the question which dominates
1:10-22, viz., who is master in one's house. רב also connects
this anticipated scene with the "abundance" of royal wine mentioned in 1:7 which led to the king's demand for Vashti in
1:10-11.[28]

The drinking (השתיה) of Esth 1:8 is אין אנס, yet remains
strictly according to royal law. We learn, however, that while
the drinking is without compulsion and within the law, Vashti's
own lack of compulsion in obeying a royal summons is very much
against the law.

In addition to this non-banquet use of שתה in Esth 1:8, we
find two further instances of its use in the book. The root
appears as an inf. cstr. in Esth 3:15, and again in Esth 7:1.
No major plot developments take place during these references
to "drinking," but we again find them ironically contrasted.

In 3:15, the king and Haman sit down "to drink" and to
celebrate the forthcoming destruction of an allegedly disobedient people. Esther 7:1 again finds Ahasuerus and Haman
drinking, this time at Esther's second banquet where the fate
of this people again arises. The earlier occasion which
brought the king and his official together "to drink" was a
joint celebration. Their joint drinking in 7:1, however,

results in an abrupt cessation of their relationship. Esther
3:15 describes the king's and Haman's response to the publication of the edict; Esth 7:1 introduces events leading to the
decree's reversal.

The last instance where שתה occurs is Esth 4:16. There,
Esther commands Mordecai to instruct the Jews of Susa neither
to eat nor drink. Again, the presence of שתה is somewhat
ironic, since it is used in the context of a fast rather than a
feast. Equally ironic is the sandwiching of this non-feast use
of שתה between two "feasts of Esther"--those held *for* and *by*
Esther (2:18; 5:4-8). The latter instance is particularly
striking since Esther's command in 4:16 not "to drink" signals
her decision to intercede with the monarch. Having fasted herself, Esther risks her life to invite Ahasuerus to a feast!

C. Fasts

The auxiliary motif of fasting contrasts and highlights
the motif of feasting in Esther. A consideration of its use in
the story clarifies the importance and function of the motif of
banquets. A brief examination of this auxiliary motif thus is
useful to our discussion.

Fasting is unusual in Esther. It therefore is not surprising that the root צום, the most common term for fasting, is
found infrequently. The term occurs only four times in the entire scroll, two of those occurrences in the previously noted
contrast of Esth 4:16. The term also appears in 4:3 and 9:31,
although the latter may belong to a later addition.

The last example cited of the non-banquet use of שתה (Esth
4:16) suggests the manner in which the author contrasts feasting and fasting. The irony of Esther's intended fast, just
prior to her invitation to Ahasuerus and Haman for a feast, is
obvious. This ironic contrast, however, is reinforced in a
subtler fashion. In 2:9, Esther earns Hegai's special favor,[29]
which includes the receipt of "portions"[30] and the appointment
of seven women to serve her. Despite the use of the singular
imperfect, אצום, in Esth 4:16, these seven servants clearly are
included in the intended fast. The reference to the servants
in this context reinforces the contrast between Esther's feasts
and fasts: in 2:9, Esther receives special foodstuffs; in

4:16, she abstains from eating.[31]

The contrast to which 2:9 and 4:16 point also illustrates
the narrator's anticipatory style. Esther's receipt of Hegai's
special favor in Esth 2:9 anticipates the king's similar reaction to her upon their meeting. Even the appointment of Esther's seven maid-servants is reminiscent of the seven servants
and wisemen who personally minister to the king. Here, we find
a hint of Esther's forthcoming coronation as queen. One wonders if the fast of Esther and her servants in 4:16 hints at
the fast which they will observe when Esther exercises her own
royal power (cf. Esth 9:31). Does their abstinence from food
in the hope of Esther's favorable reception before the king
anticipate a later fast--one whose observance is bound up in
the joyful celebration of Esther's successful intercession? If
so, we detect a further contrast between feasts and fasts.

Two problems are engendered by my suggestion. The first
of these concerns the integrity of Esth 9:29-32. Virtually all
modern commentators view this passage as a subsequent addition
to the text.[32] Strong linguistic and stylistic evidence exists
to support such a view. Nevertheless, some consideration
should be devoted to internal evidence, prior to excising these
verses as secondary.

Since the narrator highlights his use of feasts through
the contrast of fasts elsewhere, it is not surprising to find
mention of a fast in connection with the Purim feasts. To the
contrary, we expect some suggestion of fasting, particularly in
light of the correspondence between the three pairs of banquets, some of which also are contrasted with fasts. A contrast between the joy of the Purim feasts and a preceding, commemorative fast maintains the internal harmony and structure of
the narrative. Even if 9:29-32 stems from a later hand, its
author is sensitive to the style and spirit of the tale.

The other problem with my suggestion concerns the precise
nature of Esther's fast in 4:16. I have understood its character to be one of hopeful anticipation. Esther and her servants
are joined by the entire Jewish community of Susa. Her request for a communal fast is unusual, for the Jews already observed a fast (cf. 4:3).[33] The new fast, then, does not differ
with respect to its participants.

Do the fasts of 4:3 and 4:16, however, differ in their

underlying intent? The fast of 4:3 is presented as an act of
mourning, the dreaded anticipation of a forthcoming catastrophe. By contrast, the fast of 4:16 precedes Esther's acknowledgment that she will intercede with the king. Her request for
this fast, in fact, indicates Esther's agreement to plead for
her people.

The communal fast of 4:16 may be similar in its purpose to
the fast of 4:3. That is, this fast may be a sign of mourning
in anticipation of Esther's expected fate. Esther's resigned
words in 4:16, וכאשר אבדתי אבדתי ("if I perish, I perish"),
suggest that she does not anticipate a favorable reception by
Ahasuerus. But her words also suggest that she retains the
slim hope that her intercession somehow will prove successful.
The fast of 4:16 thus represents a communal response to Esther's desperate act. The Jews fast in anticipation of Esther's fate; but also in the hope that, despite the odds, Esther will succeed in averting the catastrophe that awaits them.

The fast of 4:3 lacks the hopeful aspect of the second
communal fast. In this respect, the two fasts differ. The
Jews now fast in hopeful anticipation of the future--a future
whose earlier anticipation caused their fast of mourning in
4:3.

If this understanding of Esth 4:16 is correct, Esther's
author contrasts not only fasts with feasts but also fasts with
each other. Stylistically, then, the narrator utilizes an auxiliary motif of fasts in a manner similar to his use of the
dominant motif of feasts.[34]

D. Purim

Our discussion of the motif of feasting began with the
observation that Purim is of primary importance in Esther.
Following the anticipatory style of the narrative, we may conclude our analysis of feasts with an examination of Purim's
function in the story.

The narrative suggests that the name of the festival comes
from the word פור, "lot." The infrequency of the root פור in
Esther is somewhat surprising in light of Purim's importance to
the tale. The root occurs only eight times in the entire
scroll, usually in the festal name, "Purim." Even these

occurrences are basically restricted to Esth 9:20-32, which
treats the institution and regulation of the festival. According to 9:26, the festival's name is derived from the "lot" cast
by Haman to determine a date for the destruction of the Jews.
This reference recalls the earlier notice of Esth 3:7, which
constitutes the only mention of casting lots in the main body
of the narrative. The fact that casting lots plays no significant role in the narrated events[35] and that most occurrences of
the root פור are concentrated in 9:20-32 indicates the possibility of a later editorial hand.[36]

The integrity of 9:20-32 is not easily determined. Certain discrepancies arise when this passage is compared to the
rest of the narrative, suggesting its secondary nature. For
example, Esth 9:18-19 provides an etiological explanation for
the different dates of Purim. Yet Esth 9:21,27-28 suggests
that both dates are binding upon *all* Jews.[37] Even the reference in 9:24 to Haman's casting of lots diverges somewhat from
the earlier notice of 3:7 by adding לְהֻמָּם.[38] Esther 3:7, in
fact, suggests that someone other than Haman cast lots on
Haman's behalf, הפיל פור לפני המן. On the other hand, Esth
9:24 gives the impression that Haman himself cast lots.

The correspondence between banquet pairs itself indicates
that Purim is not incidental to the story. Rather, from its
beginning, the Book of Esther anticipates its conclusion in the
two-day festival. A two-day festival, already observed by the
narrator's own time, also explains the death and hanging of
Haman's progeny on successive days (Esth 9:6-10,13-14).
Whether this two-day festival, however, was known to our narrator as "Purim" is less clear. Did the storyteller himself
name this festival? If so, of what significance are the festival and its name to his story?

Apart from the casting of "purim" in Esth 3:7 and 9:24
(cf. 9:26)--references generally regarded as secondary--the
particular name of this festival seems neither indicated nor
required by the story. 2 Maccabees 15:36 mentions a "Mordecai's Day" which suggests that the festival was known in Palestine, but not by the name "Purim."[39]

How did the commemorative observance of events detailed in
Esther, then, come to be known as "Purim"? As indicated above,
some scholars sought solutions to this question in various

extra-Israelite festivals. But no convincing model for Purim
has been found. Nor have we any indication that the narrator
himself was aware of a non-Israelite festal origin. If the
author understood the festival to have a non-Jewish provenance,
or if he thought its name derived from a non-Hebraic term, we
might expect to find the festal name as ימי הפור, "Days of the
'Pur'." We probably would not find, however, the plural ימי
הפורים (cf. 9:28, 31; also דברי הפורים in 9:32).[40]

The author's own understanding of Purim therefore is probably not to be found in extra-Israelite traditions. Rather,
his understanding can be located only through whatever clues
are preserved by his account. Fortunately, we find two such
clues: the explanation given for the festal name, and the
customs which the narrator associates with Purim's observance.[41]

If current philological analyses of the term פור are correct, the word means precisely what our narrator claims, i.e.,
פור is synonymous with גורל ("lot").[42] If פור indeed means גורל
how does the term relate to the name of the festival?

To answer this question, it is necessary first to determine those customs associated with the festal observance. We
actually find three accounts of the celebration of Purim, that
of 9:16-19, a second account in 9:20-28, and a final description in 9:29-32. According to 9:17b, the Jews outside of Susa
"rested" on Adar 14, making it a day of feasting (יום משתה) and
joy (שמחה). The Jews of Susa observed Adar 15 in an identical
manner. According to this first report, then, Purim is characterized by the concepts of משתה, נוח and שמחה.

Esther 9:20-28 gives the name of the festival, "Purim,"
and adds that the festival was a יום טוב. More importantly,
this second account mentions the custom of sending "portions,"
משלוח מנות...ומתנות לאביונים (9:22). The edict issued by Mordecai in 9:21 instructs the Jews to observe annually that which
transpired. Esther 9:22a describes the new festival as the
days "on which the Jews enjoyed relief (נוח) from their foes,"
and the month "which had been transformed for them. . . ."
Verse 22b concludes Mordecai's instructions by indicating the
form of the observance. Mordecai's edict thus prescribes
Purim's date and gives its historical foundation and mode of
observance.

The Jews' response to Mordecai's edict is detailed in
9:23-28. The Jews adopted the practices "which they had begun
to practice," אשר־החלו לעשות. This phrase suggests the manner
in which the first Purim was observed as well as the Jews' compliance with an annual celebration. The following verses summarize Esth 3:1-9:13 in a catechetical fashion, again citing the
historical basis for the festival. As a somewhat awkward conclusion, Esth 9:26 indicates that "these days"--presumably the
annual observance--were named "Purim." Both the contents of
the letter and the events they had experienced motivate the
Jews to observe Purim.[43] This obligation also extends to future generations and "all who might join them" (9:27).

In addition to a slight variance in customs, Esth 9:20-28
differs from 9:16-19 in its discussion of Purim's relationship
to the narrated events. Esther 9:16-18 describes the initial
celebration which accompanied the events of Adar 14 and 15.[44]
Esther 9:20-28, however, suggests the institution of an annual
festival whose observance was incumbent upon all Jews. If our
narrator already was familiar with an annual festal observance, we might expect some mention of it. Loewenstamm undoubtedly is correct to observe that 9:28 "obviously served to conclude the scroll of Esther irrespective of whether we ascribe
it to the author of the original scroll or not."[45]

As indicated above, scholars are divided over the integrity of Esth 9:20-28. Our results thus far permit some tenta-
tive observations regarding this problem. First, it is not
surprising to find elaborations of the festal observance, particularly when Purim's observance includes two meals. Given
the importance of feasting in Esther, it would be surprising if
the scroll did not end with some mention of Purim and its banquets. We might be more surprised, in fact, if the Purim
feasts received only the brief mention of Esth 9:17-19 without
further comment. We expect the author to elaborate upon the
significance of the banquets, if only to remark that they became an annual event. We learn something of the nature of
other banquets in Esther, e.g., those of 1:3-9, and we expect
similar treatment of Purim's feasts. Here, we learn that the
"days of feasting and merrymaking" (ימי משתה ושמחה) are

occasions when "portions" are exchanged and "gifts" sent to the
poor. As we shall see below, the narrative function of other
motifs in Esther also recommends the retention of Esth 9:20-
28--or at least a similar passage--as a part of the original
story.

Purim legislation again is provided in Esth 9:29-32 which
introduces a law of fasting into the festal observance. Unlike
the legislation of Esth 9:20-28, the acceptance and observance
of Purim by the Jews play no significant role. Rather, the
introduction of a Purim fast constitutes the primary legal emphasis of these verses. Some scholars argue that the introduction of a fast serves as the *raison d'être* of this passage.
Yet it is odd that we find only passing reference to this new
law. If the intent of this passage was to introduce a new custom, we might expect greater attention devoted to it.

The precise emphasis of Esth 9:29-32, in fact, is not
clear; but it is worth noting that Esther is mentioned specifically for the first time since 9:13. This passage both begins
and ends with references to Esther's role in establishing Purim
(קים דברי הפורים האלה, v 29; לקים את אגרת הפורים, v 32). We
find a concern to clarify Esther's part in the institution of
Purim, and this may be the primary intention of the passage.
One problem with this understanding is the mention of Mordecai
in 9:29, implying that both Esther and Mordecai confirmed his
letter.[46] Mordecai's confirmation of his own law, however,
seems odd. Stranger still is the presence of a feminine, singular verb.[47] If we retain the MT, however, Esther continues
to receive credit, albeit shared credit, for the institution of
Purim.[48]

The textual problems of Esth 9:29-32 are even more complicated.[49] The initial verb of Esth 9:30, וישלח, suggests that
the reference to Mordecai in verse 29 is not secondary.[50] Also
problematic are the last three words of 9:30 which are variously interpreted. Robert Gordis argues that the phrase דברי
שלום ואמת, "words of peace and truth," forms the letter's initial formula of greeting, probably followed by the text itself.[51] The letter perhaps recapitulated the events leading to
the institution of Purim and urged its observance. According
to Gordis, 9:30 summarizes the bulk of the letter whose length
precluded its citation *in extenso*. There was no need to cite

its entire text, since the audience was familiar with the events it recounted. On the other hand, the following verse (v 31) contains a similarly constructed expression: דברי הצמות וזעקתם. The impression given by Esth 9:31 is that these "words of fasting and supplication" are the object of the verbs קים\קימו. Consequently, the "words of peace and truth" (9:30) might refer to the letter's content, not its greeting.

If this alternative understanding is correct, Esth 9:31 commands the observation of Purim at its appointed season. Authority for this command derives from the examples of Mordecai and Esther who obligate themselves and their descendants to fasts and supplications. Mordecai and Esther thus introduced a solemn, commemorative note to the Purim festivities.[52] It is feasible, given the contrasts elsewhere between feasting and fasting, that the joy of Purim should also recall and contrast with the solemnity of a fast.[53] Esther 9:32 concludes this passage with another reference to Esther's role in establishing Purim.

Recent commentators generally delete 9:29-32 as secondary. The textual difficulties of this passage, however, advise against deletion since we do not fully understand its content. The stylistic use of fasts elsewhere in Esther suggests that 9:29-32 approximates part of the original story. My own suspicion is that the present text of Esth 9:29-32 represents a reworking of an earlier version by a redactor who wished to affirm Esther's role in the authorization of the Purim legislation.[54] This later editor perhaps also saw the need for royal confirmation of Mordecai's authority to institute such legislation.[55]

The Book of Esther, then, contains three reports of Purim's observance, the last of which perhaps reworked an earlier tradition. Using these reports, we may characterize Purim as a period of "joy" (שמחה) and "rest" (נוח) from enemies. Purim is a "holiday" (יום טוב) celebrated through joyous feasts and reciprocal exchange of "portions" (מנות) and "gifts" (מתנות). In addition, the festival recalls narrated events by contrasting the joyous feasts with solemn fasts.

To return to our earlier question of how the narrator understood Purim's function, we may focus upon those features which characterize the festal observance. We already noted a connection between the Purim feasts and others in the tale. A similar connection between the story and festival is indicated by the Purim custom of sending "portions." As suggested above, Esther's receipt of "portions" from Hegai was a sign of her special favor with him.[56] In one sense, the Jews' sending and receipt of portions symbolize the special status they possess by the story's conclusion.

Purim's customary sending of portions also continues the feast/fast contrast. Within the context of Esther's receipt of portions from Hegai, the special favor she receives anticipates the king's later reaction to her. This, in turn, results in Esther's coronation feast (2:18). Esther 2:9, however, simultaneously contrasts with Esther's later fast in 4:16. Esther and her maid-servants are joined in their fast by the entire Jewish community of Susa. This communal fast is changed into a communal feast by the story's conclusion, viz., the feast of Purim. The Purim legislation contains two other occurrences of the term מנות (9:19, 22), and the limited use of this term contributes to the fast-feast contrast.[57] The exchange of portions also underscores the communal nature of Purim. With the feasts, it provides a suitable commemoration of the narrated events.

Gerleman notes that sending portions also characterizes the celebration mentioned in Neh 8:10-12. He speculates that sending portions represents a typical mode of celebration in the Jewish diaspora.[58] More importantly, he suggests a connection between sending portions and the festal name. The narrator refers to Purim as a plural form, ימי הפורים, rather than as a singular, i.e., ימי הפור. If the name of the festival, "Purim," relates to the sending of portions, מנות, its plural form makes sense.

Abraham Cohen offers a different explanation for the festal name. Commenting upon Y. Kaufmann's observation that biblical writers frequently subscribed to a dual causality of events (natural and divine), Cohen remarks:

> In the words of the megillah, *pur hu hagoral*, i.e., the *pur* is the lot, and it is the symbol of chance-fate. . . . God acts behind the veil of causality and chance, on behalf of the people of Israel. It is specifically to accentuate this point that the name of God is not mentioned in the megillah, while all the events are 'cast' to give the appearance of

chance-occurrences, or, *purim*.[59]

Cohen's observation that we attend to the narrator's own explanation for the meaning of פור, and presumably thus of "Purim," is not without merit. To this, we might add Gerleman's explanation for the festal name, which also seems reasonable, and ask: Is there any correspondence or connection between the terms מנות and גורל?

One such relationship is hinted, albeit negatively, by Jer 13:25. There we read: זה גורלך מנת־מדיך מאתי נאום־יהוה. Psalm 16:5 similarly juxtaposes the two terms: יהוה מנת־חלקי וכוסי אתה תומיך גורלי.[60]

Is it possible that the term מנות had a secondary meaning of "fate" (גורל)? Since "Purim" is characterized by the sending of "portions," the narrator--or a later editor--explained the name of the festival by reference to the other meaning of מנות, i.e., גורל ("fate" = פור, "lot"). He thus is correct to tell us that פור and גורל are synonyms and that the reversal of the Jews' "fate" is properly commemorated by sending "portions," מנות.

"Portions" (מנות) often signify special favor,[61] and sending portions in observance of Purim symbolizes the privileged status of the Jews in Ahasuerus' empire. This status is attained through the reversal of the Jews' גורל. Sending portions, then, suitably characterizes the celebration of the "Feast of Lots."

The reports of Esth 9:16-19 and 9:20-28 view Purim as a period when "rest" (נוח) was obtained from the Jews' enemies. We again may ask how obtaining "rest" relates to a festival called "Purim."

A linguistic connection between the concept of "rest" and the festal name is difficult to establish. But just as פור is related to מנות through the concept of גורל, the latter term may provide a link between נוח and פור. The terms נוח and גורל appear together in Ps 125:3 and Dan 12:13. The latter passage, in particular, points to "rest" as the גורל of the elect.[62] The "Feast of Lots," i.e., of פורים and גורלות, perhaps also suggests "rest" as the "fate" awaiting the Jews.[63]

In addition to the "rest" associated with Purim's celebration, we find two further uses of the root נוח in the Book of Esther. The first is found in Esth 2:18, in connection with

Esther's coronation. Esther's accession to power provides the occasion for a banquet, משתה, and for a הנחה[64] and the giving of משאת כיד המלך (= foodstuffs?; cf. Jer 40:5). Similar features characterize Purim, viz., feasting, rest and portions. It is striking that Purim symbolizes the Jews' empowerment, and the use of the infrequent term נוח in Esth 2:18 draws our attention to the parallel fates of Esther and her people.[65]

To summarize our discussion of the narrator's apparent understanding of Purim, the festival is the feast *par excellence* of the story. The connection between Purim's name and its mode of observance is not entirely clear although the stylistic use of the term "portions" suggests a possible link. The evidence also indicates that the festal name was no arbitrary choice and that "Purim" is aptly named.

Internal evidence also suggests that the festal legislation is integral to the story. Purim both commemorates, and at the same time symbolizes, events narrated in the rest of the book. Both the story and the festival portray the fate of the Jews: the former tells how the Jews were saved by the efforts of Esther and Mordecai; the latter celebrates their success and the defeat of the Jews' enemies. Purim's place in the story becomes particularly apparent when we note the narrator's use of a motif of feasts. Through this motif, he establishes a vital link between the events which lead to the institution of Purim, and its annual observance.

[1]Anderson, "The Book of Esther," 824.

[2]I shall argue below that feasting is one custom associated with the festal observance.

[3]The Purim feasts are considered in greater detail in the discussion which follows.

[4]The large number of guests invited to this banquet may not be an exaggeration. Neh 5:17 suggests that Nehemiah daily fed 150 Judeans and other guests; cf. Neh 5:14-18. Also see Herodotus' report that the Greeks who received Xerxes' army were forced to pay 400 talents daily to cover the cost of food (*Hist.* 7.118-119).

[5]The precise translation of בירה is difficult. The word is late and probably derives from the Assyrian *bîrtu*, "fortress" (cf. the Persian *bāru*). The Hebrew term is translated most commonly as "palace," "capital city" or "acropolis, citadel."

The suggested translation of "palace" is too limited for the setting of the narrated events, particularly since we often find בית מלכות or בית המלך to denote the palace structure. Compare also the use of ביתן in Esth 1:5; 7:7. The latter term may be equivalent to the Persian *apadana*, "throne room," referring to the public portions of the palace structure.

The translation, "capital city," is possible since Susa was a royal capital and spring residence by the time of Darius. This interpretation is particularly appropriate to Esther, since extensive renovations of the palace structures--implying more extensive use as a royal capital?--were undertaken by Xerxes.

The meaning, "acropolis, citadel," however, seems most applicable in Esther. A distinction is made between the בירה and the "city" in Esth 3:15; 4:1,6; 8:15. "Acropolis," which would encompass the palace structures, seems the best general understanding of the term בירה in Esther.

[6]The phrase, למגדול ועד־קטן, is translated in various ways: e.g., the *RSV*, "both great and small," similarly, the *KJV*; the *NEB*, "both high and low"; Moore, *Esther*, "for both the important and the unimportant alike"; Gordis, *Megillat Esther*, "whatever their position"; Dommershausen, *Die Estherrolle*, "vom Grössten bis zum Kleinsten," similarly Bardtke; Gerleman, *Esther*, "hoch und niedrig." The precise meaning of the phrase, however, is almost irrelevant. It is the all-inclusive nature of the invitation which the narrator stresses.

[7]Note the use of גם in Esth 1:9. The separate women's banquet presents an historical problem. We have no evidence that the ancient Persians secluded their women during banquets, a custom not introduced until the Islamic period. According to Plutarch, wives could be present at a banquet but would leave

50

when the drinking began. Perhaps related to this is Herodotus' suggestion that concubines, as well as wives, sat next to the men at Persian banquets. An obvious explanation for the women's banquet, however, is that it serves as a useful plot device.

[8]See the remarks of Bardtke, *Das Buch Esther*, 243; Dommershausen, *Die Estherrolle*, 128-129.

[9]This distinction is due to a second day of attack in Susa against the enemies of the Jews. This attack results in a one-day delay in the celebration of Purim, which then falls on Adar 15. This explanation probably is an etiological account of a custom already prevalent in the author's own time. We shall examine this possibility more fully below.

[10]But cf. Esth 9:20-21, which implies that Purim is to be observed by all Jews on *both* Adar 14 and 15.

[11]Esth 9:15-18 does not distinguish between the "acropolis" and "city" of Susa. Purim, like Ahasuerus' second banquet, has an all-inclusive nature; cf. Esth 9:23-32.

[12]One might argue that this judgment applies to all the characters in the story. Yet we receive glimpses of Mordecai apart from his conflict with Haman, e.g., in his dealings with Esther and the other Jews, and even with Ahasuerus. We similarly learn about Esther--certainly about her beauty and her obedience--prior to her appearance at court.

[13]Such an understanding is implied by the LXX, *b. Meg.* 11b and *Tg. Esth I*. See also Bardtke, *Das Buch Esther*, 278, n. 3.

[14]We are not told what became of Vashti. She apparently ceased to concern the author as an independent figure after her disenthronement. The fact that we are not told of her death has led to the suggestion that Vashti was not eliminated in this fashion; hence, the need to ban her further appearance before the king. But one could as easily speculate the converse, i.e., that she was killed. The notice of Vashti's banishment perhaps represents a humorous accommodation of imperial law to suit Vashti's crime. See also the comment of D. N. Freedman, cited by Moore, *Esther*, 14: "There is some irony in the fact that this decree [1:22] by which the king establishes the supremacy of the male in his own household initiates a story whereby the king having got rid of one recalcitrant wife ends up with one who controls him completely." Equally ironic is the fact that Ahasuerus, master of the Persian realm, is himself mastered by wine; cf. *kĕ* + inf. cstr. of *ṭôb* in Esth 1:10.

[15]The word used in Esth 2:1 is כְּשֹׁךְ, an inf. cstr. of שכך, "subside, abate." A similar usage is found in Gen 8:1, regarding the subsiding of floodwaters. A form of שכך, viz., שככה, occurs in Esth 7:10. These are the only occurrences of this root in Esther.

[16]The integrity of this passage is discussed below. The correspondence between the three pairs of banquets elsewhere

recommends serious consideration of the originality of this passage.

[17]See Chapter III.

[18]Dommershausen, *Die Estherrolle*, 24, suggests the importance of this motif in his analysis of the structure of 1:1-9. He finds a chiastic alternation of the roots שתה, מלך and עשה. After careful study, I am unable to detect any significance attached to the root עשה in Esther, although I concur with Dommershausen as to the importance of the roots שתה and מלך.

[19]Gerleman, *Esther*, 60.

[20]This word play also is noted by Jones, "Two Misconceptions about the Book of Esther," 174.

[21]This example of paronomasia anticipates events forthcoming in the narrative. Elsewhere, we shall note other uses of the author's anticipatory style. This particular play on words indicates that the Vashti traditions are integral to the narrator's account, *contra* Bardtke's view.

[22]Dommershausen, *Die Estherrolle*, 22, remarks that השתיה and דת serve as good introductions to that with which a Jew would be unfamiliar, viz., Persian drinking customs.

[23]The LXX apparently read כדת as a cstr., without the definite article. Moore, *Esther*, 7-8, follows the sense of the LXX by adding a negative. He translates: "the drinking was not according to the law, without compulsion."

[24]Gordis, *Megillat Esther*, 22-23. The principle of "no compulsion" is further explained by the words which follow, לעשות כרצון איש־ואיש ("to comply with each one's wishes"). The sense is that one could drink as he wished without compulsion to drink more nor restraint to drink less.

[25]Paton, *The Book of Esther*, 146; cf. Ezra 8:36.

[26]That the law of "no compulsion" results from Ahasuerus' personal decree adds an artistic touch: the audience associates the monarch with the concept of unlimited drinking, an idea which lies behind the events of Esth 1:10-22.

[27]Note the use of כי־כן throughout the Book of Esther.

[28]Note the syntax of the phrase, כטוב לב־המלך ("when the king was merry"; Esth 1:10). This clause is similar to that of Esth 1:2. The presence of the inf. cstr. in Esth 1:10 suggests the underlying cause of the king's disposition to be the abundant wine.

[29]The verb used to indicate Esther's receipt of Hegai's favor is נשא. A more common verb is מצא and the expression מצא חן ("find favor") is almost a stock-phrase. Some scholars argue that the use of נשא rather than מצא in this instance conveys a more active nuance than "finding favor." Moore, *Esther*, 21, notes that when Esther speaks to Ahasuerus in Esth

52

8:3,5, מצא is used as a self-demeaning, and thus flattering, expression. Esther depends upon the king's good will and reflects proper court etiquette. But in describing Esther's effect upon others, as in Esth 2:15,17; 5:2, the narrator employs נשא to indicate that Esther herself earned the deserved favor.

[30]More is said below concerning the use of מנות, "portions."

[31]The only other reference to Esther's servants occurs in 4:4, again within the context of fasting; cf. 4:1-3.

[32]The most thorough discussion of Esth 9:29-32 is found in Samuel E. Loewenstamm, "Esther 9:29-32: The Genesis of a Late Addition," *HUCA* 42 (1971) 117-124. See also Bruce William Jones, "Rhetorical Studies in the Book of Esther: The So-Called Appendix," paper delivered to the Society of Biblical Literature, Chicago, October 31, 1975. Jones takes exception to the view that Esth 9:20-10:3 is a late addition to the text. I am grateful to the author for a copy of his paper.

[33]Compare the language used to describe the fast of Esth 4:3 and the feast of Esth 8:17:

ובכל-מדינה ומדינה	ובכל-מדינה ומדינה
מקום אשר דבר-המלך	ובכל-עיר ועיר
ודתו מגיע	מקום אשר דבר-המלך
אבל גדול ליהודים	ודתו מגיע
צום ובכי ומספד	שמחה וששון ליהודים
	משתה ויום טוב
(Esth 4:3; cf. Joel 2:12)	(Esth 8:17)

The striking similarity of wording suggests that the fast of 4:3 finds its antithesis in the feast of 8:17.

[34]Is this pair of fasts (Esth 4:3,16) meant to correspond to the pairs of banquets? Crucial plot developments take place in connection with these banquet pairs. It thus is significant that Esther's crucial decision to intercede with the king is sandwiched between these two fasts.

[35]See the remarks of Bardtke, *Das Buch Esther*, 317; Gerleman, *Esther*, 92; Dommershausen, *Die Estherrolle*, 132; Abraham D. Cohen, "'Hu Ha-goral': The Religious Significance of Esther," *Judaism* 23 (1974) 88. The reference to the casting of lots in Esth 3:7 is not clear until the explanation of 9:24. This fact indicates a connection between the two verses.

[36]Divergent opinions are expressed with respect to the origin of these verses. While allowing for some glosses, the following scholars accept the integrity of Esth 9:20-32: Bardtke, *Das Buch Esther*; Gerleman, *Esther*; Anderson, "The Book of Esther"; Dommershausen, *Die Estherrolle*; Moore, *Esther*. Jones, "Rhetorical Studies in the Book of Esther: The So-Called Appendix," retains the passage on rhetorical-stylistic grounds. Scholars who reject Esth 9:20-32 as secondary include Paton, *The Book of Esther*, André Barucq, *Judith, Esther* (La Sainte Bible; Paris: Cerf, 1959); Loewenstamm, "Esther

9:29-32: The Genesis of a Late Addition."

[37]Bardtke, *Das Buch Esther*, 392, thinks Esth 9:20 retains a distinction between Susa and the provinces. This is not clear from the text and could not apply, in any case, to Esth 9:27-28.

[38]Is לַהֲמָם an intentional play on the villian's name?

[39]The reference to "Mordecai's Day" in 2 Macc 15:36 raises questions concerning its relationship to Purim and/or Nicanor's Day. The latter commemorates the Jews' victory over their foes and is observed on Adar 13. We should note that Purim is not celebrated on the dates of the actual battles, but on the following days, viz., Adar 14 and 15.
The possible connection between Purim and Nicanor's Day is examined by H. E. del Medico, "Le cadre historique des fêtes de Hanukkah et de Purim," *VT* 15 (1965) 254-267; and Schneider, "Esther Revised According to the Maccabees," 190-218. Schneider concludes that the events narrated in Esther originally were recalled on Adar 14 by some Jewish groups and on Adar 15 by others. Later, legislation was added to transform the festival into a two-day general observance. Schneider reaches his conclusion on the basis of 1 and 2 Maccabees. Unfortunately, I am unable to discover similar evidence in those texts.

[40]Gerleman, *Esther*, 27.

[41]These two starting points for an investigation of Purim are suggested by Würthwein, *Die Fünf Megilloth*, 170-172. My findings, however, differ substantially from those of Würthwein.

[42]Virtually all scholars now accept the basic thesis of J. Lewy, "Old Assyrian *puru'um* and *pūrum*"; see also, idem, "The Feast of the 14th Day of Adar." Lewy finds a double etymology for "Purim"--one from the Assyrian *purruru*, "to destroy," and a second from *pùru*, "to cast lots." Lewy also notes that most occurrences of *pūrum*, or the variant *puru'um* in Assyrian texts are found with accompanying references to nuisance or danger. The term *pūrum* thus "has the sense of 'ill fortune' or 'great calamity' which is attaching also to English 'lot' and German 'Los'" ("Old Assyrian *puru'um* and *pūrum*," 121).
See also the discussions of Bea, "De origine vocis פּוּר," 198-199; Würthwein, *Die Fünf Megilloth*, 170-171. Würthwein suggests that the philologically correct correspondence between פּוּר and גּוֹרָל indicates only linguistic knowledge at one level of transmission. It does not denote a connection between the casting of lots and the festival's name. Rather, the festal name was no longer understood by the narrator's own time, nor during that of the redactor responsible for the etiologies of Esth 3:7; 9:24,26. A similar opinion is held by Hayyim Schauss, *The Jewish Festivals* (Cincinnati: Commission on Jewish Education of the Union of American Hebrew Congregations and the Central Conference of American Rabbis, 1938), 312, n. 288.

[43]Note the order of the cited reasons: Purim's observance is based upon the letter, then upon the historical experience. This order is closer to that suggested by Esth 9:20-23 than to

the sequence of events narrated in the story.

[44]This evaluation, of course, is not applicable to the etiology of Esth 9:19. The MT lacks any information regarding the celebration of Purim in walled cities. This information is supplied by the LXX which indicates that city dwellers celebrate Adar 15 in a similar fashion, i.e., by exchanging "portions" with their neighbors. Schneider, "Esther Revised According to the Maccabees," 200, n. 27, notes that the word for "fourteen" in the Greek verse which corresponds to the MT is written in full. The following number, "fifteen," however, is in figure form.

[45]Loewenstamm "Esther 9:29-32: The Genesis of a Late Addition," 117.

[46]Moore, *Esther*, 95-96, interprets this passage differently and thinks Mordecai's name resulted from an unwillingness to minimize his importance. One might hold both views concurrently and argue that both Mordecai and Esther are to be credited with Purim's institution and regulation. The plausibility of such divergent views underscores the obscurity of this passage.

[47]Many scholars transpose the words מרדכי היהודי after תקף, or eliminate them completely. Loewenstamm, "Esther 9:29-32: The Genesis of a Late Addition," 117, objects to such emendations on the grounds that they are unsupported by the LXX. But the text of the LXX differs from the MT throughout Esth 9:29-32. Verses 28-32 are lacking in the Lucianic and the Old Latin omits vv 30-32. Because of the divergences among the ancient versions, their reliability as witnesses to the Hebrew text is limited.

[48]Perhaps Mordecai is cited along with Abihail as part of Esther's family tree. Such a reading diverges from the genealogy given in Esth 2:15. Yet a later editor could understand Esther to be the daughter of both men--Abihail, her natural father, and Mordecai, her adoptive father.

[49]The content of the document also is subject to dispute. The phrase, את-כל-תקף, generally is understood in an adverbial sense, e.g., "emphatically," "forcefully," "mit allem Nachdruck." Paul Haupt, "Critical Notes on Esther," *Old Testament and Semitic Studies* ([Festschrift William Rainey Harper], 2 vols.; ed. Robert Francis Harper, Francis Brown and George Foot Moore (Chicago: University of Chicago, 1908) 2.190-191, believes that such expressions are represented in Hebrew by the phrase בכל תקף.

Loewenstamm, "Esther 9:29-32: The Genesis of a Late Addition," maintains that Haupt's observation never was refuted in a convincing manner. Both scholars view the construction of תכתב...את as anticipating the object of the verb. Loewenstamm begins his own analysis with this feature in mind and suggests that the word sequence of the phrase את אגרת הפורים הזאת recalls the words פורים and האגרת הזאת (9:26). He argues that 9:29 takes up v. 26 with the information that "this Purim epistle" was written by both Esther and Mordecai, not by Mordecai alone. He continues his argument by comparing the MT and LXX of 9:29. This comparison suggests to him that the term תקף

points to something written, i.e., to a "deed of legal
strength." Such an understanding is confirmed by a secondary
meaning of the Akk. *dannatu* and some Nabataean inscriptions.
        Haupt's suggested reading strikes the ear as a convention-
al manner of expression. Nevertheless, the imposition of a
prescriptive norm for Esther's Hebrew, which abounds in *hapax
legomena* and idiomatic expressions, is a dangerous procedure
without solid support from the ancient versions. Loewenstamm's
suggestions of such proof are problematic. He places too great
a value on the LXX which, as indicated above, diverges substantially from the MT of Esther 9. Loewenstamm thus conveniently
deletes the words לקים and שנית. In addition, Loewenstamm's
translation of תקף ignores the usages found in Dan 11:17 and
Esth 10:2 (parallel with גבורתו), which recommend the usual
reading. Finally, Loewenstamm himself acknowledges on 119, n.
11, that his suggested interpretation of תקף in the Nabataean
inscriptions is disputed.

        [50]This verb, however, is often emended: Dommershausen,
Die Estherrolle, 133, retains the form of the MT but interprets
the verb impersonally; G. R. Driver, "Problems and Solutions,"
VT 4 (1954) 237, emends to a niphal, cf. the Vulgate and
Syriac; Haupt, "Critical Notes on Esther," 190-191, reads a qal
fem. sing. imperf.

        [51]Gordis, "Studies in the Esther Narrative," *JBL* 95 (1976)
57-58.

        [52]Many think this fast alludes to Esth 4:3, 16. For exam-
ple, Loewenstamm, "Esther 9:29-32: The Genesis of a Late Addition," 123-124, understands Esth 9:31 to imply that "as the
Jews were ready to fast in the days of their distress, they
should be willing to rejoice on the anniversary of their deliverance in accordance with the decree of Esther and Mordecai."
Loewenstamm cites--and ignores!--Rashi's observation that the
fasts of Esth 4:3 and 4:16 considerably precede Adar 13, when
the new fast is observed. But Rashi's cogent objection loses
force if we attend to the stylistic use of fasting in Esther.
The fasts of Esth 4:3, 4:16 and 9:31 anticipate or recall each
other, and contrast with various feasts. The purpose of Esth
9:31 is not the institution of a fast as part of the Purim observance so much as a continuation of the contrast between
fasting and feasting. Both commemorate narrated events. Such
an understanding perhaps explains the limited attention to the
"institution" of a fast.

        [53]Esth 9:29-32 perhaps presupposes knowledge of Zech 8:19.
The latter passage connects the command to love "peace and
truth" (cf. Esth 9:30) with the reversal of days of fasting into days of joyous celebration. Zech 8:19, too, indicates a
contrast between feasting and fasting with the institution of
new holidays.

        [54]But see the argument of J. C. H. Lebram, "Purimfest und
Estherbuch," *VT* 22 (1972) 208-222.

        [55]As I hope to demonstrate below, the original narrator
would not need to secure royal authorization for Mordecai's
law. Other evidence which points to a late date for Esth

9:29-32 consists of the omission of any reference to fasting in the LXX, Josephus or the Old Latin. The plural form, צֹמֹות, is not found elsewhere in the MT, although Marcus Jastrow lists its use in post-biblical Hebrew; see *A Dictionary of the Targumim, the Talmud Babli and Yerushalmi, and the Midrashic Literature* (New York: Title, 1943) 1267. The cumulative weight of the evidence indicates that Esth 9:29-32 stems from a later hand. Yet the later redactor preserves the contrast between feasting and fasting. This fact suggests a familiarity with an earlier tradition at this point.

[56]מנות also is used elsewhere to indicate special favor, e.g., 1 Sam 9:23; 2 Kgs 25:30; Dan 1:1-5; and negatively, Jer 13:25. The passage in 2 Kings is of particular interest with its notice that Jehoiachin ate at the Babylonian king's table as a sign of favorable treatment. In addition to the fact that Mordecai is identified as one exiled with Jeconiah in Esth 2:6, the absence of further comment upon 2 Kgs 25:30 suggests that dietary laws were not incumbent upon Jews at a foreign court. Such a view contrasts with the portrayal of Daniel 1 which perhaps arose in a circle of Jews especially concerned with such matters.

[57]Moore, *Esther*, liv, writes that Esther's "Hebrew vocabulary is scarcely what might be called rich," and that the narrator repeatedly uses the same verbal roots in his narration. The repetition of less common terms at key points thus deserves our notice. Their infrequency itself reinforces the juxtaposition of earlier and later incidents.

[58]Gerleman, *Esther*, 25-27.

[59]Cohen, "'Hu Ha-goral': The Religious Significance of Esther," 89. More is said below regarding "chance-occurrences" in the story.

[60]Reference perhaps can be made to Isa 65:11. Neither term occurs in this passage, but we do find the word מני. BDB, 584b, refers this term to a god of fate, probably related to the god מנותו of the Nabataean inscriptions.

[61]See above, n. 56.

[62]The concept of election in the Book of Esther is discussed below in Chapter VI.

[63]The concept of "rest" frequently accompanies Israel's conquest of its enemies; cf. Deut 25:19; Josh 21:44; 2 Sam 7:10-11; 1 Kgs 5:18; Isa 63:14; 1 Chr 22:9; 2 Chr 14:6. Deut 25:19 is particularly significant since the attainment of rest from the enemies is linked to the destruction of Amalek. As we shall see below, Israel's conflict with Amalek plays a role in the confrontations between Mordecai and Haman. Gerleman, *Esther*, comments on Esth 9:15-19 that Purim does not recall the battle between the Jews and their enemies. The storyteller refers only to "resting" after the siege. The link between the conquest of enemies and the concept of rest explains the narrator's lack of reference to the battle itself.

[64]הנחה occurs only here and could be patterned after an Aramaic causative infinitive. Not surprisingly, its translation varies. See the remarks of Moore, *Esther*, 25. Herodotus, *Hist.* 3.67, reports a suspension of taxes and military conscription with the coronation of the false Smerdis. He also suggests the Persian custom of releasing debts owed to the crown when a new king came to power (*Hist.* 6.59).

[65]The hiph. of נוח appears again as a part of Haman's accusation against the Jews (Esth 3:8). Haman charges that it is not beneficial for Ahasuerus להניחם. Discussion of this third and final use of נוח in Esther must be postponed to Chapter IV below.

CHAPTER III

DOMINANT MOTIFS: KINGSHIP AND
OBEDIENCE/DISOBEDIENCE

A. *The Motif of Kingship*

The motif of banquets is central to the Book of Esther,
and feasts provide the setting for major plot developments. Of
particular interest are three banquet pairs which both compare
and contrast with each other.

In Chapter II, I argued that the Purim feasts, like those
of Ahasuerus and Esther, were hosted by royalty. In the Masoretic account, Esther plays a role in issuing the Purim legislation (cf. 9:29-32). In addition, the scroll depicts Mordecai
as a quasi-royal figure. We now may examine these claims in
detail to determine the sense in which the feasts of Purim represent "royal" banquets.

The Book of Esther clearly is concerned with the concept
of kingship, and the story itself is presented as a court tale.
The importance of this motif is indicated by the frequency of
the root *mlk* which occurs over 250 times in the 167 verses of
Esther.[1] The most frequent use of this root is in the titles
"king" and "queen." These titles regularly occur without an
accompanying proper name, the context clarifying the referent.[2]

The title "king," however, does not always apply to Ahasuerus. For example, Esth 2:6 refers to "Jeconiah, king of
Judah," who was exiled by "Nebuchadnezzar, king of Babylon."
Similarly, Esth 10:2 mentions the annals of the "kings of Media
and Persia," against which the audience is invited to check the
story's veracity. These references to other kings show that
kingship is not restricted to the reigning monarch.

The word *malkût* is frequent in Esther, most often in con-
struct with some other term (e.g., wine, palace, diadem, word,
law, throne). *Malkût* is common as an adjective to denote
either possession or a royal quality. But the author sometimes
uses the word *malkût* in a remarkable fashion. For example,
מלכותה occurs in Esth 1:19, again referring royal power to

someone other than the reigning king. This reference is set
within the context of Memukhan's advice that Vashti's position
be given to another. The use of מלכותה here introduces the
prospect of Esther's coronation and suggests her possession of
royal authority.

Esther's royal power, anticipated by Esth 1:19, becomes a
central issue in the tale. This matter again arises in Esth
4:14, when Mordecai asks, ומי יודע אם־לעת כזאת הגעת למלכות
("who knows whether you have attained to royal position for
just such a time"). Mordecai's question draws our full attention to the issue of Esther's power and sets the stage for subsequent scenes where Esther's power plays a significant role.
His question also reminds the audience that Esther, who thus
far appears as a passive, obedient figure, possesses power in
her own right.

Esther's power becomes evident in the king's reception of
her (Esth 5:1-5). Unsummoned appearances before the king normally warrant death. Yet Esther is not punished at all; instead, she is rewarded by the king's promise of up to half the
kingdom (malkût).

Esther's influence becomes increasingly apparent with the
progression of the tale.[3] For example, when Esther eventually
indicates her request to Ahasuerus that her people be spared,
the king's initial response is one of outrage--not at Esther's
petition, but at the villain who presumes to jeopardize the
queen (7:5).

Haman further enrages the king by what appears to be a
personal attack against Esther. Despite his office and personal influence with Ahasuerus, Haman dies for his actions. That
Esther's standing with the king is responsible for Ahasuerus'
response is evident from the king's indifference to the fate of
other threatened persons (cf. 3:8-11; 9:12-14). Esther even
receives permission to destroy the Jew's powerful enemies and
to authorize a second day of attack.

Esther, too, is personally responsible for Mordecai's promotion: ומרדכי בא לפני המלך כי־הגידה אסתר מה־הוא לה ("Mordecai
came before the king, for Esther had revealed how he was related to her"; 8:1). She, not Ahasuerus, transfers Haman's
possessions to Mordecai. Esther 1:19 and 4:14 correctly hint at
Esther's power. Stylistically, their use of the root mlk also

suggests a contrast: the former anticipates Vashti's disempowerment; the latter, Esther's increasing power, evidenced by
subsequent events. Esther's power and her participation at
Purim's institution suggest that the festal meals indeed are
royal banquets.

Another unusual use of *malkût* appears in Esth 3:8. Haman
addresses Ahasuerus in the second person (מלכותך) and his inti-
macy with the monarch indicates Haman's favored status. The
king again is addressed in the second person in Esth 7:3, this
time by Esther. These unusual instances of second person address provide an interesting contrast: in Esth 3:8, Haman requests the destruction of the Jews; in 7:3, Esther asks that
they be spared. These two examples also underscore the contrast in the speaker's power. Despite Haman's standing with
Ahasuerus, Esther clearly holds greater influence.

Of particular interest is the use of *malkût* in reference
to clothing. The phrase כתר מלכות applies to Vashti's regalia
(Esth 1:11) and symbolizes Esther's new status (Esth 2:17).
The application of the phrase to both queens heightens the contrasts between them.

The phrase, כתר מלכות, also occurs in Esth 6:8, a difficult verse not yet satisfactorily explained. The general context of Esth 6:8 suggests that the phrase, ואשר נתן כתר מלכות
בראשו, describes a horse. Yet it seems odd that the horse, not
its rider, wears a crown. Not surprisingly, several ancient
versions solve this problem by deletion.

Those commentators who retain this passage explain it in
various ways. Bardtke cites the Assyrian palace reliefs at
Nineveh and Chorsabad which display a horse bedecked with
crown.[4] In light of these palace reliefs, Bardtke argues that
the crowning of a horse in Esth 6:8 is reasonable.[5] One nevertheless expects the wearer of the king's clothing and the bear-
er of the royal diadem to be identical. Gerleman sees the in-
definite nuance of the relative particle as the root of our
difficulty.[6] He follows the Syriac and interprets אשר tempo-
rally (cf. Gen 40:13; 1 Kgs 8:9; Jer 29:19; Ps 139:15; 2 Chr
35:20). In this manner, Gerleman understands Haman to request
the requisition of a royal robe like that worn by the king, and
the horse upon which the king rode at the time of his coronation.

A different interpretation is offered by Oswald T. Allis,[7] who interprets אשר as a substantive which contains its pronominal antecedent.[8] He finds an allusion to the coronation regalia and translates, "even he upon whose head a royal diadem was placed." In a word, Haman asks for a garment and a horse used by the king, the wearer of the crown. He does not ask to wear the diadem itself, but would have a robe and horse that a crowned king has used.

From the perspective of linguistic usage and intelligibility, both referents (horse and man) are possible. At present, it remains difficult to determine which is more appropriate. More importantly, it does not seem necessary. The question of who wears the crown in Esth 6:8 is insignificant since both meanings have identical force. To wear the king's robe and ride the king's horse signals the great favor in which an individual stands.[9] A crown upon a horse or a crown upon the man clearly indicates that the individual wears the regalia.[10]

Of greater concern is the significance of Mordecai's reward. Does Mordecai's public appearance in the king's robes imply only a great honor? Probably not. Even in Persian times, the king's robe was considered to be uniquely his own, imparting his aura. An etiological legend known to Xenophon relates that Cyrus received the Median king's crown and robe when he married the king's daughter. These were more than the symbols of kingship, and in later times we find reference to the "Robe of Cyrus" as possessing supernatural, magical powers. This garment was thought to have been worn by Cyrus at his coronation at Parsargadai, later described by Plutarch as teletē. Plutarch's characterization almost suggests a mystery rite with an implied metamorphosis of the king.[11] Similarly, when Cyrus the Younger plotted to murder his recently crowned brother, he refused to let the blow be struck while Artaxerxes wore the coronation robe.[12] The talisman-quality of the king's robe was retained even when the garment was worn out. Plutarch tells of Teribazus' crime, viz., his wearing of Artaxerxes' torn robe.[13] Even in an imperfect condition, the king's robe retained its special power.

In the Greek period, a similar significance was attached to the king's garment. Alexander insisted upon wearing Median dress, if not the robe of a Persian king, to convince the

Persians that he possessed the attributes of a Persian monarch.
1 Maccabees 6:15 reports that Antiochus IV bequeathed his crown
and robe to the regent responsible for raising his successor.
The significance of the king's robe thus was known in some Jewish circles.

The belief that a king's garment possessed special significance, if not magical power, was widespread in the ancient
world. The manner by which Mordecai is honored in Esther 6
thus suggests more than a simple reward of his deed. This impression is strengthened by the similar phraseology employed in
Esth 6:8 and 2:17. כתר מלכות בראשו ("a royal diadem upon his
head") in Esth 6:8 recalls כתר־מלכות בראשה ("a royal diadem upon her head") of Esth 2:17, the only occurrences of such
phrases in Esther.

We must ask, however, whether it is plausible that Ahasuerus would allow someone to wear his robes if they possessed
such great significance. Some commentators think Ahasuerus ex-
emplifies a capricious fool,[14] and perhaps Esth 6:8 provides a
further example of the monarch's personality.[15] Even if this
is not the case, Mordecai's reward is not implausible when we
recall the audience to which Esther was addressed. A Jewish
audience, living under foreign rule, undoubtedly delighted in
any allusion to royal power secured by the Jews at the expense
of the ruling administration. Moreover, Esth 6:8 is no less
plausible than other events of the story, e.g., the decree
ordering all men in the empire to be masters of their homes
(1:22), the permission, given a full year in advance, to destroy an entire people (3:12-15), or the king's return to Esther's banquet at the precise moment that Haman is prostrate
upon Esther's couch (7:8). One could also point to the implausible "coincidences" which lead to Mordecai's honor: the
king's insomnia (6:1); the reading of the specific passage concerning Mordecai's service to the king (6:2); Haman's early
appearance at court (6:4); and Haman's assumption that the
honor applies to himself (6:6).[16] In short, the implausibility
of Mordecai's reward is no greater than that of other narrated
events.[17]

Esther 6:8 intimates that Mordecai's appearance in the
regalia signifies "royal" status. This impression is reinforced by Esth 8:15, where Mordecai again appears in regal

attire (בלבוש מלכות). Unlike the earlier report of Esth 6:8,
Mordecai clearly wears a crown (עטרת זהב גדולה).[18] What appears to be ambiguous in Esth 6:8 is made clear in Esth 8:15:
Mordecai appears in his own לבוש מלכות.[19] Moreover, this portrayal follows the notice that Mordecai issued his own edict
with full royal authority. Mordecai both looks and acts like a
king. It is only as we look back from the later to earlier
passages that the implications of Esth 6:8 become clear.

Mordecai's appearance in royal garb is not the only indication of his status. Rather, our narrator hints early in his
tale that Mordecai is of royal descent. Esther 2:5 introduces
Mordecai as בן יאיר בן־שמעי בן־קיש איש ימיני ("son of Jair, son
of Shimei, son of Kish, a Benjaminite"). Mordecai's relationship to these other figures is not clear. Josephus, *Megilla*
and the Targumim, however, understood Shimei and Kish to be his
remote ancestors. This view is followed by most commentators,
despite our uncertainty whether the ancient interpreters were
correct.[20]

"Shimei" is mentioned several times in the Bible, notably
as an opponent to David's kingship (cf. 2 Sam 16:5). "Kish"
also occurs often, although the name is best known as that of
Saul's father. Both names recall the figure of Saul, and their
occurrence together in Esth 2:5 reinforces the impression that
Mordecai descends from this Israelite king.

We know of no familial connection between Shimei and Kish.
Nevertheless, Esther's author cites their relationship, suggesting either a fabrication of Mordecai's genealogy or a tradition with which we are unfamiliar. If Mordecai's genealogy
is fictitious, we can only wonder at the narrator's choice of
ancestors. He could easily have assigned Mordecai a direct
Saulide descent[21]--or for that matter, any other. On the other
hand, the narrator's choice of ancestors seems more reasonable
if he merely cites a tradition known to him. An examination of
the biblical genealogies suggests one manner by which such a
tradition could have developed.

The names "Shimei" and "Kish" were common in ancient Israel. For example, 1 Kgs 4:18 mentions a Benjaminite Shimei
(cf. 1 Chr 8:21), perhaps referring to the figure cited in
1 Kgs 1:8 (cf. 1 Chr 3:10-19). This Shimei, like the figure
mentioned in 2 Samuel, was embroiled in a dispute over the

monarchic succession. In this instance, Shimei supported Solomon in his conflict with Adonijah. It is striking that both cases involved a Benjaminite Shimei in a succession controversy.

Shimei, however, also is found as a descendant of the tribes of Simeon (1 Chr 4:24-26), Reuben (1 Chr 5:4) and Levi (Exod 6:17; Ezra 10:23, 33; 1 Chr 6:2; 23:7; 2 Chr 29:14; 31:12-13). The Joseph tribe is represented indirectly by 2 Sam 19:21 where the anti-Davidic Shimei--a few verses earlier described as a Benjaminite--refers to himself as a member of the house of Joseph. The Chronicler supports this view, for before citing the Reubenite Shimei, he notes that Reuben's birthright was given to Joseph (1 Chr 5:4). The Chronicler also mentions a Shimei of Ramath (1 Chr 27:27), although it is not clear if this Shimei is identical to some other identified by him.

Certain of these genealogies are of particular interest. For example, 1 Chr 3:10-19 lists Shimei as the great-grandson of Jeconiah, the exiled king with whom Mordecai is associated in Esth 2:6. 1 Chronicles 4:34-43 reports that the sons of Shimei destroyed the Amalekites.[22] This notice demonstrates continued interest in Israel's conflict with Amalek during a later period.[23]

The identity of Kish also is obscure. 1 Sam 14:51 lists the Benjaminite family of Saul, citing Ner as the brother of Kish, the father of Saul.[24] This tradition coincides with that of 1 Samuel 9. The Chronicler, however, offers a slightly different list in 1 Chr 9:35-44. He cites Ner as Saul's grandfather, not uncle (cf 1 Chr 23:21; 2 Chr 29:12). It also is striking that 1 Chr 9:35-44 lists Kish and Saul as Levites, not Benjaminites. These genealogical references suggest a confluence of traditions surrounding Kish.

The Levitical Kish again is cited in 1 Chr 23:21, and 1 Chr 23:7-11 includes Shimei among Kish's ancestors (cf. Exod 6:17; 1 Chr 6:17).[25] Although the Levitical Kish of 1 Chronicles 23 is not listed as Saul's father, one nevertheless wonders if a confluence of traditions blurred the distinction between the Benjaminite and Levitical figures. The identification of Saul and his father as Levites in 1 Chr 9:35-44 then seems less surprising.

Our narrator possibly understood Shimei and Kish to be

related and to be Mordecai's remote, Benjaminite ancestors.[26]
Mordecai's other ancestor, Jair, perhaps also refers to Mordecai's early family history,[27] or, as easily, to his father.
The question of Jair's relationship to Mordecai is not clarified by other biblical references. Occurrences of the name
outside Esther consistently identify Jair as a Manassite from
Gilead (cf. Num 32:41; Deut 3:14; Josh 13:30; 2 Sam 20:26; 1
Kgs 4:13; 1 Chr 2:22-23; cf. also Judg 10:3-5).[28] Nor do we
find any anti-Davidic or pro-Saulide associations with this
name.

Unfortunately, the narrator does not indicate Mordecai's
precise relationship to these other individuals. Yet whatever
the narrator's own understanding, these genealogical possibilities undoubtedly occurred to various audiences. This fact
seems certain in light of the interpretations of Josephus,
Megillah and the Targumin.

The probability that Shimei and Kish refer to Mordecai's
remote ancestors is strengthened by Esth 3:1. There, Mordecai's opponent is described as an "Agagite." This term is interpreted variously by commentators. Ringgren finds reference
to an otherwise unknown Persian family.[29] C. F. Keil views it
as a *nomen dignitatis*,[30] while Haupt sees a designation for a
"northern barbarian."[31]

The LXX renders האגגי as *bougaion*. Haupt cites the term
as a reproach which also accounts for the use of "Macedonian"
in the Greek of Esth 9:24 (cf. the LXX addition, E 10).[32] The
variant reading simple substitutes a contemporaneous allusion
for a Jewish audience familiar with the Macedonian conquests.
As Carey Moore observes,

> . . . symbolic or allegorical names loomed large in
> Jewish literature such as found at Qumran, for exam-
> ple, the use of the phrase "the House of Absalom" in
> 1QpHab to designate contemporary enemies of Qumran.
> Thus, while the MT used "Agagite" as a name suggest-
> ing the implacable archenemy of the Israelite days,
> so Greek editors used meaningful contemporary terms
> for their Greek-reading Jews, for example, Macedo-
> nian.[33]

Most modern commentators follow Josephus, the Talmud and
the Targumim which view Haman as descended from Agag, the
Amalekite king opposed by Saul (cf. 1 Sam 15).[34] If the latter
view is correct, the narrator again cites a genealogy which

points to the figure of Saul.

The term "Hammedatha" also is problematic. Most often, the word is understood as a Persian name, although its derivation is not clear. Perhaps like "Jair" in Mordecai's genealogy, "Hammedatha" simply refers to Haman's immediate ancestor and is part of his family name.

We remain uncertain of the significance attached by the narrator to Mordecai's and Haman's genealogies; yet both recall the figure of Saul. These Saulide associations also explain the odd remarks of Esth 9:10,15-16, that the Jews took no booty from their enemies. This notice is quite unusual since Esth 8:11 gives the Jews express permission to plunder their foes. This situation provides an antithesis to events narrated in 1 Samuel 15.[35] There, Saul's contingent plunders the Amalekites, despite the ritual ban (ḥerem). This plundering of Israel's foes provides one explanation for Yahweh's removal of Saul's kingship. The issues of plundering and of royal authority, juxtaposed in 1 Samuel 15, are again raised in Esther 9. In Esth 9:10,15-16, the Jews honor the obligation ignored by their ancestors. In addition, Esth 9:20-23 pictures Mordecai's institution of Purim as royally sanctioned.[36] That is, Mordecai receives royal power and acts as a king. In short, Esther 9 reverses the situation portrayed in 1 Samuel 15.[37]

The genealogies of Mordecai and Haman recall an earlier conflict between Saul and Agag. This allusion, in turn, illuminates the logic of Mordecai's refusal to bow before Haman. Esther 3:4 indicates that Mordecai would not bow before Haman because he was a Jew: ‏ויהי באמרם אילו יום ויום ולא שמע אליהם‎ ‏ויגידו להמן לראות היעמדו דברי מרדכי כי־הגיד להם אשר־הוא יהודי.‎ No further explanation is offered. But if the conflict between Mordecai and Haman mirrors an earlier conflict between their ancestors, Mordecai's confrontation with Haman was more than personal. Saul and Agag were kings of two nations which were age-old enemies (cf. Exod 17:8-16; Num 24:7; Deut 25:17-19). Like their ancestors before them, Mordecai and Haman are the leaders of their respective peoples. In light of the national enmity between Israel and Amalek, Esth 3:4 offers a "logical" reason for Mordecai's refusal, viz., because he was a Jew. Conversely, this nationalistic antagonism clarifies Haman's desire to avenge Mordecai's refusal by destroying the entire

Jewish people.[38]   The Book of Esther thus portrays Mordecai as
a quasi-royal figure. A king's direct descendant, he wears the
robes of a reigning king. This portrayal supports the earlier
claim that the Purim feasts were instituted by royalty. If we
retain those passages describing Esther's role in Purim's institution, there is no doubt that the story's final pair of
banquets is authorized by two types of royal power, i.e., those
of Persia and of Israel.

We may note in passing that the motif of kingship, like
that of feasts, exhibits an adumbrative style of narration. It
is only from the perspective of the completed story, with its
institution of Purim, that we discern the significance of earlier allusions to Mordecai's kingship. The adumbrative style
also indicates why Mordecai's Saulide descent is not related
more clearly in the narrative.

Undoubtedly, other factors also contribute to the absence
of any clear, Saulide genealogy for Mordecai. Moore suggests
that Mordecai's genealogy argues in favor of Mordecai's historicity. "Had he been a totally fictitious character, the author of Esther could easily have made him a direct descendant
of Saul, thus setting up a perfect parallel with Haman, who was
a descendant of Agag. . . ."[39] The nature of Mordecai's genealogy, however, lies with the author's style and perhaps also
with his religio-political views. By portraying Mordecai's
royal status covertly, the narrator avoids any implied threat
to the sovereignty of the reigning monarch. The disapora situation itself necessitated such a covert portrayal since the
Jewish communities remained under foreign domination. A covert
portrayal of Mordecai's kingship is particularly appropriate to
a story which does not envision or promote the return of Jews
to Palestine.

Yet the fact that Mordecai is given a Saulide ancestry remains surprising. Considering the number of traditions concerning the Davidic monarchy during the post-exilic period--
traditions which were overwhelmingly favorable--it is amazing
that Mordecai is not of Davidic descent. At present, we only
can speculate as to the reasons for the narrator's choice of
ancestors. First, we must remember that David indeed was
viewed favorably during the post-exilic period. But later traditions also are sympathetic toward Saul.[40] John Van Seters

recently argued that the court history of David is less sympathetic toward the monarch than often thought. Van Seters maintains that the court history calls into question "the traditional royal ideology of the Davidic covenant and the picture
of good king David which is basic to that ideology."[41] In
addition, the hope for the restoration of Israel as a politi-
cally independent, sovereign and autonomous state is central to
the Davidic traditions. Perhaps the narrator found the Palestinian orientation of these Davidic traditions inappropriate
to a tale of Jewish life in the diaspora.

Davidic ancestry for Mordecai might be inappropriate in
another sense. Since a part of the people remained in "exile"
after the "restoration" of Ezra and Nehemiah, the narrator may
have understood the permanency of the Jewish diaspora as given.
David's throne was not re-established immediately after the
restoration, and the narrator possibly questioned the primacy
of Davidic kingship. This understanding is not unique during
the post-exilic period. For example, in a comment upon Isaiah
24-27, 34-35, 40-66, W. S. McCullough remarks:

> It is notable that there is no reference to a kingly
> figure who will give guidance to the restored commu-
> nity. . . . This indifference to the tradition about
> a future Davidic ruler suggests that some Jewish
> circles set little store by this tradition (as in
> Daniel, the Assumption of Moses, 3 Baruch). Even in
> 2 Esdras 7 where "my son the Messiah" appears and
> lives for four hundred years before he dies, he has
> no vital function to perform, and in the subsequent
> resurrection and judgment he plays no role at all.[42]

James D. Newsome, Jr., similarly argues that "no breath of roy-
alist or messianic hope stirs in Ezra-Nehemiah."[43] Even in
Palestine, the importance of the Davidic dynasty was not uni-
versally held, and Esther's author may come from a community
which was indifferent to Davidic traditions.

This understanding does not appear improbable: in the
Book of Esther, Israel defeats its enemies despite the lack of
an independent, autonomous monarchy. Even under foreign rule,
the Jews' power increases to the extent that they inspire fear
among the peoples of the empire (cf. 8:17; 9:3-4). In effect,
the Jews obtain all the benefits and privileges associated with
an independent, Davidic-ruled monarchy--without it. The probability that a Davidic ancestry for Mordecai was inappropriate
to a diaspora tale, and the fact that Saul continued to be

viewed favorably by later traditions, perhaps account for the narrator's choice.

We have noted the function of royal apparel in the narrator's portrayal of Mordecai as a quasi-king. But references to royal clothing are not restricted to Mordecai. For example, Vashti's refusal to appear in her כתר מלכות in Esther 1 precipitates ensuing events. Her refusal results in Vashti's disenthronement as queen. This in turn anticipates Esther's coronation in 2:17. The latter further anticipates, through almost identical phrasing, the reference to כתר מלכות in Esth 6:8.

An unusual reference to royal apparel is found in Esth 5:1. The author here portrays Esther as putting on her *malkût*, not the expected לבוש מלכות. Clearly, the queen's regalia is implied, but does the appearance of *malkût* without additional qualifiers hold special significance? Perhaps the author intends a subtle comparison of the queen's power with that of Ahasuerus, whose own authority is indicated through the repetition of the root *mlk* in this verse.[44] The repetition of *mlk* in Esth 5:1 directs our attention to the question of "kingship"—an issue raised by Mordecai in Esth 4:14, the last occurrence of *malkût* prior to Esth 5:1. Esther's assumption of her *malkût* in 5:1 thereby constitutes a suitable response to Mordecai's challenge.

The story indeed promotes an indirect comparison between Esther's and Ahasuerus' power.[45] In Esth 5:1, the queen defies an "irrevocable" law, yet she is not punished for her action. Rather, Ahasuerus promises her that her request will be granted, "up to half the *malkût*" (5:3). Esther's *malkût* thus appears to overpower the authority of the imperial law. A similar situation occurs in Esth 7:4-10, where Esther's desire again supercedes a royal edict. A counter-edict is required to save Esther's people, yet the story does not indicate that Esther's personal safety depends upon it. Ironically, Mordecai's observation, ואת ובית-אביך תאבדו ("you and your father's house shall perish," 4:14), seems incorrect. Esther 8:8 presents a further irony: the king himself cannot rescind a royal decree, yet *Esther's* actions transcend the law. *Esther and Mordecai*—not Ahasuerus—are responsible for reversing Haman's decree (cf. 8:8-14).

The root *mlk* sometimes occurs as a verbal form and again

points to Esther's royal power. For example, in Esth 2:4, the king's servants repeat Memukhan's advice that Ahasuerus choose a queen to "rule" in Vashti's stead. It is significant that *mlk* is not used to refer to Vashti, apart from her title, המלכה. The one exception is מלכותה in Esth 1:19, but this reference is set within the context of Memukhan's advice that Vashti's *malkût* be given to another. Vashti's successor is found and in Esth 2:17, and Ahasuerus makes Esther queen (וימליכה).

The narrator clearly intends us to associate the concept of royal power with Ahasuerus.[46] Excluding the introductory ויהי,[47] הַמֶּלֶךְ is the first verb encountered in the story. It functions as a verbal adjective, indicating the continuing state of Ahasuerus' reign. הַמֶּלֶךְ thereby serves to introduce the audience to Ahasuerus, the powerful king. This initial perception is reinforced by 1:1b which refers to the extent of Ahasuerus' empire. The narrative setting is given through references to the royal holdings, כשבת המלך אחשורוש על כסא מלכותו אשר בשושן הבירה ("when king Ahasuerus occupied his royal throne in the acropolis of Susa"). Narrative action commences at the king's first banquet, held during the third year of his reign, לְמָלְכוּ.

Esther 1:4 relates the great wealth which accompanies Ahasuerus' power: בהראתו את־עשר כבוד מלכותו ואת־יקר תפארת גדולתו ("he displayed the vast wealth of his kingdom and the glorious splendor of his majesty"). In this verse, גדולתו ("greatness," here "majesty") is set in parallel with מלכותו ("kingdom"). This parallel lies dormant through most of the story but re-emerges at its conclusion. Esther 9:4 describes Mordecai's power in terms of his "greatness": כי־גדול מרדכי בבית המלך...כי־האיש מרדכי הולך וגדול ("for Mordecai was influential in the king's palace . . . as the man Mordecai grew increasingly powerful"). Esther 10:2-3 similarly refers to Mordecai's "greatness" (גדלת מרדכי אשר גדלו המלך).[48] Moreover, this characterization of Mordecai applies not only to his position at court, but also to his standing within the Jewish community (וגדול ליהודים). Again, Mordecai is not openly portrayed as a royal figure but the root *mlk* indirectly is applied to him.

Stylistically, the parallel between *mlk* and *gdl* provides

72

a balance to the story. The Book of Esther begins by reference
to Ahasuerus' royal power and concludes with the suggestion of
Mordecai's "greatness." The emphasis upon Ahasuerus' royal
power in Esther 1 ironically acquires its greatest significance
only in retrospect, where we find a similar emphasis upon Mordecai's power. The issue of royal power also become crucial in
the middle chapters of the story which relate Mordecai's honor
and Esther's increasing power. The parallel between *mlk* and
gdl is implied by Esth 6:3 where the king asks, מה־נעשה יקר
 וגדולה למרדכי. His question juxtaposes יקר and גדל, recalling
the earlier juxtaposition of Esth 1:4, where גדולתו and מלכותו
also are parallel.[49]   In terms of its occurrence and its centrality, the motif of kingship thus is parallel to that of
feasts.

B. *The Motif of Obedience/Disobedience*

Ahasuerus' empire was governed strictly according to imperial law. Once issued, in fact, the king's law could not be
rescinded (Esth 1:19, 8:8; cf. Dan 6:8,12,15).[50] The law's
importance is indicated by the frequency of the word דת in Esther, which occurs only twice elsewhere (cf. Deut 33:2; Ezra
8:36).[51] The narrator introduces his audience early in his
story to the importance of law. At the banquet of Esth 1:5-9,
we learn that even noncompulsory drinking is regulated by law:
והשתיה כדת אין אנס (1:8).

Soon after, Vashti precipitates a legal crisis by refusing
to appear before Ahasuerus. The king consults his advisers
concerning the dictates of the law (cf. 1:13-15). These legal
advisers are described as חכמים ידעי העתים (1:13).[52] The word
ʿēt here is unusual; but an indication of its meaning is gained
by reference to 1 Chr 12:33. There, the tribe of Issachar is
described as יודעי בינה לעתים לדעת מה־יעשה ישראל. Both passages probably refer to astrologers, but Chronicles equates the
"time-knowers" with those who know what actions to take. Esther 1:13 similarly suggests that the "wisemen who are time-
knowers" are כל־ידעי דת ודן, i.e., those who know the laws and
consequently which actions are legally permitted. Both passages imply juridical competence.[53] Esther 1:13-15, then, suggests that the king presents a legal question to advisers who

are knowledgeable in the law and who consequently know what to
do.[54] Even the king is limited by law in his response to his
wife's actions![55]

Vashti's refusal to appear before Ahasuerus is not the
only instance where disobedience to royal laws precipitates
major plot developments. An individual's response to the law
is crucial in the Book of Esther and an issue around which the
plot-line develops.

Following Vashti's disobedience, the king decides to
search for a new queen. It is at this point of the narrative
that we are introduced to Mordecai and Esther. The latter is
taken with the other women to Susa where, in accordance with
the royal edict of Esth 2:8, she is placed under Hegai's care.
Esther's introduction to court life thus stems indirectly from
Vashti's disobedience and directly from Esther's compliance
with the king's decree.

Esther 2:10 relates our first information about Esther a-
part from a notice of her physical beauty: Esther is obedient.
She did not reveal her people or national origin just as Mordecai commanded her. Esther's obedience provides an apt contrast to Vashti's disobedience--and ironically, unlike Ahasuerus, Mordecai is master of his household![56] Esther's silence
concerning her origin is repeated in Esth 2:20,[57] and the narrator reminds us that Esther continued to obey Mordecai.

This portrayal of an obedient Esther serves several functions in the story. As suggested above, it sharply contrasts
with Vashti's disobedience in chapter one. It further prepares
the audience for Esther's response to Mordecai in Esth 4:16,
itself underscored by Esth 4:17: Mordecai did "everything
which Esther commanded him." Finally, Esther's obedience contrasts with her later disobedience to the king's law (Esth
5:1-5). The latter provides for continued dramatic suspense
and raises the question of whether Esther will obey Mordecai's
instruction to intercede with the king (cf. 4:8-17).[58]

Esther 2:21-23 relates Mordecai's act of loyalty when he
saves the king's life. The following verses unexpectedly report the promotion of Haman, not Mordecai.[59] The king commands
all his servants to kneel before Haman; only Mordecai refuses.

Haman decides to avenge this insult by seeking the destruction of Mordecai and his people (cf. 3:6). He determines

a favorable day to accomplish his goal (3:7) and initiates his
plan by securing Ahasuerus' permission to rid the empire of
these undesirable inhabitants.

    We should note that Haman initiates his plans for the Jews'
destruction prior to receiving permission to dispose of them
(cf. 3:8-11). He demonstrates a similar hybris when he erects
gallows to hang Mordecai (5:14) *before* seeking royal permission
to do so (6:4). In both instances, Haman's plans radically
miscarry: Haman indeed determines a day favorable to the destruction of a people (cf. 3:7-8), but those annihilated are
Haman and his supporters, not the Jews.[60] Haman builds a gallows because of Mordecai's refusal to rise (5:9)--an ironic
contrast to Mordecai's earlier refusal to bow (3:2-6). This
gallows becomes the instrument by which Haman himself is elevated (cf. 7:10)! Haman's presumptuous actions suggest that
he, not the Jews, usurps royal prerogatives and hence poses a
threat to the king.[61] The motif of obedience/disobedience sur-
faces throughout Haman's dealings with Mordecai.

    This motif also proves central to Haman's accusation a-
gainst Mordecai's people (cf. 3:8). The fact that the Jews are
scattered throughout the empire presumably is accurate, although probably not in itself criminal. That their laws differ
from those of others also is partially accurate[62]--and here,
one thinks also of the Purim ordinances in chapter nine, fore-
shadowed by this accusation. The differing laws and customs of
the Jews pose a danger to the Persian administration only if
they conflict with those of the state. Haman addresses this
concern in his third accusation: this people does not obey the
king's laws.[63] Again, this accusation is partially true since
Mordecai has disobeyed the king's law. Its inaccuracy lies in
its generalization to all Jews and to all laws. Despite the
fact that Mordecai already demonstrated his loyalty to the king
(cf. 2:21-23), Haman charges him and his people with injurious
conduct.

    Haman receives permission to deal with the offending peo-
ple. In Esth 3:12-13, the scribes dutifully record Haman's
edict, as Haman directed (ככל־אשר־צוה המן). Haman's edict is
written in the king's name and sealed with the royal signet-
ring, i.e., it has the authority of imperial law. The edict
is promulgated throughout the empire with its content given in

detail.[64]

That Haman's decree will be carried out seems assured. A-
part from its interest to a Jewish audience, the detailed content of the letter ensures that all subjects of the empire will
know the full letter of the law. This fact, along with the
letter's royal seal, guarantees compliance to Haman's law. In
addition, earlier acts of disobedience to imperial law, viz.,
those of Vashti and Mordecai, suggest that disobedience is not
tolerated by the Persian administration. The audience thus can
have no doubt that Haman's edict will be enacted, and the motif
of obedience/disobedience provides the central crisis in the
story.[65]

Mordecai and his people learn of the new edict in Esth
4:1-4. Any doubt as to the desperate plight of the Jews in the
minds of the audience is dispelled by their response to the
edict. Mordecai publicly mourns, tearing his clothes and don-
ning sackcloth and ashes. He thereby observes traditional Jewish mourning customs. Mordecai, however, also observes Persian
customs.[66] He proceeds as far as the king's gate without en-
tering, "for there was no admittance to the king's gate in
sackcloth" (4:2). The irony of this statement is twofold:
Mordecai now obeys a custom necessitated by his earlier disregard of Persian law. In addition, he is forbidden entry to
the place where he habitually is found, viz., at the king's
gate.[67]

Esther learns of Mordecai's behavior, although she remains
unaware of its reason (cf. 4:8). Greatly distressed,[68] she
sends Mordecai fresh apparel which is refused without explanation. Esther then sends her servant, Hatakh, with the command
that Mordecai explain his actions: ותצוהו על־מרדכי לדעת מה־זה
ועל־מה־זה. Mordecai complies readily but returns his own command to Esther via Hatakh. He demands that Esther intercede
for her people.[69]

This initial exchange is related through a simple, third-
person narration. Subsequent dialogue, however, relates the
actual words of Mordecai and Esther reported by Hatakh. These
direct quotations point to the special significance attached by
the author to this discussion.

Esther responds to Mordecai with an additional order,
ותצוהו אל־מרדכי (4:10), although no instructions to him are

indicated. Esther does not defy Mordecai's command; rather,
she indicates the impossibility of compliance. The initial
words of Esth 4:11, "every servant of the king and [each] people of the king's provinces," implies a common knowledge of the
law which Mordecai seems to forget! There is one law which
governs *all* unsummoned appearances before the king, and that law
carries a death penalty. Esther adds that she has not been
called to the king for a month,[70] indicating the improbability
of a summons in the near future. Esther's remark further implies that she will not be exempted from the law.

Mordecai suggests that Esther has placed her personal
safety before that of her people (cf. 4:13). Her position does
not guarantee immunity from Haman's edict (4:13), but may prove
helpful in averting disaster (4:14d). If Esther remains silent, however, another source will aid the Jews while Esther
and her father's house will perish.[71]

There is considerable discussion regarding the meaning of
מקום אחר. Several commentators see the phrase as a veiled allusion to God.[72] Bardtke, however, correctly observes that
such an interpretation conflicts with the tenor of the narrative.[73] The most judicious reading of Esth 4:14 is that of
Peter Ackroyd.[74] Ackroyd argues that too little notice is
taken of the adjective אחר. If מקום is a metonym for God, we
are forced into the untenable reading, "from another God." "It
is much more natural to the sense to take מקום in a non-reli-
gious sense and to see in Mordecai's words the expression of
the conviction that if Esther fails in her divinely appointed
task, God will choose some other instrument for it."[75] The
thrust of Ackroyd's remarks is correct, although it is not necessary to refer to divine assistance in any form. Mordecai
suggests less concern for the source of assistance than the
assurance that help is forthcoming.

Esther's final response to Mordecai signifies her acquiescence to his command of 4:8. In Esth 4:16, she instructs Mordecai to assemble the Jews of the Susa acropolis. Along with
Esther and her servants, they are to fast for three days.[76]
Following this fast, Esther will go before the king although
her action is against the law, לא כדת. This scene ends ironically with the remark that Mordecai did everything which Esther
commanded him.

The exchange between Mordecai and Esther in Esth 4:4-17 centers upon the motif of obedience/disobedience. The always-obedient Esther, whom the audience expects, is replaced in this scene by a queen who issues her own commands. Mordecai, by contrast, does "everything which Esther commanded him" (4:17). Yet Esther agrees once more to obey Mordecai--although obedience to Mordecai entails disobedience to the king's law.

Esther's intended violation of the law, like that of her mentor (cf. Esth 3:2-4), does not disregard the law. Rather, Esther's noncompliance with the law stems from her inability to separate her own destiny from that of her people (cf. 4:13). To place her own safety above theirs produces only negative results: if Esther does not intercede for her people, she and her father's house will perish, even should some other assistance for the Jews appear. The disobedience of Esther, like that of Mordecai, directly results from her membership in the larger Jewish community.

Esther's decision to disobey the law, thereby linking her fate to that of her people, begins an unexpected reversal in the fortunes of the *dramatis personae*.[77] This reversal becomes evident almost immediately with Esther's appearance before the monarch (Esth 5:1-5). Previous administrative responses toward law-breakers, e.g., Vashti and Mordecai, suggest that Esther's infraction will not be tolerated. But Esther's unlawful act produces an unusual exception to the law. She wins Ahasuerus' favor, symbolized by the extension of his scepter.[78] In addition, Ahasuerus promises Esther that her petition will be granted.

In Esth 5:4, Esther invites Ahasuerus and Haman to a banquet she has prepared "for him." The king readily agrees, and during the banquet he again asks what Esther desires. Ahasuerus once more assures Esther that he will grant her request, up to half the kingdom. But Esther invites her guests to a second banquet, promising to obey the king on the following day: ומחר אעשה כדבר המלך (5:8).

Esther's delay in stating her actual request troubles many commentators. Gordis attributes Esther's delay to psychological motives.[79] He argues that Esther wished to present her request at a time when the king's good humor was assured. She invites Ahasuerus to a banquet where abundant wine could

favorably influence him. Yet it is difficult to understand how
Gordis' explanation accounts for the delay, particularly since
the king already promised that Esther's request would be
granted. Other scholars view the delay as a literary device to
increase dramatic suspense [80] and to permit the introduction of
additional information, e.g., Haman's self-aggrandizement (Esth
5:11-12) and Mordecai's reward (Esth 6:6-11). D. N. Freedman
notes the stylistic effect of Esther's delay. She presents her
petition only after Ahasuerus has asked three times what she
wishes.

> The third time is the charm in literary accounts. It
> is like the acrobat or magician who deliberately fails
> twice in trying to perform his most difficult feat,
> before succeeding on the third try. This enhances the
> suspense and the expectation of the audience, as well
> as winning for the performance the applause he deserves
> but is not likely to get if the audience thinks that
> there is no danger or limited need of skill to
> succeed.[81]

To these explanations, we may add that this delay provides
an additional example of Esther's disobedience. By refusing to
tell Ahasuerus her real request, Esther continues to disobey
the king (cf. 5:8). She disobeys Ahasuerus twice: by her unsummoned appearance, and by her continued refusal to state the
reason for her first crime.

At this point, the audience wonders if Esther will reveal
her true identity. She twice risked her life by disobeying the
king. Will she now endanger herself by obeying Mordecai? And
will Esther's request come soon enough to avert disaster?[82]

Mordecai's demand that Esther assume responsibility for
her co-religionists is a major concern of the narrative. In
the next chapter, the theme of Jewish solidarity will be examined. For the present, we may note that Mordecai's words to
Esther in 4:13-14 alternate the ideas of (A) Jewish identity
and (B) responsibility for the Jews:

> Do not imagine that you, of all the Jews, will escape
> with your life by being in the king's palace (A). On
> the contrary, if you keep silent in this crisis, re-
> lief and deliverance will come to the Jews from an-
> other quarter (B), while you and your father's house
> will perish (A). And who knows, perhaps you have
> attained to royal position for just such a crisis (B).

Esther 5:8-9 indicates Haman's delight at his invitation
to Esther's second banquet. Yet Haman's high spirits prove

short-lived: he encounters Mordecai who refuses to rise before
him. Neither Haman's personal fortune nor previous honors
shown him by the king compensates for Mordecai's lack of deference.[83] Following the advice of his wife and counselors, Haman
erects a gallows for Mordecai.[84]

Rather presumptuously, Haman plans to hang Mordecai before
receiving permission to do so, and it seems fitting that his
plan immediately miscarries. Wishing to secure permission to
execute his foe, Haman arrives at court precisely when the king
contemplates how to honor Mordecai. Haman, again presumptuously, assumes that the man whom the king wishes to honor must be
himself. He therefore unwittingly suggests not only the mode
of Mordecai's reward but also becomes the means for its execution. Again, Haman receives his just deserts and his participation in Mordecai's reward presages his impending fall--a fact
acknowledged by Haman's wife and advisers.[85] In both instances,
Haman does not disobey the king's law; but he consistently
usurps royal prerogatives--hardly the image of the king's loyal
and obedient servant! The ironic results of Haman's presumptuous behavior indirectly support the view that disobedience is
not tolerated in Ahasuerus' kingdom.

In 6:14, Haman is whisked off to Esther's second banquet.
There, Ahasuerus repeats his question to Esther, asking the
nature of her petition and again promising its fulfillment.
Esther responds to the king's two-part question, מה־שאלתך...ומה־
בקשתך ("what is your request? . . . what is your desire?"),
with a two-part response. The latter is prefaced with solici-
tous formulae of court etiquette.[86]

Esther finally presents her petition to the king in Esth
7:3-4 and asks for her own life and those of her people.[87] We
should note that Esther's request for her own safety is placed
within the context of her people's welfare. This aspect is
underscored by the words להשמיד להרוג ולאבד, which paraphrase
Haman's edict.

Esther's intercession elicits the response hoped for by
the Jewish community. Ahasuerus' question in Esth 7:5 suggests
that harm to his queen is antithetical to his wish. Ahasuerus'
question also indicates his ignorance of the source of this
threat. Esther, however, clarifies any question the monarch
had concerning the culprit by singling out Haman.[88] Her

response to the king's twofold question again is in two parts,
המן הרע הזה and איש צר ואויב.

Hearing Esther's words, the furious monarch momentarily
retires to the palace garden. Meanwhile Haman remains to plead
(literally, "stand") with Esther: עמד לבקש על־נפשו מאסתר
המלכה. This "coincidental" situation seals Haman's fate with
an ironical flourish. Alone with the queen, Haman *falls* upon
Esther's couch, just as the king returns to the banquet.
Haman's supplication reverses the very actions refused by Mordecai as acts of deference (prostration, rising). Ironically,
it is Haman who bows before a Jew, as Esth 6:13 presaged!

Ahasuerus interprets this scene as an attempted rape[89] and
orders Haman's execution upon the gallows intended for Mordecai. This irony appears even greater when we recall that this
gallows prompted Haman's earlier appearance at court, an appearance which initiated the reversal in Haman's personal fortunes.

Haman's property and office are transferred to Mordecai
(8:1-2), and Mordecai and Esther no longer stand in personal
danger.[90] But the other Jews remain in danger and Esther's
petition is not yet granted. The remainder of the book addresses these problems.

Esther again beseeches Ahasuerus to rescind Haman's edict
(8:3),[91] and Esth 8:4 reports that Ahasuerus extended his
scepter to her. This notice perhaps implies that Esther has
repeated her initial crime, viz., appearing uninvited before
the king. Esther's repetition of her crime brings about the
battle against the Jews' enemies and, ultimately, the Purim
celebration. It is striking that these results of Esther's
second unsummoned appearance also are subject to repetition,
i.e., a second day of battle and its commemoration in a second
day of Purim ("Shushan Purim").

Esther's second appearance before Ahasuerus is as successful as her first. Although the outcome of Esther's disobedience suggests otherwise, Ahasuerus reminds her that imperial
laws are irreversible (8:8). Esther and Mordecai, however, are
permitted to issue a new decree in the king's name. This new
edict authorizes the Jews to defend themselves against their
adversaries and is intended as a counterpart to Haman's earlier
decree. This is clear from the new law's wording, almost

identical to Haman's decree, and from the notices regarding the
scribes, date and messengers which also accompanied the earlier
decree (8:9-14; cf. 3:12-15).[92]

Ensuing events relate the Jews' victories over their enemies. Of particular interest is the Jews' restraint from taking booty. Their restraint probably results from the narrator's attempt to reverse the situation described in 1 Samuel
15. But the fact that the Jews do not plunder their enemies
when they are so authorized implies a further disregard of the
king's law.

The story concludes with the Purim legislation which bears
the weight of imperial law.[93] The Jews willingly obey these
ordinances, as they are charged by Mordecai and Esther. The
tale thereby ends with the suggestion that the Jews obeyed laws
issued by Jews--a contrast with the story's beginning where a
Persian queen disobeys her king.

An analysis of Esther's plot indicates that the motif of
obedience/disobedience pervades the story and frequently inspires narrated events. It is striking that only the disobedience of Jews yields favorable results. Also of interest is the
fact that each instance of *Jewish disobedience* to the law concerns the issue of Jewish identity. Moreover, Mordecai's and
Esther's civil disobedience *always* entails personal risk. The
storyteller does not equate civil disobedience with a disregard
for the law. To the contrary, the concept of law is taken seriously, with a respect for the consequences of disobedience to
it.[94] But the narrator places even greater weight upon the individual's commitment to the Jewish community. Not even the
law takes precedence over the community's welfare. Cognizant
of the consequences, each Jew nevertheless must disobey the law
and sacrifice personal safety on behalf of the community. To
do otherwise, as Mordecai warns in 4:13-14, presents even
greater danger.

An objection to this understanding seems indicated by Esther's initial silence concerning her own Jewish identity. If
the storyteller wished to establish a relationship between obe-
dience/disobedience and Jewish identity, why was Esther commanded by Mordecai to conceal her Jewish identity? Further,
why did Esther prove obedient regarding this command and not
others? Would we not expect both a different command and a

different response to it?

The issue of Jewish identity and the question of Esther's obedience to Mordecai are central to Esth 4:13-17. The importance of this passage should not be underestimated, for it is only after Esther's agreement to betray her identity and intercede with Ahasuerus that the fortunes of the *dramatis personae* begin their astonishing reversal. The fact that Mordecai twice instructs Esther to remain silent (2:10,20) gives the impression that Esther's silence concerning her Jewish identity is important to the narrator. This impression is strengthened by his emphasis upon Esther's obedience to Mordecai. The significance of Esther's revelation that she is a Jewess is enhanced by her earlier silence. Finally, Esther's silence is required as a plot device. Haman presumably could not issue a decree against the Jews were it known that the queen was Jewish.

Mordecai's refusal to bow to Haman is based upon his identity as a Jew. His action holds consequences for the entire Jewish community and results in a problem which dominates the plot. Mordecai's Jewish identity presents dangers; Esther's Jewish identity resolves them. It is either the queen's silence or the admission of her identity which will determine the fate of *all* Jews.

Like other dominant motifs of the story, obedience/disobedience governs Esther's plot and recurs at crucial points of the narrative. As with feasting and kingship, the narrator contrasts earlier and later occurrences of this motif, giving the story symmetry and balance.

NOTES

[1] Moore, *Esther*, liv.

[2] Not surprisingly, royal titles appear frequently in Esth
1-2. Dommershausen, *Die Estherrolle*, explains this frequency
as a desire to portray the great wealth and power of the king.
    These titles sometimes are used ironically, e.g., in Es-
ther 1. Prior to Memukhan's advice in Esth 1:19 that Vashti be
removed as queen, her name always appears with the title,
"queen." From 1:19 onward, however, Vashti's name appears
without the accompanying title.

[3] It is fitting that by the story's conclusion, Esther
herself introduces a Purim law, viz., that concerning a Purim
fast.

[4] Bardtke, *Das Buch Esther*, 348.

[5] Gerleman, *Esther*, 116-117, disputes this evidence since
these reliefs date from the time of Tiglathpileser III. The
fact that these images were preserved without alteration suggests that Bardtke's point be taken seriously.

[6] Ibid. See also the review of Gerleman's study by P.
Wernberg-Møller, *JSS* 20 (1975) 241-243. Wernberg-Møller refers
the reader to Ps 144:12 and to uncited passages in the Manual
of Discipline which he claims indicate that אשר does not always
function as a relative particle. He interprets the phrase אשר
נתן as equivalent to a consecutive perfect.

[7] Oswald T. Allis, "The Reward of the King's Favorite
(Esth 6:8)," *Princeton Theological Review* 21 (1923) 630-631.

[8] Such usage occurs elsewhere in Esther, e.g., 2:1,15;
8:9; 9:23. If present in 6:8, we find a touch of adulation
appropriate to this context.

[9] Allis, "The Reward of the King's Favorite (Esth 6:8),"
629, notes the personal element introduced into the idea of the
reward by Haman's suggestion: "Perhaps also it was because of
this very personal element so dextrously introduced by Haman
that the king, his gratitude increased by the thought of his
neglect, regarded it as a suitable tribute to pay to one who
had shown his devotion to the king's person by exposing a conspiracy against the king's life--Mordecai, the Jew."
    Xenophon, *Anabasis*, 1.9, similarly indicates the impor-
tance of a personal touch in royal gifts. He reports that
Cyrus the Younger frequently sent half-used flagons of wine or
partially eaten food to friends. A message accompanied these
gifts, stating that Cyrus himself so enjoyed these items that
he wished to honor his friends by sharing them.

[10] The suggestion that someone other than the reigning king
could wear the regalia appears questionable at first. But

83

Herodotus, *Hist.* 7.15-16, reports that Xerxes desired his adviser, Artabanus, to wear his royal attire. Reference also can
be made to Gen 41:42 and 1 Samuel 18 which indicate that a living king could honor someone through a gift of his clothing.

[11]Samuel K. Eddy, *The King is Dead* (Lincoln: University
of Nebraska, 1961), 45.

[12]Ibid.; cf. Xenophon, *Cyropaedia* 8.5, 18; Plutarch, *Art.*
3. Eddy views the magical qualities of the king's robe as the
key to an anecdote related by Herodotus, *Hist.* 9.108-113. Herodotus tells of Xerxes' promise to give his mistress, Artaÿnte,
whatever she desires. She requests his robe, a gift from
Xerxes' wife, Amestris. Xerxes unsuccessfully attempts to sub-
stitute other gifts but is held to his promise. Amestris subsequently learns of this gift and mutilates Artaÿnte's mother
and husband. Eddy suggests that Artaÿnte's husband desired the
crown, and the king's robe was an essential requirement for
this. Amestris presumably obtained her revenge and simultaneously protected her husband's--and her own--royal standing.

[13]Plutarch, *Art.* 5.2, possibly a paraphrase from Ctesias'
The Persians [Persica].

[14]E.g., Anderson, "The Book of Esther," 862; Browne, *Esther*, 384. According to Jerald M. Brown, "Rabbinic Interpretations of the Characters and Plot of the Book of Esther (as Reflected in Midrash Esther Rabbah)" (Rabbinical thesis, Hebrew
Union College--Jewish Institute of Religion, Cincinnati, 1976),
3-20, the later midrashim view Ahasuerus as a fool.

[15]Brown, *Esther*, remarks that "it may have been intentional to make the king such a fool that he forgot the name of the
man who saved his life. . . ." Perhaps the nature of Mordecai's honor is meant to reinforce Ahasuerus' foolish behavior
toward Mordecai.

[16]The "coincidences" of the story are discussed more fully
in Chapter IV.

[17]In addition, later Jewish interpreters understood Esth
6:8 to refer to the regalia, with the implication that Mordecai
became "king" of the Jews. Cf. *Est.Rab.* 10.12; *Tg. Esth II*
6:8; *Pirq.R.El.* 50.

[18]That Mordecai does not bear the king's diadem is clear
by the use of עטרה; cf. 6:8, כתר. But the significance of Mordecai's appearance in his own large, gold crown should not be
overlooked.

[19]The ambiguity of Esth 6:8 perhaps was intended, for Mordecai returns to his usual place at the king's gate following
his honor. Allis, "The Reward of the King's Favorite (Esth
6:8)," 632, finds a different kind of ambiguity in Esth 6:8.
He remarks that Haman's request to the king was phrased so that
Haman might hope, presumptuous as it appears, that the king
would allow him to wear a royal diadem. Haman couched his
suggestion in language through which he could claim that he
asked only for reflected glory in case the king demurred.

[20]The Hebrew text offers no clues as to the author's intention. Since the earliest interpreters of the text held this view, it is not inconceivable that other early audiences understood Mordecai's ancestry in a similar fashion.

[21]Moore, *Esther*, 19-20.

[22]Here, the Chronicler presumably refers to the Shimei of Simeon; cf. 1 Chr 4:24-26. 1 Chr 5:4 relates the Reubenite Shimei to "Gog"--a name applied to Haman in the Lucianic recension of the LXX. In the latter instance, the similarity of names may be coincidental; cf. the "Gog" of Ezek 38-39.

[23]I argue below that Haman's ancestry is traced to the Amalekites. If this understanding is correct, we find the interesting suggestion that Mordecai's and Haman's ancestors came into conflict. Surprisingly, we do not yet find Edom as the paradigm of Israel's enemies. This understanding is evident by the rabbinic period and already began in the post-exilic period. See the discussion of Peter R. Ackroyd, *Exile and Restoration* (OTL; Philadelphia: Westminster, 1968) 224, 230-231.

[24]Cf. 1 Chr 26:28.

[25]According to 1 Chr 6:16-18, Levi fathered Gershom, whose son was Shimei. Shimei also appears a few verses later (cf. 1 Chr 6:29-30) as the son of Merari, Gershom's brother. Presumably the Chronicler applied the latter references to different, albeit related, individuals than those he cites in 1 Chr 6:2. 1 Chr 23:7-11 similarly lists Shimei as descended from Merari.

[26]The order of Mordecai's ancestors remains problematic. Some traditions suggest Shimei as Kish's ancestor, i.e., in an order opposite that of Esth 2:5.

[27]If a remote ancestor was intended, the narrator perhaps saw a connection between Mordecai's Benjaminite descent and a Manassite ancestry of Shimei, via the house of Joseph.

[28]Judg 10:3-5 mentions a Jair who judged Israel for 22 years. Apart from the fact that both Jair and Mordecai were recognized leaders of their people, it is difficult to discern any connection between these individuals.

[29]Ringgren, *Das Buch Esther*, 387.

[30]*Biblischer Kommentar über die nachexilischen Geschichtsbücher: Chronik, Esra, Nehemia und Esther*; cited by Moore, *Esther*, p. 35.

[31]Haupt, "Critical Notes on Esther," 141-142.

[32]Ibid.

[33]Moore, *Esther*, 36.

[34]See the various commentaries and especially the discussion by McKane, "A Note on Esther IX and I Samuel XV," 260-261.

[35]Ibid. See also the remarks of Bardtke, "Neuere Arbeiten zum Estherbuch," 525-526. Bardtke argues that the diaspora situation plays a significant role in the narrator's interpretation of 1 Samuel 15.

[36]The accounts given in Ezra and Nehemiah indicate that Esth 9:20-23 is not the only occasion when Jewish religious practices were authorized by a Persian monarch. The Jews' peculiar abstention from plundering their enemies implies one reason for the reinstatement of royal authority in the Saulide line.

[37]*Est.Rab.* 4:9 suggests another type of reversal of 1 Samuel 15. Here, a connection is seen between 1 Sam 15:28 and Esth 1:19 which suggests that Saul forfeited his crown because of his behavior toward Amalek while *Esther* won it back!

[38]Anderson, "The Book of Esther," 847, states that Esther "may be regarded as the inexorable working out of the divine curse against Amalek." Elias Bickermann, *Four Strange Books of the Bible* (New York: Schocken Books, 1967), 197, holds a similar view and adds, "Haman's descent from Amalek explains his hatred of Israel and further provides assurance that Mordecai ultimately will triumph over Haman. . . ." See also the remarks of Robert R. Wilson, "The Old Testament Genealogies in Recent Research," *JBL* 94 (1975) 169-189, who argues that multiple or conflicting genealogies often result from an intent to express more than actual biological ties. This certainly is the case with the genealogies cited for Mordecai and Haman!

[39]Moore, *Esther*, 19-20.

[40]See the post-biblical traditions concerning Saul cited by Louis Ginzberg, *The Legends of the Jews*, (6 vols.; Philadelphia: Jewish Publication Society of America, 1939), 4.65-77, especially 67; 6.233-238. These traditions indicate both a continued and a favorable interest in Israel's first monarch.

[41]John Van Seters, "Problems in the Literary Analysis of the Court History of David," *JSOT* 1 (1976) 23. Van Seters, 29, n. 25, indicates a fuller treatment of this theme in his forthcoming study of Israelite historiography, *Histories and Historians of the Ancient Near East*, ed. J. W. Wevers (Toronto: University of Toronto).

[42]W. S. McCullough, "Israel's Eschatology from Amos to Daniel," *Studies on the Ancient Palestinian World* ([Festschrift F. V. Winnett], ed. J. W. Wevers and D. B. Redford; Toronto: University of Toronto, 1972) 89. Otto Eissfeldt, "The Promise of Grace to David in Isaiah 55:1-5," *Israel's Prophetic Heritage* (ed. Bernhard W. Anderson and Walter Harrelson; New York: Harper & Bros., 1962) 196-207, argues that Second Isaiah held little hope for the continuation of the Davidic dynasty.

[43]James D. Newsome, Jr., "Toward a New Understanding of the Chronicler and His Purposes," *JBL* 94 (1975) 214. Frank Moore Cross, "A Reconstruction of the Judean Restoration," *JBL* 94 (1975) 13, attributes the lack of emphasis upon the Davidic

dynasty in the so-called Chronicler's work to a later editor (Chr$_3$).

[44] בית המלך ("king's palace") occurs twice; כסא מלכות ("throne") and בית מלכות ("palace") each occur once.

[45] The treatment of Esther's two banquets suggests a subtle indication of the queen's power. During the first meal, Esther's name appears without the royal title, המלכה. But the corresponding description of the second feast, where Esther's power is put to its critical test, refers to her as אסתר המלכה ("Queen Esther"). The narrator clearly intimates that Esther's power over the king is bound up with her own royal authority, indicated by the use of *mlk*.

[46] See Dommershausen's structural analysis of Esther 1; *Die Estherrolle*.

[47] ויהי frequently begins the historical books and suggests that events which follow continue a preceding account. Such is not the case, however, in the Book of Esther. ויהי also begins the Books of Ezekiel and Jonah, usages analogous to that of Esth 1:1. Striedl, "Untersuchung zur Syntax und Stilistik des hebräischen Buches Esther," 73, perhaps is correct to argue that ויהי contributes to the narrator's archaizing intent.

[48] Again, it is not clear whether Esth 10:1-3 constitutes an addition to the text. See the remarks of Daube, "The Last Chapter of Esther," 139-147, and Jones, "Rhetorical Studies in the Book of Esther: The So-Called Appendix," who argue that Esther 10 is part of the original tale. We should note that Esth 9:4, whose integrity is not disputed, portrays Mordecai in a similar fashion.

[49] *Gdl* also is applied to Haman. Esth 3:1 and 5:11 refer to Haman's "greatness," and both occasions provide the basis for a conflict between Haman and Mordecai. Haman's exalted position in Esth 3:1 results in the king's order that others bow before him. In Esth 5:11, Haman relates to his companions how the king promoted him. Haman is advised to ask permission to hang Mordecai, and his attempts to follow this advice result in Haman's honoring of Mordecai. *Gdl* thus refers to Haman infrequently but with great irony. References to Haman's "greatness" result in significant plot developments and contrast with Mordecai's eventually exalted position.

[50] No extra-biblical source suggests the irrevocability of Persian law; cf. Herodotus, *Hist*. 9.109; Plutarch, *Art*. 27. But J. Stafford Wright, "The Historicity of the Book of Esther," *New Perspectives on the Old Testament* (ed. J. Burton Payne; Waco, Texas/London: Word Books, 1970), 39-40, cites a passage from Diodorus Siculus which he argues supports the irrevocability of Persian law. Moore, *Esther*, 11, maintains that this understanding of the nature of Persian law does not reflect sound historical knowledge. If Moore is correct, presumably the authors of Esther and Daniel 6 wrote at a time somewhat removed from actual experience of Persian rule.

[51]The word דת occurs 20 times in Esther. In addition, the phrase דבר־המלך frequently has the sense of royal edict; cf. Esth 2:8; 3:15; 4:3; 8:17; 9:1. Surprisingly, the term צוה is infrequent in Esther. It is striking that this term occurs most often in passages which concern the revealing or concealing of one's Jewish identity; cf. Esth 2:10,20; 3:3; 4:8,17.

[52]The word חכם occurs only here and in Esth 6:13. The latter is usually emended, despite the lack of substantial textual support. If חכמיו is retained in 6:13, its sense is similar to that of 1:13, i.e., "advisers." But in 6:13, the word attains an ironical nuance since Haman's advisers can discern the "times" in a manner which Haman cannot.

[53]The Book of Daniel also suggests a connection between "knowing" the times and undertaking suitable actions. For example, Dan 2:9 reads: "for you have agreed to speak to me a false and deceptive word until the times change." Similarly, in Dan 2:21: "he changes times and seasons. . . ; he gives wisdom to the wise and knowledge to those who have understanding."
The relationship between knowing the times and taking legal actions advises against the emendation of העתים to הדתים. For example, Moore, *Esther*, 9, writes that the wisemen who knew the times "could hardly be regarded as 'knowers of the law and government.'" But it is precisely this knowledge of legal matters which permits them to recommend legal actions which are an appropriate response to the "times."

[54]The *RSV*, *NEB*, Moore, and Gordis translate דבר־המלך in Esth 1:13 as "the king's custom, practice." The precise nuance of the phrase is rendered better by the more usual meaning of דבר, "word, matter." Esth 1:13 thus refers to the king's entreaty, i.e., the specific legal question he asks in Esth 1:15.

[55]Note the delightful correspondence between Vashti's crime and its punishment: since Vashti refuses to appear before the king, it is to be recorded in the laws (בדתי) that she not appear before the king!

[56]The narrator digresses in 2:11-12 to report that Mordecai visited Esther every day. He gives detailed information of life in the harem, all of which was regulated כדת נשים.

[57]In *b. Meg.* 13a, R. Judah suggests that Esther's name derives from the concealment of her identity (מסתרת).

[58]These examples of Esther's obedience or disobedience are discussed more fully below. The portrayal of Esther in chapter two perhaps serves a further purpose. Does Esther's obedience imply that the Jews normally were an obedient people? Mordecai's refusal to bow before Haman presupposes a traditional enmity between Israel and Amalek, i.e., it represents a special circumstance. Mordecai's act of disobedience follows his saving of the king's life (cf. 2:21-23). The story suggests that under "ordinary" circumstances, the Jews were loyal subjects of the king. Jeremiah's advice to the exiles (cf. Jer 29:4-7) characterizes the stance which Esther's author seems to take. See the remarks of Humphreys, "The Motif of the Wise Courtier

in the Old Testament," 282-284; idem, "A Life-style for Diaspora: A Study of the Tales of Esther and Daniel," 211-212.

[59]The extent of Haman's promotion is indicated by the remark that his כסא was exalted above other nobles. The word כסא
occurs only two other times in Esther, both times referring to
the king's throne (cf. 1:2; 5:1).

[60]Kaufmann, תולדות האמונה הישראלית [The Religion of Isra-
el], 8.446, observes that the "omen" Haman received was correct
and that Adar 13 proved a favorable day. But Haman suffered a
fate shared by others in the ancient world. The sign Haman
received was ambiguous and consequently misunderstood. Haman's
wife and advisers eventually discern Haman's error (cf. 6:13),
although he seemingly does not.

[61]Haman's genealogy suggests that he was not a Persian
but, like Mordecai and Esther, a member of a subject people.

[62]Haman's second accusation ironically brings to mind such
regulations as the dietary laws and the prohibition against
intermarriage--matters which do not otherwise seem to concern
the narrator. Haman's accusation undoubtedly applies to other
peoples subject to Achaemenian rule and does not seem particularly condemnatory.

[63]Note the emphatic position of the words ואת־דתי המלך.

[64]Here, the less elaborate notice of Esth 1:22 should be
compared.

[65]The eleven-month delay between the promulgation and the
fulfillment of the decree presumably allows the non-Jewish subjects of the empire to prepare (עתדים) for the destruction of
the Jews. The choice of Adar 13 for the destruction of the
Jews, however, has further significance. Dommershausen, Die
Estherrolle, 66, thinks the narrator's choice of dates depends
upon "unlucky" associations with the number thirteen. More
probable is that a Jewish audience would note the edict's date,
promulgated just prior to the commencement of the Passover observance. Hence, Purim is celebrated exactly one month before
Passover. The significance of the story's various dates is
indicated more fully below.

[66]The explanatory note of Esth 4:2 suggests a Persian, not
Jewish, custom. Mordecai presumably no longer feared any punishment for acts of disobedience--he already faced a disastrous
fate! Yet Mordecai honors this Persian custom, again promoting
the view that he is an obedient subject of the empire.

[67]The "king's gate" may denote an official post held by
Mordecai; cf. Herodotus, Hist. 3.120; Xenophon, Cyropaedia
8.1-6. See also O. Loretz, "šᶜr hmlk--'Das Tor des Königs'
(Esth 2, 19)," Die Welt des Orients 4 (1967) 104-108; Hans P.
Rüger, "Das 'Tor des Königs'--der königliche Hof," Bib 50
(1969) 247-250; Moore, Esther, 30; Gordis, "Studies in the Esther Narrative," 47-48. In some ways, Haman's edict already
proves disadvantageous to the king by preventing the continued
service of a subject who saved the king's life.

[68]This seems to be the sense of התחלחל (4:4). The hith-
palpel of חיל occurs only here. Moore, *Esther*, 48, follows the
LXX and reads "perplexed."

[69]Dommershausen, *Die Estherrolle*, 71-72, suggests that
Mordecai's command to Esther is constructed around a series of
inf. cstrs. which appear in Esth 4:8. The words לצות and
לבוא are central and framed by pairs of infinitives which precede and follow. The narrator, however, structures the command
on the pattern of 3 + 3. The initial set of three infinitives
presents the grounds for Esther's expected actions, the latter
suggested by the second set of infinitives. The second set is
dependent logically upon the first and indicates Esther's "appropriate" response to Mordecai's information. Also note the
loose correspondence between the verbs through their contrasting concepts, לבקש\לצרות; להגיד\להתחנן.

[70]B. Wolff, *Das Buch Esther* (Frankfurt am Main: J. Kauffmann, 1922), 25-26, argues that an audience is possible under
two conditions: (1) the audience is pre-arranged through a
formal request; (2) the king agrees to the audience, indicating
his consent by the extension of his scepter. The phrase לבד
כל־איש ואישה אשר יבוא־אל־המלך אל־החצר מאשר ירשיט־לו המלך follows
הפנימית אשר לא־יקרא and thus suggests that the extension of the
scepter symbolizes an exception to the law, not a part of it.
A similar regulation regarding audiences with the king is
indicated by Josephus, *Ant.* 11.205, but is limited to the royal
family. But Herodotus, *Hist.* 1.99; 3.72,77,84,118,140 (cf.
2.68), suggests comparatively easy access to the Persian monarch. Several commentators are puzzled by the fact that Esther
did not utilize the eleven months before the enactment of the
decree to seek an audience. Moore probably is correct in view-
ing Esther's self-endangerment as vital to dramatic suspense.

[71]Paton, *The Book of Esther*, and Bardtke, *Das Buch Esther*,
interpret these verses as a factual statement. Hoschander, *The
Book of Esther*, sees them as an implied threat. Hoschander's
view strikes me as more probable in light of Mordecai's suggestion that some other assistance for the Jews would be forthcoming. Mordecai, in effect, seems to suggest, "if you are not
for us, you are against us."

[72]For example, Paton, Vischer, Ringgren, Gerleman, Talmon,
Moore, Humphreys; also, L. H. Brockington, *Ezra, Nehemiah and
Esther* (Century Bible, New Series: London: Thomas Nelson &
Sons, 1969). Several of these scholars understand מקום to be a
metonym for God, as it may be in the rabbinic literature.
Brown, "Rabbinic Interpretations of the Characters and Plot of
the Book of Esther (as Reflected in Midrash Esther Rabbah),"
52, however, argues that מקום does not refer to Yahweh in the
midrashic literature.

[73]Bardtke, *Das Buch Esther*, 333.

[74]Peter R. Ackroyd, "Two Hebrew Notes," *ASTI* 5 (1967) 82-
86.

[75]Ibid., 83-84.

[76]Fasting as a religious response to calamity, impending or actualized, was not limited to Jews. Nevertheless, for a Jewish audience, Esther's instructions suggest "traditional" Jewish behavior in times of danger. Her intended fast implies Esther's recognition of her membership in the Jewish community--an acknowledgment which her fast, to some extent, makes public.

Despite the great attention devoted toward discovering "religious" elements in the Book of Esther, the significance of Esth 4:16 has been ignored. As suggested earlier, this fast contrasts with the preceding fast of 4:1-3 and was undertaken in the hopeful anticipation of a favorable outcome to Esther's audience with Ahasuerus. I find it difficult to interpret the fast of Esth 4:16 as anything but a "religious" act.

[77]More is said concerning this reversal in Chapter IV below.

[78]Note the use of נשא חן (not מצא חן) as in Esth 2:17.

[79]Gordis, *Megillat Esther*, 42.

[80]For example, Bardtke, Dommershausen and Moore. Gerleman, *Esther*, 108-109, understands Esther's delay to be modeled after Exodus 7-10 where Moses repeats his demand to Pharaoh that Israel be freed. The parallel, however, is not convincing. In Exodus, an Israelite repeats his demand to the monarch; in Esther, the monarch repeats his question to an Israelite.

[81]Quoted by Moore, *Esther*, 58.

[82]Adding to the suspense is the fact that Mordecai stands in personal danger; cf. Esth 5:14. Esther's intercession yet may save other Jews; but does her request come too late to save Mordecai?

[83]Haman is not content with Mordecai's recognition of him. In one sense, Haman already honors Mordecai by his concern with the Jew.

[84]The exaggerated height of the gallows--50 cubits!--also implies Haman's regard for Mordecai. Mordecai already was subject to the edict against the Jews. Only a formidable adversary requires special consideration, and particularly, a gallows of such stature.

[85]Esth 6:13 clarifies that Haman's imminent defeat stems from Mordecai's Jewish ancestry. Haman's downfall results also from Esther's revelation of her Jewish identity. The observation by Haman's wife and advisers in 6:13 thus proves correct: Haman cannot succeed against a Jew.

[86]Again, note Esther's use of second person address. Ahasuerus' question in 7:2 recalls those of 5:3,6. It also anticipates the later, twofold question of 9:12. Esther's response to the question in 7:2 ultimately results in the Jews' self-defensive battle on Adar 13. Her response to the later question of 9:12 also is twofold and permits the extension of

the battle to Adar 14; cf. 9:13: ‏ינתן גם־מחר...ואת עשרת בני־‎
‏המן.‎

[87]Esther's request to the king for the lives of her people
does not mention them by name. This parallels the form of
Haman's request for the lives of her people in a different
sense: neither Haman nor Esther refers to "this people" by
name.

[88]Esther designates Haman as solely responsible for the
edict against the Jews; she ignores the king's participation.
But Ahasuerus authorized Haman's edict which was sealed with
the royal signet-ring. Does Esther single out Haman as the
culprit only for psychological or political reasons? We shall
return to this question in the following chapter.

[89]Haman's alleged rape attempt, not his authorship of the
edict against the Jews, results in his downfall. This fact,
which troubles many commentators, perhaps is to be explained on
historical grounds. Seth Bernardete, *Herodotean Inquiries* (The
Hague: Martinus Nijhoff, 1969) 72, suggests that Persian custom
forbade even the king from killing someone for a single cause.
Rather, the king had first to determine if that individual rendered more benefits than injustices to the empire; cf. Herodotus, *Hist*. 1.136-137; 7.194.1-2. The Book of Esther may supply
additional support for Herodotus' understanding of Persian law.
On the other hand, the narrator appears more concerned with the
interpretation of Haman's action than with its motive. He suggests no reason for this charge against Haman nor why it is
this alleged attempt at rape and not Esther's identification of
Haman as her foe which accomplishes his demise. The explanation perhaps is stylistic. Haman's downfall is figuratively
and literally accomplished through an ironic use of ‏עמד\נפל‎.

[90]Cf. Esth 8:6, where the queen expresses concern only for
the safety of her people. She no longer seems concerned with
her own welfare as she did in 7:4.

[91]This scene may presuppose a new setting. The initial
word of Esth 8:3, ‏ותוסף‎, suggests the continuation of Esther's
discussion with the king at her banquet. On the other hand,
8:1-2, along with the mention of the royal scepter in 8:4, indicate a setting of the throne room.

[92]The counter-edict may quote a portion of Haman's earlier
edict; see the remarks of Gordis, "Studies in the Esther Narrative," 49-53. Gordis also argues cogently that the new edict
is intended as a self-defensive measure by the Jews. Note the
response of the Jews and of the Susa acropolis to the new edict
and to Mordecai's appearance in regal attire (‏לבוש מלכות‎; 8:15-
17). Not only the edict itself, but the public response to it,
reverses the situation portrayed in Esther 3.

[93]In addition to Mordecai's and Esther's roles in establishing the festal observance, the use of ‏ספרים‎ in Esth 9:20
suggests imperial law; cf. 1:22; 3:13; 8:5,10. "Scribes" record the edicts of 3:12 and 8:9, again indicating the juridical
nuance of ‏ספר‎ in Esther. Do the chronicles of 2:23, 6:1 and

10:2, with which Mordecai is associated, also suggest legal records?

[94]A similar understanding is suggested by the treatment of Purim, which is considered binding upon all Jews.

CHAPTER IV

THEMES AND STRUCTURE

Preceding chapters of this study suggested some of Esther's dominant motifs. These motifs pervade the narrative, recurring at key points, and sometimes are highlighted by auxiliary motifs. The dominant motifs help to unify the Book of Esther by potently anticipating or recalling their other occurrences through conscious uses of parallel and contrast. These motifs also appear interdependent and provide a balance between the beginning, middle and conclusion of the story.

This chapter discusses the implications of the narrator's use of motifs. When taken together, Esther's dominant motifs suggest a particular understanding of the situations its narrator portrays. The motifs point to certain implicit concepts or "themes" which the storyteller presumably sought to convey. Esther's themes thus represent fundamental loci of meaning which the motifs, jointly considered, articulate. In short, the narrator's method of presentation indicates his narrative's messages.

The presence of certain themes in Esther does not demand that it was intended as a didactic work. The storyteller perhaps wished only to present a charming and entertaining tale. By presenting his story as he did, the narrator nevertheless directs our attention to specific narrative themes. These themes may constitute the narrator's assumptions and presuppositions; or they may indicate something which he sought to prove. In either case, these themes express ideas and concepts held by the storyteller. More importantly, they suggest concerns which the author singled out for our consideration through his narrative style. The Book of Esther may be considered a didactic work, even if its primary purpose was to entertain.

96

A. Themes

1. The Theme of Power

   The Book of Esther begins with two banquets hosted by
Ahasuerus. The story concludes with two feasts instituted by
the quasi-royal figure, Mordecai, as part of the Purim celebration. The king's banquets in Esther 1 anticipate the later
Purim feasts. But they also serve another function: they indicate the extent of Ahasuerus' great wealth and power.[1] This
function seems especially clear in Esth 1:4 where Ahasuerus
displays his extensive wealth.[2] Gunkel argues that the storyteller describes only the second of the two feasts in detail
since he narrates as one invited to that banquet.[3] Yet the
author's silence concerning the details of the first banquet
permits another interpretation. Ahasuerus' first banquet honors the officials of the empire and lasts 180 days. We assume
that it probably was more elaborate than the banquet given for
the Susa populace. In light of the splendor of the second banquet (cf. 1:6-7)[4] and the abundance of provisions, we can only
imagine the even greater opulence and wealth witnessed at the
first banquet.

   If Esth 1:1-9 portrays the wealth and power of the Persian
court, the parallels between Ahasuerus' banquets and Purim's
feasts presumably transfer some vestige of this wealth and
power to Mordecai, who instituted the festal meals. Esther
10:3 articulates such a transference: "for Mordecai the Jew
ranked next to King Ahasuerus and was great among the Jews."[5]
Mordecai's power, however, stems not only from his position in
Ahasuerus' administration, but also from his own royal descent.
Mordecai's royal power is highlighted by the narrator's portrayal of him as a quasi-king. Mordecai thus comes to represent not only the greatness of the Persian court but also that
of Israel.

   The Book of Esther concludes with the suggestion of Mordecai's power. This portrayal, however, contrasts with our initial views of him. Mordecai is introduced as an individual of
presumably low social standing within the dominant society.
The repeated use of the root גלה, "to exile," in Esth 2:6
leaves little doubt regarding Mordecai's status: he is a

Jewish exile whose king was defeated by the Babylonian monarch.[6] The initial verses of the book make clear that Mordecai
remains subject to a foreign king, living as an exile in a foreign land.

The status of Mordecai's ward parallels his own. We have
noted the power possessed by Esther whose personal influence
with Ahasuerus is directly responsible for saving her people.
Yet we are introduced to Esther as an orphan whom Mordecai
adopted. She thus holds little social status within both Persian and Israelite societies. We do not initially perceive
Mordecai and Esther to be outstanding, and we certainly do not
expect them to attain the highest positions available to them
within the Persian empire. They are distinctive only in their
representation of the lower rungs of the social ladder. At
best, Mordecai and Esther are quite ordinary diaspora Jews, not
individuals whom we expect to achieve greatness.[7]

It is striking that the Book of Esther does not limit the
possession of power to its Jewish protagonists, Mordecai and
Esther. Rather, the entire Jewish community shares their
power. Esther 8:17 relates that other Jews, like Mordecai, inspired fear in their enemies, and this point is important
enough to be repeated in Esth 9:2. Esther 9:5 presents a similar image by its suggestion that the Jews were authorized to do
whatever they wished to their enemies. Their power is such
that other peoples מתיהדים ("became Jews" [?]; 8:17), a term
which occurs only here.[8] The Jews' power coincides with the
increase in Mordecai's stature. Esther 10:3 indicates that
Mordecai used his increasing authority to benefit his people:
דרש טוב לעמו ודבר שלום לכל־זרעו ("he sought the good of his
people and interceded for the welfare of all his kinsmen").
The empire's Jews thus share indirectly in Mordecai's power.[9]

Like Mordecai and Esther, other Jews do not possess power
at the beginning of the book. They appear powerless in the
face of Haman's edict. Yet by the story's conclusion, their
fate is dramatically reversed. They hold a favored status in
the empire and inspire "fear" among their enemies. The for-
merly powerless have become the powerful. Just as the feasts
of Esther 1 depict the power of the Persian administration, the
Purim banquets symbolize and commemorate the power of Mordecai
and the Jews.[10]

The motifs of feasting and kingship thus point to a reversal in the status of Jews in Ahasuerus' empire. The narrator
utilizes these motifs to contrast the former powerlessness of
the diaspora Jews with their later power.[11] The story's motifs
suggest this theme and also indicate the reason for the dramatic change in the Jews' status and fate, viz., their loyalty.

2. The Theme of Loyalty to the Jewish Community

The impending destruction which threatens the Jews
throughout most of the Book of Esther results directly from
Mordecai's refusal to bow before Haman. Mordecai clearly disobeys the king's law. On the other hand, Haman's edict itself
is averted by acts of disobedience, viz., Esther's unsummoned
appearances before Ahasuerus. Esther's initial disobedience of
royal law, in fact, begins a reversal in the Jews' fortune.
This reversal is indicated initially by the king's response to
Esther's crime: instead of punishing Esther, Ahasuerus promises that he will grant her petition. Shortly thereafter,
Haman builds the gallows upon which he eventually is hanged and
unwittingly earns a key role in the king's honoring of Mordecai. The latter scene initiates the reversal in Mordecai's
personal fortune, soon followed by a reversal in the fate and
fortune of the entire diaspora Jewish community.

Esther's disobedience in chapter 5 thus initiates a series
of reversals in snowball fashion. The significance of her action is marked by a shift in the author's focus upon his protagonists. Prior to chapter 5, Mordecai is the prime mover of
events; with Esther's appearance before the king, she becomes
the main initiator of action.[12]

Mordecai's and Esther's disobedience is based upon their
Jewish identities. Esther 3:4 indicates that Mordecai's refusal to bow before Haman was "because he told them he was a
Jew." Esther similarly disobeys a royal decree and identifies
herself with the Jewish community, a fact suggested by Esth
4:13-16. Yet the disobedience of the Jewish protagonists is
out of character with their usual law-abiding nature: Mordecai
already has demonstrated his concern for the crown by saving
the king's life; and Esther's crime in 5:1-5 differs sharply

from her previous image as the always-obedient woman.

It is particularly striking that only the disobedience of
Mordecai and Esther yields favorable results. This fact becomes more apparent when we recall the respective fates of
Vashti and Haman after their crimes. More importantly, Mordecai's and Esther's disobedience is grounded upon a voluntary
acknowledgment or awareness of their identities as Jews. The
favorable results of their insubordination, the reversal in the
fate of the Jews, and their attainment of great power cannot be
dissociated from the heroes' loyalty to their co-religionists.
The loyalty of Mordecai and Esther to their community is such
that, if necessary, they prove willing to accept the consequence of their disobedience to the law.

Mordecai's and Esther's disobedience of royal law suggests
that the narrator values loyalty to the Jewish community above
any allegiance to the civil government. Yet the Book of Esther
envisions no conflict by this ordering of priorities. The narrator portrays Mordecai as a minor court official[13] who even
saves the king's life. That his Jewish identity occasions
civil disobedience does not affect Mordecai's loyalty to the
crown, a loyalty the king himself acknowledges in Esther 6.
Ahasuerus not only rewards Mordecai with special honors, but
invests his faithful servant with Haman's former position of
power (cf. 8:2; 10:3).

Esther disobeys the law by her unsummoned appearances and
her delay in stating her request. Yet her petition clearly
suggests that the annihilation of the Jews would prove a dis-
service to the king (cf. 7:3-4). Esther indicates that she
disobeys civil law because of her concern both for her people
and for her king.[14]

The narrator hints elsewhere that no conflicting loyalties
are engendered by placing allegiance to the Jewish community
above the civil administration. In Esther 3, Haman's decree is
accompanied by the report in verse 15 that "the city of Susa
was dumbfounded." Mordecai's promotion and his counter-edict,
however, elicit a different response from Susa's populace:
"the city of Susa rang with joyous cries" (8:15). The Jews'
fate obviously concerns their Persian compatriots who respond
appropriately to the imperilment or empowerment of the Jews.
The response of Susa's citizens to the two decrees implies that

they, as well as the Jews themselves, display a certain loyalty to the Jewish community.

Haman accuses the Jews of being "scattered and dispersed among the other peoples in all the provinces of your [Ahasuerus'] realm" (3:8). The narrator stresses the truth of Haman's accusation by repeated references to the Jews' location throughout the empire (cf. 8:11,17; 9:2,12,16,19,20,28).[15] Most of these notices appear relatively late in the story, after Mordecai and Esther already have proven loyal to the king. The author seemingly does not want the physical separation of the Jewish communities to imply a spiritual dispersion or lack of concern among Jews for their co-religionists.

Communal solidarity also is expressed through the fasts of 4:3,16. It is important to note that Esther's request for a communal fast marks her agreement to intercede with the king. One could view even Mordecai's personal concern for his ward in Esth 2:7,11 as an expression of the theme of loyalty on a personal level.[16]

The motif of obedience/disobedience thus points to the value of loyalty to the crown and to the importance of Jewish solidarity. The latter, in fact, supercedes the former, even in the cases of usually obedient and law-abiding Jewish citizens. This ordering of priorities, however, provokes no conflict of interests. On the contrary, loyalty to one's Jewish compatriots benefits the civil administration as well.

The clearest expression of this view occurs in Esth 7:4. Here, Esther requests that Ahasuerus spare the Jews and gives the reason for her request: כי נמכרנו אני ועמי להשמיד להרוג ולאבד ואלו לעבדים ולשפחות נמכרנו החרשתי כי אין הצר שוה בנזק המלך. Esther's reasoning presumably was clear to the narrator and his audience; but for us, "her rationale is far from clear."[17] Moore attributes our confusion to the corrupt state of the MT, as does Paton.[18] For Gordis, however, the crucial question is whether the second clause of Esther's statement relates directly to the first. Is there an ellipsis between the two clauses?[19] Most modern commentators do not assume an ellipsis. If we accept this view, Esth 7:4 nevertheless permits two different interpretations of the concluding clause (כי אין הצר שוה בנזק המלך): (A) the Jews' affliction would be less injurious to the king if Esther's people were threatened only with slavery; or, (B) Esther would not trouble the king if only slavery were at issue.[20]

Esther 7:4 has elicited a wealth of discussion in the commentaries; Esther's response remains enigmatic nonetheless. None of the suggested readings of this verse, including the two mentioned here as most favored among recent commentators, resolves the dilemma indicated by Moore: Esther's response seems to lack any logic. We may restate the problem to which Moore points as follows: How does the difference between slavery or annihilation explain Esther's request?[21]

We may begin by noting Esther's quotation of the precise words of Haman's edict. להשמיד להרוג ולאבד ("to destroy, massacre and exterminate"). She obviously alludes to the impending destruction of the Jews which Haman's edict authorizes. But what is the referent of the alternative treatment of the Jews which Esther mentions, viz., their "sale" into servitude? The storyteller clearly does not wish his audience to miss Esther's reference to this "sale" for he repeats the word נמכרנו ("we are sold") within this one verse.

The only point in the story where the Jews seemingly are "sold" occurs in Esth 3:8-9. Here, Haman requests that the king issue an edict for the Jews' destruction, יכתב לאבדם. In exchange, Haman offers 10,000 talents of silver.[22]

Most interpreters understand the phrase יכתב לאבדם to refer to the destruction of the Jews. But the term אבד sometimes possesses a broader meaning. For example, Deut 26:5 reads: ארמי אבד אבי, frequently rendered, "a wandering Aramean was my father."[23] A similar sense for אבד is suggested by Isa 27:13, האבדים בארץ אשור, "the homeless ones in Assyria." The juxtaposition of לבקש and לאבד in Qoh 3:6 indicates for the latter a sense of "to lose."[24]

This alternate interpretation of אבד does not appear suitable to the Book of Esther, especially when אבד is linked with הרג and שמד. The more usual rendering, "to destroy," seems appropriate, particularly in reference to Haman's decree. But in Esth 3:9, the word אבד occurs alone, without the qualifying הרג and שמד. There exists a possibility that an alternate sense of אבד was intended here.

That אבד in Esth 3:9 may refer to something other than the destruction of the Jews is supported by the reason offered by

Haman for his request: אין שוה להניחם. B. Wolff suggests that
initially Haman suggests something involving "their rest."[25]
From the standpoint of the association of ideas, נוח, "rest,"
finds its contrast in the concept of עבד, "work" or "servitude." Does the storyteller play on words here? That is, does
he suggest that Haman allows the king to think he speaks of
לעבדם, "cause them to work" or even לאבדם, "cause them to become dispossessed, homeless"? Does Haman allow the king to
think that he refers to the selling of the Jews into servitude
while Haman, as well as the audience, knows that he intends
לאבדם, "to destroy them"? Such a play on words at least clarifies Haman's odd remark concerning the 10,000 talents of
silver--a remark which makes little sense if Haman *unambiguously* requests the destruction of the Jews.

A play on the senses of אבד and עבד also explains Esther's
statement in 7:4, where she refers both to the destruction and
the servitude of the Jews. Her words themselves present a play
on the two terms in chiastic fashion: כי נמכרנו אני ועמי
להשמיד להרוג ולאבד ואלו לעבדים ולשפחות נמכרנו החרשתי כי אין
שוה בנזק המלך.

Finally, support for this suggested example of paronomasia
is found in Ahasuerus' response to Esther's words. Esther 7:5
indicates Ahasuerus' ignorance regarding the planned destruction of the Jews or its instigator. As frequently noted by
commentators, the king's innocence here makes little sense
since he assented to Haman's plan. But Ahasuerus' ignorance is
understandable if the plan he believed himself to have authorized concerned the selling into servitude--not the wholesale
destruction--of a people (cf. 7:4, להשמיד להרוג ולאבד).[26]

The logic of Esther's remarks in 7:4 thus becomes clear:
she requests that the Jews be spared since their destruction
runs counter to the king's best interests. If only the sale of
Jews into slavery were at issue, Esther would remain silent.
Such treatment of her people accords with the king's wishes;
their destruction, however, does not. Esther breaks her silence on this matter[27] because of her concern for herself and
her people, but also because of her loyalty to the crown. Her
words imply that the Jews' enemy, Haman, is one who attempts to
deceive the king and threatens his rule.

This interpretation conforms with the portrayal of Haman

throughout the Book of Esther. In comparing the actions of
Mordecai and Esther to those of Haman, Humphreys notes that
Haman's concerns are limited only to those which prove *person-
ally* beneficial.

> The basic dichotomy between Haman's stated purpose
> and his real intent is made apparent in the climac-
> tic seventh chapter. He had presented his plan to
> the king, with a certain cleverness, in terms of the
> king's own interest and benefit (3:8-11); his ploy
> to destroy the Jews is presented in terms of pro-
> tecting the kingdom from the dangerous influence of
> a lawless people and of enriching the coffers of the
> king. However, his hatred of Mordecai led him to
> later give up this plan and to seek a more immedi-
> ate fulfillment of his purpose by erecting a huge
> gallows upon which to hang Mordecai. This dichot-
> omy becomes clear to all in the seventh chapter;
> the pretended royal benefactor is (ironically enough,
> wrongly) accused of attempting to violate the queen
> (7:8; cf. 5f.).[28]

Haman thus deceives the king--if not by the ambiguous request
לאבד, then by the concealment of his actual intentions in presenting his request in 3:9 as a concern for the king.

The motif of obedience/disobedience suggests the value the
narrator placed upon a theme of Jewish loyalty. In the Book of
Esther, allegiance to the Jewish community supersedes even loyalty to the king. Yet the narrator does not portray his Jewish
protagonists as unconcerned about the welfare of the state. On
the contrary, Esther and Mordecai are loyal and responsible
citizens of the empire. They demonstrate both a concern for
their co-religionists and, unlike Haman, a genuine regard for
the king's well-being.

3. The Themes of Inviolability and Reversal

Inherent to the themes of power and loyalty in the Book of
Esther is a subsidiary theme, the inviolability of the Jewish
people. The clearest statement of this theme is found in Esth
6:13. Here, Haman's wife and advisers note that Haman cannot
succeed against Mordecai. The "logic" of their appraisal is
based upon the fact that Mordecai is a Jew: אם מזרע היהודים
מרדכי.[29] The inviolability of the Jews already is signaled
with their introduction into the narrative. In Esth 2:5-6, we
meet Mordecai. His genealogy suggests the long history of the

Jewish people (2:5), and his "personal history" indicates the
continued survival of the Jews despite their captivity and
exile (2:6). Another hint of this theme is found in Esth. 4:14,
where Mordecai asserts that assistance to the Jews would derive
from another source if Esther failed to intercede with Ahasuerus.[30] Whatever its source, Mordecai knows that assistance for
the Jews will appear.

Scholars often note the remarkable series of "coincidences" reported in Esther.[31] For example, Mordecai chances to
overhear the plot to assassinate the king; Ahasuerus has insomnia and "coincidentally" is read the report in the royal chronicles describing Mordecai's loyalty; Haman enters the court at
the moment the king ponders the question of how to reward Mordecai; the king returns to Esther's banquet while Haman, having
fallen upon Esther's couch, begs for his life. These "coincidences" fall within the realm of possibility but nevertheless
strain the laws of probability. These coincidences surely
seemed as remarkable to an ancient audience as they strike us.
Their very improbability itself underscores the fact that the
Jewish people cannot be destroyed. The coincidences of the
plot demonstrate the truth of Mordecai's assurance: assistance
for the Jews indeed would appear. The author of the story
thereby affirms his own belief that, despite the great dangers
which threaten the diaspora Jewish communities, the Jews are
inviolable.[32]

Some scholars attribute the series of remarkable coincidences found in Esther to the story's underlying religious elements.[33] Such views in principle accept Y. Kaufmann's argument
that Esther cannot be understood as a "secular" document.[34]
Kaufmann maintains that biblical narratives are characterized
by a dual causality, i.e., a natural causation itself guided by
a program of divine providence. It is through the natural
order that God effects His plans. Even if a clear reference to
God is lacking in Esther, the story nonetheless displays divine
control of the created order.

Michael Fox similarly argues that the Book of Esther displays "an ordering principle, something which makes sense out
of the events."[35] This ordering principle is displayed in the
series of fortunate coincidences, all of which suggest a pattern to history. This pattern is that of reversal, or more

specifically, peripety.[36] According to Aristotle's *Poetics*,
peripety is a fundamental element in tragedy, occurring when an
action or state of affairs produces the opposite of the expected result. The peripetetic principle expresses the frustration of human expectations and demonstrates that the course
of human lives is influenced by forces beyond human control.
In the biblical literature, the force behind peripety is always
God. Moreover, peripety is not limited to tragedy in the
Hebrew Bible.[37]

The series of astonishing coincidences in the Book of Esther amply illustrate the peripetetic principle. For example,
through a series of coincidental events, Haman unwittingly vol-
unteers the method by which his arch-enemy, Mordecai, is honored by the king. Yet Haman had come to court to seek the
death of Mordecai! Later, Haman's inopportune plea for his own
life occurs at the precise moment the king returns to Esther's
banquet. This coincidence leads to the death of Haman upon the
gallows he intended for Mordecai. In both cases, peripety is
at play and leads to a situation the opposite of what we initially expect.

The fact that the series of coincidences in Esther point
in a certain direction, viz., that of reversal, indicates that
they cannot be attributed to mere chance. If Kaufmann and Fox
are correct, these coincidences point to the divine activity
which lies beneath the surface of events. The Book of Esther
thereby displays an implicit "theology" despite the absence of
any clear references to Yahweh.[38]

The theme of reversal is evident throughout the Book of
Esther. For example, we already have noted that the low social
status of the Jewish protagonists is radically altered by the
story's conclusion. Similarly, the initially powerless Jews
attain great power with the denouement of the tale. Reversals
also are evident in the story's motifs, where occasions which
initially prompt Jewish fasts are transformed into joyous cele-
brations accompanied by feasts. Even actions which normally
warrant punishment, e.g., Esther's unsummoned appearances before Ahasuerus, are reversed and instead merit rewards.

The theme of reversals is explicitly stated in Esth 9:1.

In the 12th month, the month of Adar, on the 13th day,
when the king's command and decree were to be carried

> out--on the very day when the Jews' enemies hoped
> to gain control over them--the opposite happened
> (ונהפוך הוא) and the Jews gained control over their
> enemies.

The theme of reversal similarly is stated in Esth 9:22,25.[39]

The theme of reversal is so important in the Book of Esther that the narrator even structures his story according to
this principle. It consequently is helpful to examine the
literary architecture of the Book of Esther prior to considering the implications for the themes of inviolability and reversal.

B. Structure of the Book of Esther

The structure of the Book of Esther is ordered according
to the theme of reversal. The narrated events are organized

> . . . as a symmetrical series of theses and antitheses,
> situations and their reversals. The theses are situa-
> tions portending disaster for the Jews and success for
> their enemies, situations which could be expected to
> lead, in the natural course of events, to the Jews'
> destruction. But events do not run their natural
> course, but lead to the antitheses, which are the ex-
> act opposites of the result potential in the theses.[40]

The series of theses/antitheses is built into the architecture
of Esther, beginning

> . . . after the preparatory matters of chapters 1 and
> 2 and continues until the end of the book. The thesis
> series proceeds to 6:9, at which point the antithesis
> series begins. The turning point is bracketed between
> Esther's two banquets, the first of which swells
> Haman's pride, the second of which crushes him. Haman
> ironically starts his own downfall by pronouncing Mor-
> decai's reward, so that by his own actions he begins
> to reverse his scheming upon his own head.[41]

To ensure that his audience does not miss the careful
structuring of the antithetical pairs, the narrator uses identical, or nearly identical, phraseology in most of the pairs.
His repetition of similar phrases both establishes the link between earlier and later events and emphasizes the counterpoint
between them. We may compare the following pairs:[42]

3:1	גדל המלך אחשורוש את־המן בן־המדתא האגגי וינשאהו וישם את־כסאו מעל כל־ השרים אשר אתו	10:3	כי מרדכי היהודי משנה למלך אחשורוש וגדל ליהודים
		(cf. 9:3)	(מנשאים את־היהודים)
3:7	הפיל פור הוא הגורל	9:24	והפיל פור הוא הגורל

3:8	ולמלך אין־שוה להניחם	7:4	כי אין הצר שוה בנזק המלך
3:10	ויסר המלך את־טבעתו מעל ידו ויתנה להמן בן־המדתא האגגי צרר היהודים	8:2a	ויסר המלך את־טבעתו אשר העביר מהמן ויתנה למרדכי
3:11b	והעם לעשות בו כטוב בעיניך	8:8a	ואתם כתבו על־היהודים כטוב בעיניכם
3:12-13	ויקראו ספרי המלך בחדש הראשון בשלושה עשר יום בו ויכתב ככל־ אשר־צוה המן אל אחשדרפני־ המלך ואל־הפחות אשר על־ מדינה ומדינה ואל־שרי עם ועם מדינה ומדינה ככתבה ועם ועם כלשונו בשם המלך אחשורש נכתב ונחתם בטבעת המלך: ונשלוח ספרים ביד הרצים אל־כל־מדינות המלך להשמיד להרג ולאבד את־כל־היהודים מנער ועד־זקן טף ונשים ביום אחד בשלושה עשר לחדש שנים־עשר הוא־חדש אדר ושלֹלם לבוז	8:9-11	ויקראו ספרי־המלך ... בחדש השלישי הוא־חדש סיון בשלושה ועשרים בו ויכתב ככל־ אשר־צוה מרדכי אל־היהודים ואל האחשדרפנים־והפחות ושרי המדינות אשר מהדו ועד־כוש שבע ועשרים ומאה מדינה מדינה ומדינה ככתבה ועם ועם כלשנו ואל־ היהודים ככתבם וכלשונם: ויכתב בשם המלך אחשורש ויחתם בטבעת המלך וישלח ספרים ביד הרצים...אשר נתן המלך ליהודים אשר בכל־עיר־ ועיר להקהל ולעמד על־נפשם להשמיד ולהרג ולאבד את־כל־ חיל עם ומדינה הצרים אתם טף ונשים ושללם לבוז (cf. 8:12)
3:14	פתשגן הכתב להנתן דת בכל־מדינה ומדינה גלוי לכל־העמים להיות עתדים ליום הזה	8:13	פתשגן הכתב להנתן דת בכל־ מדינה ומדינה גלוי לכל־ העמים ולהיות היהודיים עתודים ליום הזה
3:15	הרצים יצאו דחופים בדבר המלך והדת נתנה בשושן הבירה והמן והמלך ישבו לשתות והעיר שושן נבוכה	8:14-15b	הרצים רכבי הרכש האחשתרנים יצאו מבהלים ודחופים בדבר המלך והדת נתנה בשושן הבירה: ...והעיר שושן צהלה ושמחה (ויבא המלך והמן (cf. 7:1) לשתות)
4:3	ובכל־מדינה ומדינה מקום אשר דבר־המלך ודתו מגיע אבל גדול ליהודים וצום ובכי ומספד שק ואפר יצע לרבים	8:17a	ובכל־מדינה ומדינה ובכל־ עיר ועיר מקום אשר דבר־ המלך ודתו מגיע שמחה וששון ליהודים משתה ויום טוב

Yehudah T. Radday also finds the Book of Esther to be constructed according to a pattern of reversals, but in stricter fashion.[43] Radday argues that Esther is structured according to a chiastic principle, a common feature of literature from the early periods of Israelite history. According to Radday, Esther's chiastic structure represents a conscious attempt to archaize.

108

The chiastic arrangement of Esther's ten chapters "strikes the eye even of the cursory reader." Unlike Fox, Radday sees the conscious structuring of the narrative encompassing the book as a whole, and he suggests the following schematic overview:[44]

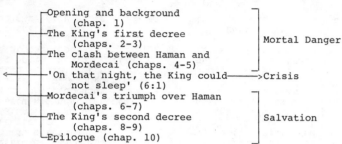

As this schematic summary of the story suggests, Radday considers Esth 6:1 to be the crucial turning point of the narrative.[45]

Esther's author adheres to "the chiastic tradition which he had inherited from his predecessors,"[46] to the extent that the second part of the scroll repeats the first not only in content and structure, but also in its episodes, keywords, idioms and stylistic techniques. For example, three banquets are found prior to the central verse of 6:1, just as three feasts follow. We find three references to the royal chronicles at the beginning (2:23), middle (6:1) and end (10:2) of the scroll. In addition several key words occur the same number of times in the first and second halves of the scroll, although Radday cites only the example of "Susa" (29 times).[47] Radday seemingly would concur with Fox that Esther's author intended to underscore the inverse symmetry of his story by informing the audience in 9:1 that "the opposite happened."

The Book of Esther, however, diverges from a "classical" chiasm.

> Classical chiasm would have demanded that in Esther . . . certain stylistic elements occur, for the sake of symmetry, twice only: once before and once after ch. 6,1, and, as far as possible, in inverse order. It must be conceded that the author of Esther did not follow this rule. Instead of the expected 'dislegomena', we find a number of 'trislegomena'. Yet when these are disregarded, and they number no more than half a dozen, we still find 48 elements in Part I

which re-occur in Part II, i.e., ten elements per
chapter, on the average.[48]

Both Fox and Radday, despite the differences in their
arguments, find a pattern of reversals to govern the structure
of Esther.[49] The evidence, however, suggests that the series
of reversals depends as much upon the content of events as upon
their order. The sequence of events does not present a precise
chiasm; rather, the reversals are of a general nature. The
"antithesis" of each pair may occur at a point in the narrative
preceding or following what would be its position in a strict
chiasm. The structure of Esther also manifests a narrative
style apparent in its motifs. Just as each occurrence of a
dominant motif potently anticipates or recalls its other appearances, each member of the antithetical pairs recalls the
other.

The Book of Esther was constructed according to a precise
pattern that manifests the theme of reversal. The general
thrust of Fox's and Radday's theses seems warranted by the evidence; their specific arguments nevertheless pose some problems. For example, Radday's methodology may not suit the Book
of Esther. Its narrator conveyed his ideas through the recurrence of motifs and themes which bring to mind situations and
events recounted elsewhere in the tale. Repetitions are common
throughout Esther and facilitate the comparison of incidents
and events. But can these repetitions be taken as evidence for
a chiastic structure? Even were a chiastic structure present
in Esther, can we assume with Radday that this chiasm was the
narrator's starting point in composing his story? Is Esther's
chiastic structure due merely to an inheritance from the past?

The type of statistical analysis offered by Radday is
valuable since it uncovers features of the story which might
not otherwise be discerned. It is interesting to discover that
words such as "Susa" appear an equal number of times in both
halves of the story. Such findings lend support to the analysis of Esther suggested above on other grounds. On the other
hand, Radday's statistical analysis also possesses a wooden
artificiality.[50] It tends to ignore the content of episodes,
overemphasizing data which may result from stylistic and rhetorical techniques, idiomatic expressions and even the uncon-
scious or accidental choice of words. Radday's approach to

Esther implies that its content was determined largely by a
premeditated plan of construction. The content and structure
of events in Esther indeed are integral and governed by the
theme of reversals; but they are not necessarily identical.

Radday also points to the interesting feature of "trislegomena" in Esther.[51] This phenomenon is not unique to Esther, but is found elsewhere in the Hebrew Bible. For example,
we find Pharaoh's advisers unable to interpret his dream on
three occasions in the Joseph story (cf. Gen 41:8c, 15a, 24b).
This threefold notice should probably be connected with Ahasuerus' thrice-asked question regarding Esther's petition (cf.
Esth 5:3,6;7:2).[52] Examples of "trislegomena" also abound in 1
and 2 Samuel. For example, Yahweh calls Samuel twice (1 Sam
3:4-8) before Eli recognizes the source of the divine summons
on its third occasion (1 Sam 3:8).[53] "Threeness" can be found,
e.g., in Gen 18:2 (three men); 22:4 (third day); 42:18 (third
day); Exod 19:16 (third day); Num 24:10 (Balaam's three bless-
ings); Josh 2:16 (three days); Jonah 2:1 (three days and three
nights); Ezra 8:15 (three days); cf. Hos 6:2 (on the third day).[54]

The phenomenon of "trislegomena" is not unique to Esther.
Its presence in the scroll probably derives not from the
story's chiastic structure, but from a common rhetorical
trait--even a motif--of ancient Israelite storytelling.

Presumably, Radday's designation of Esth 6:1 as the turning point of the tale stems from his statistical analysis.
That is, Esth 6:1 is preceded and followed by an equal number
of identical words or expressions. But does this turning point
mirror the reversals in the actual content of the events? Is
the king's insomnia, which this verse relates, the central
point of the narrative?

I suggested above that the critical turning point of the
story occurs at 4:13-14--a passage which scholars frequently
cite as crucial, if not central. Esther 4:13-14 marks a transition in the course of events, the point at which the series
of "theses" ends and the sequence of "antitheses" begins.[55]
Here, Mordecai obeys Esther, reversing our images of the protagonists. Esther becomes the initiator of events, and this
transition is marked by Ahasuerus' rewarding, not punishing,
her crime in 5:1-5. Esther 6:1 initiates the reversal of Mordecai's personal fortunes, but the transition between thesis

and antithesis has already begun with Esther's decision to aid
her people.

The content and structure of events in the Book of Esther
suggest that history is not a sequence of random events. Rather, it is ordered and this knowledge undoubtedly provided reas-
surance to diaspora audiences who lived in "exile" and often
were subject to forces over which they had little control. Fox
indicates that ancient audiences were reassured by the *pattern*
of events more than by their successful conclusion. Even when
no pattern in everyday events is discernible, the Book of Esther illustrates that history is not dependent solely upon
human forces. To the contrary, the peripetetic principle governing history depicts the frustration of human expectations.
We learn that events can assume a direction radically different
from--even opposite--what we anticipate.

It is at this point that Fox's thesis strikes me as most
problematic. If "history" depicts the frustration of human expectations and demonstrates that humanity cannot determine the
course of events, where is the control of history to be
located? What role does humanity play in shaping the course of
history? One could attribute *complete* control of history to
Yahweh. Yet the Book of Esther lacks any direct reference to
Yahweh's role in the narrated events. Would not the argument
for the reversal of life's expectations be clearer and more
easily apprehended if Yahweh were portrayed as unambiguously
and undeniably in control of history? Fox notes the careful
avoidance of references to the deity. He argues, however, that
an ancient audience would not deny the possibility of Yahweh's
control of history; rather, it would assume His control. Such
a view strikes me as correct. But at the same time, this
understanding suggests that the narrator was *not* interested in
demonstrating to his audience that Yahweh controls history.[56]
In fact, God's control of events, while assumed, probably is not
stated precisely so that the roles of Mordecai, Esther and the
other Jews might take center stage.

That the narrator did not seek to demonstrate Yahweh's
control of history is supported by other examples of peripety
in the Hebrew Bible. As Fox observes, peripety frequently is
found in the psalmic literature, where it is used to praise
God's justice and to express the psalmist's faith that the

righteous and the wicked receive their appropriate recompense.
But nowhere in the psalms does peripety serve as the psalmist's
argument *per se*. Rather, peripety suggests the certainty that
God's justice will prevail, despite the expected outcome of
events. The psalms only indirectly present a theme of reversal; the psalmists were more concerned to make faith statements
regarding God's justice. Their statements are framed by a
peripetetic theme, but the affirmations of the psalmists direct
our attention elsewhere.

Throughout the Hebrew Bible, the reversal of human expectations provides the means to some other end. The arguments of
the biblical writers cannot be characterized as intending to
prove a theme of reversals. On the contrary, this theme often
is assumed and perhaps constitutes a common mode of expression.

What distinguishes the Book of Esther from other biblical
writings is the fact that the content and pattern of the narrated "history" indicates peripety to be a central thematic
concern. But this theme is integral to others. The theme of
reversal illustrates the possibility--even probability--of the
themes of power, loyalty and inviolability. At the same time,
the theme of reversal makes sense only in light of the presence
of these other themes; in a sense, it derives its meaning from
them.[57]

I have suggested that the Book of Esther is built around
pairs of opposites whose comparison is promoted by similarities
in content and/or phrasing. At the same time, we also may note
some differences between the members of each pair. For example, the edict mentioned in Esth 8:9-12 is similar to that of
3:12-13, and even may quote the earlier passage.[58] But Esth
8:9-12 adds the explanation that the Jews assembled to "fight
for their lives" against "those attacking them" (8:11). Esther
8:13 similarly indicates the self-defensive nature of the Jewish attack, להנקם מאיביהם. This phrase was added to the almost
identical passage of 3:14. Other examples of differences in
phrasing are found in 10:3, where we read that Mordecai was
"great among the Jews" (cf. 3:1), and in 8:2a, which refers to
Haman's former possession of the monarch's ring. These slight
differences contrast the pairs and, at the same time, underscore the relationship between the disempowering of Haman and
Mordecai's promotion.

The reversal of events, then, constitutes an important
theme in Esther. But the successful outcome of events, as well
as their pattern, is crucial.[59] The fortunate conclusion of
Esther's "history" affirms that the reversal of events proceeds
in a particular manner. The theme of reversal serves as a com-
pass, pointing beyond itself to the themes of power and inviolability. We learn that despite the expectations of the Jews
in Ahasuerus' empire, they will prove successful. They will
ascend to the highest positions of power permitted by diaspora
life because history will reverse itself in their favor. But
such a reversal depends upon the "correct" human response to
history--a response which the narrator suggests by his theme of
loyalty.

The themes of inviolability and reversal hold implications
for Esther's function as a festal scroll. Purim commemorates
the defeat of those who sought to destroy the Jews because "the
opposite happened"; its "historical" prelude indicates how this
feat was accomplished by the Jews' own efforts. The festival
serves as a reminder to future generations that even "hopeless"
situations can be transformed by the proper human response.
The course of history, despite the odds, can be reversed. In
spite of their expectations, the people of Israel can remain
inviolable.[60]

This discussion of Esther's themes may be concluded with a
final observation. One question raised in Chapter I concerned
the narrator's understanding of history. The themes of inviolability and reversal provide a response. If Esther's author
understood history to consist of something more than a random
series of occurrences, the presentation of his tale as a "history" provides the logical expression of his belief. Although
the narrated events did not actually take place, they nevertheless indicate where history leads. The Book of Esther presents
a particular historical period from the perspective of its successful conclusion. From this perspective, one can see that
history, despite its expected course, can radically realign
itself in a favorable direction.

NOTES

[1]Anderson, "The Book of Esther," 835; Bardtke, *Das Buch Esther*, 276; Gerleman, *Esther*, 56; Moore, *Esther*, 12.

[2]The wealth and power of the Persian court were renowned in the ancient world; cf. Herodotus, *Hist.* 3.95-96; 7.27; 9.80-81; Aeschylus, *Pers.* 161. Also see the discussions of *Tg. Esth I, II* and *Est.Rab.* on Esth 1:4.

[3]Gunkel, *Esther*, 4.

[4]The abundance of unusual and rare words in Esth 1:6 suggests the somewhat exotic nature of the decor. The description of the garden canopy in Esther 1 is reminiscent of the portrayal of the tabernacle in Exodus 26-27, 36. A clear dependence, however, does not seem indicated. Gordis, *Megillat Esther*, 22, compares the description of the garden canopy to the technical catalogues of Isa 3:18-22 and Cant 4:13-14, where the luxurious and exotic also are intended.

[5]Also cf. Esth 9:3-4 which indicates the "fear" inspired by Mordecai's *growing* power: כי־גדול מרדכי...ושמעו הולך...כי־ האיש מרדכי הולך וגדול.

[6]Mordecai's royal status is implied in the genealogy of Esth 2:5. The implications of this verse, however, are not developed until later in the tale. Here it primarily serves an anticipatory function.

[7]Esther's beauty, of course, is distinctive. The audience surely delighted in the fact that a Jewess "won the admiration of all who saw her" (2:15). The notable feature here, however, is that a *Jewess*--not this particular individual--surpassed all other women of the empire in beauty.

[8]Does מחיהדים suggest a period when Jewish proselytism was not unusual? The narrator does not expand upon the meaning or significance of this term, perhaps suggesting that neither he nor his audience considered such conversions unusual.

[9]Esther, too, uses her power to benefit her people. The story demonstrates this by Esther's intercession to obstruct Haman's decree.

[10]The newly acquired status of the Jews is not entirely a result of the efforts of Esther and Mordecai. The participation of other Jews in the important fast of 4:16-17 indicates their role in the reversal of their fate.

[11]A connection between the motifs of feasts and kingship and the theme of power already is suggested by Esther's coronation and subsequent banquet (2:17-18). Esther's attainment of royal power in chapter 2 foreshadows the power which Mordecai and the other Jews will achieve.

115

[12]This shift also is noted by Talmon, "'Wisdom' in the Book of Esther," 449-453, and by Humphreys, "The Motif of the Wise Courtier in the Old Testament," 299, 305.

[13]Loretz, "$\check{s}^c r$ $hmlk$--'Das Tor des Königs' (Esth 2,19)" 104-108; Hans Wehr, "Das 'Tor des Königs' im Buche Esther und verwandte Ausdrücke," *Islam* 39 (1964) 247-260.

[14]Esther's petition in Esth 7:3-4 and its implications are discussed below.

[15]Many of these notices occur in passages whose integrity is undisputed. Similar notices also appear in 9:20-28. If this passage is secondary, the later editor indeed was perceptive in his understanding of the story.

[16]Also compare Esther's personal concern for Mordecai in Esth 4:4, set within the context of communal mourning.

[17]This opinion is expressed by Moore, *Esther*, 70. Similar views are held by Paton, *The Book of Esther*, 258-259; Torrey, "The Older Book of Esther," 36; and Gordis, "Studies in the Esther Narrative," 55-56.

[18]Paton, *The Book of Esther*, 258, finds two beginnings to the verse, "due doubtless to a combination of alternate readings." The ancient versions also seem confused by Esther's response in 7:3-4 and their readings widely diverge. They consequently are of limited value in resolving the difficulties of this verse. On the interpretations of the ancient versions, see Haupt, "Critical Notes on Esther," 164-167, and Gordis, "Studies in the Esther Narrative," 55.

[19]Gordis, "Studies in the Esther Narrative," 55-56, considers various grammatical possibilities in Esth 7:4.

[20]Gordis finds the second interpretation preferable, as do Gerleman and Moore; see also the *RSV*, *NEB*, and Humphreys, "The Motif of the Wise Courtier in the Old Testament." In a review of Gerleman's study, P. Wernberg-Møller, *JSS* 20 (1975) 241-243, argues in favor of the second interpretation of this verse.

[21]The explanation of Esth 7:4 proposed here is based upon the suggested understanding of Esther's narrative style. That which is stressed at any particular point in the story frequently anticipates or recalls some other portion of the narrative. This description suits the narrator's stylistic use of motifs. I have assumed that a similar narrative style also applies to lesser details of the story. The scope of the present study does not permit a complete analysis of narrative style in Esther. Consequently, the following remarks can be offered only tentatively.

[22]In this passage, we also find the words ולמלך אין־שׁוה, להניחם, reminiscent of Esther's statement in 7:4, כי אין הצר שׁוה בנזק המלך. Apart from these two passages, the word שׁוה occurs in Esther only in 5:13. That this term, infrequent in Esther, occurs in both 3:8 and 7:4 lends support to the suggestion that 3:8-9 underlies the "sale" mentioned in 7:4. The

narrator's choice of שוה in 3:8 and 7:4 is remarkable if he intends to play on the word שבה, "take captive." The discussion
below concerns a play on the words אבד and עבד. שבה\שוה contributes to the paronomasia.

[23]But cf. *m.Gen.Rab.* on Deut 26:5 where the rabbis accept
the more common rendering of אבד.

[24]Benedikt Otzen, "אָבַד '*ābhadh*," *TDOT* 1 (1977) 20, writes:
"Only in the qal do both principal meanings, 'to perish' and
'wander off,' occur in the OT." The use of אבד in Esther, however, may require qualification of this assertion. At any rate
the piel of אבד in Esther does not affect any play between אבד
and עבד, nor any play on an alternate meaning of the root.

[25]Wolff, *Das Buch Esther*, 22. See also Chapter I above
and the remarks of Bardtke, "Neuere Arbeiten zum Estherbuch,"
526-527, regarding the concept of obtaining rest and the Purim
legislation. Again note the use of אין שוה in both Haman's
reason (3:8) and in Esther's (7:4).

[26]This explanation of Esth 7:4 raises a question of plausibility: Could Haman actually deceive Ahasuerus with a clever
play on words? One could respond by agreeing with those who
see the king as a dupe, notably Talmon, "'Wisdom' in the Book
of Esther," 441-443. More importantly, the explanation offered
here is able to account for other problems in the story which
otherwise remain unexplained. While my remarks are offered
only tentatively, I think that they account better for the
"data" of Esther than other theories proposed thus far. And in
the final analysis, how much less plausible is Haman's ability
to deceive Ahasuerus than many other situations narrated in the
story?

[27]The use of חרש in 7:4 recalls Mordecai's words of 4:13-
14, reinforcing the link between his command and Esther's eventual obedience to it. Ironically enough, Esther's obedience to
Mordecai begins with her disobedience to the king in 5:1-5.

[28]Humphreys, "The Motif of the Wise Courtier in the Old
Testament," 302. See the discussion of David Daube, "The Last
Chapter of Esther," *JQR* 37 (1946-1947) 140-141, who argues that
Esth 10:1 places the activity of Mordecai and Esther in the
context of the king's welfare.

[29]This same rationale, viz., that Mordecai is a Jew,
ironically constitutes the reason behind Mordecai's refusal to
honor Haman (3:4).

[30]Again, Esth 4:14 is less concerned with the source of
assistance than with Mordecai's assurance that it is forthcoming. See Chapter III above.

[31]Many see in these remarkable events the hidden hand of
God, and Kaufmann's discussion at this point is helpful; see
below. The suggestion that the "coincidences" in Esther express the divine control of history is discussed below. I
shall only note here that such interpretations must be quali-
fied. The omission of references to Yahweh in the Book of

118

Esther is intentional and serves a function in the narrative.

[32]The theme of inviolability perhaps accounts for the intense, chauvinistic fervor which some critics of the story find.

[33]For example, Anderson, "The Place of the Book of Esther in the Christian Bible," 36, writes: "As the Septuagint and the Targums interpret, every seemingly 'accidental' development in the plot is actually an expression of purpose: God's intervention on behalf of his people." Dommershausen, *Die Estherrolle*, 157-158, discerns signs of the transcendental deity in the story's "Zufälligkeiten." The author further expresses his religious beliefs by alluding to other scriptural passages where God is depicted clearly as the cause of events. These views go against the earlier opinion of Paton, *The Book of Esther*, 96-97, who saw the scroll as "so conspicuously lacking in religion that it should never have been included in the canon of the OT." Pfeiffer, *Introduction to the Old Testament*, 742-744, likewise understands the book to be a secularistic document suiting the period of John Hyrcanus' reign. Gerleman, *Esther*, does not term Esther as "secular" *per se* but places the book within a secularization process which began with the Succession Narrative. Talmon, "'Wisdom' in the Book of Esther," explains the absence of any religious elements in the story as due to its wisdom character.

[34]Kaufmann, תולדות האמונה הישראלית, 8.445-447. See also the discussion of Isac Leo Seeligmann, "Menschliches Heldentum und göttliche Hilfe" in *TZ* 6 (1963) 385-411.

[35]I wish to thank Prof. Fox, who graciously provided me with a copy of his unpublished manuscript, "The Theology of the Book of Esther." This section of the dissertation was completed prior to my receipt of the final draft of Fox's study. Consequently, not all of my criticisms of his position apply. Fox's revised study will appear as "The Structure of the Book of Esther" in the forthcoming Festschrift to I. L. Seeligmann.

[36]Ibid.

[37]Fox cites examples of peripety in the Hebrew Bible outside the Book of Esther. Among these are Pss 7:11-18; 9:16-17; 35:7-9; 54:6-7; cf. Pss 37:14-15; 57:7; 141:9-10. Also cf. Prov 1:16-19; 26-27; Job 5:13; Qoh 10:8-9; and Sir 27:25-27. Peripety is found in the prophetic literature, both as forms of punishment and salvation, e.g., Jer 30:16; Isa 14:25; Ezek 17:24. While peripety often is found in connection with God's justice, the reversal of expectations illustrates divine control even when reward and punishment are not in question. Peripety thus underlies the choice of the youngest son, e.g., Isaac, Jacob, Ephraim, David and Solomon. Peripety also lies behind the motif of a long-barren woman's giving birth to a great leader.

[38]The "theology" of the Book of Esther is discussed in Chapter VI below.

[39]Esth 9:22: ". . . the month which was changed (אשר נהפך) for them from sorrow to joy and from mourning to celebration";

9:25: "But when the matter came before the king, he commanded in writing that [Haman's] wicked scheme . . . should be reversed upon his own head (ישוב...על-ראשו), and they hanged him and his sons on the gallows." If these verses are secondary, the theme of reversal was prominent enough to be recognized by a later editor.

[40]Fox, "The Structure of the Book of Esther."

[41]Ibid.

[42]The following comparison of passages from the Book of Esther basically follows that suggested by Fox. But not every pair compared by Fox is equally convincing; consequently, his list is not cited in its entirety. For example, Fox compares Esth 6:6-9/6:10 and 5:14a/6:13b-14. I find these pairs to be closer in his English translation than in the MT. Since my examples diverge somewhat from Fox's, I have cited them in Hebrew. In some cases, the similarity in phrasing is clearer in Hebrew than in the translation; in others, the similarity between the passages is primarily in terms of content.
   Compare the language and content of Esth 4:1/8:15a. Also note the reversal in roles played by Mordecai and Esther. In the first part of the story, Mordecai is the chief protagonist and the guardian whom Esther obeys. In the course of the narrative, Esther rises from Mordecai's ward to become his benefactor (cf. 8:1-2). In chapter 5 and thereafter, Esther becomes the primary initiator of events, and it is her actions which result in the reversal of the Jews' status and fate.
   Finally, note the ironical role of Harbona, who appears in 1:10 and 7:9. He was among those sent to bring Vashti, thus beginning the series of events that led to Esther's rise. He reappears later in the narrative to suggest the means for Haman's demise. He thereby plays his own small role in reversing the fortunes of the main characters.

[43]Yehudah T. Radday, "Chiasm in Joshua, Judges and Others," *LB* 3 (1973) 6-13.

[44]Ibid., 9. Fox thinks the pattern of reversals begins only in chapter 3. But is it plausible that all of chapters 1-2 were intended only as an introduction to the rest of the tale?

[45]Radday, 9. On the other hand, Fox finds the turning point at Esth 6:9.

[46]Radday, 9.

[47]Ibid. Radday remarks: "The numerical side of the literary character of Esther deserves . . . a more detailed treatment: here the one example given above should suffice, together with the remark that such numerological literary devices which look artificial to the modern reader, are quite common in the Hebrew Bible and serve there rather specific purposes."

[48]Ibid.

[49]Another recent examination of Esther's literary structure is offered by N. A. van Uchelen, "A Chokmatic Theme in the Book of Esther." Van Uchelen notes some repetition of terms (בקש, חלה, ישלח יד, שׁוב) and of content (Esth 3:6-14/8:11-9:2), but offers no systematic or integrated analysis of Esther's structure. Rather, he argues only that these repetitions suggest the presence of a "chokmatic theme" which "supplied the key-motifs for the story as a whole" (136). These "key-motifs" focus upon "the inner connection between deeds and their consequences" which demonstrate the awareness of an orderly design in the world (135). This concern for order, according to van Uchelen, is most characteristic of the wisdom literature.

[50]Radday's statistical analysis is tied directly to the Masoretic version of Esther. It is interesting to speculate in what ways his statistics and/or argument for chiasm would change if textual changes, e.g., glosses, editorial expansions, and textual errors, were established on other grounds.

[51]Not too much weight should be attached to Radday's gematria. As Fox remarks in a private communication, "Is there any number that is *not* significant? I'm sure that one can find quadlegomena and quintlegomena without much trouble."

[52]Chapter V discusses the nature of Esther's dependence upon the Joseph story.

[53]Schildenberger, *Literarische Arten der Geschichtsschreibung im Alten Testament*, 12, lists numerous examples of "trislegomena" in the Books of Samuel. He notes that in the Succession Narrative, "spielt die Dreizahl eine bedeutsame Rolle."

[54]Some of these references, of course, call to mind the "third day" of the New Testament resurrection traditions. Also see the discussions of Alfred Jeremias, *Das Alte Testament im Lichte des Alten Orients* (Leipzig: J. C. Hinrichs, 1930), 336, n. 1, 820.

[55]The series of "antitheses" is set into motion by Esther's agreement to go before the king; cf. Esth 4:15-16. Esther makes her decision in spite of the utter helplessness of the situation and the presumed futility of her actions. Thus, the poignant וכאשר אבדתי אבדתי (4:16).

Manès Sperber, "Hurban or the Inconceivable Certainty," . . . *Than a Tear in the Sea* (New York/Tel Aviv: Bergen Belsen Memorial Press, 1967), xi, also indicates the necessity for an active response to events, despite the futility of one's efforts. He maintains that it was not hope but despair which inspired the Warsaw ghetto uprising. Despite the obvious differences between Sperber's view and that of the Book of Esther, his observation suggests points of contact with the desperate and hopeless situation confronting Jews in an earlier period.

[56]I shall argue in Chapter VI that, to the contrary, humanity's role in shaping history is most important. This understanding is partially demonstrated by the fact that the reversal of events begins only when Esther agrees to aid her people. This fact, in turn, also suggests an interdependence of the themes of loyalty and reversal.

[57]That reversal is not as central as Fox and Radday imply also is indicated by the fact that הפך is limited to Esth 9:1,22, with the parallel, ישוב על־ראשו, appearing only in 9:25. In addition, the pairs of opposites occur primarily in the central chapters of the story. While the theme of reversal is important, other themes are no less significant.

[58]Gordis, "Studies in the Esther Narrative," 53.

[59]I therefore disagree with Fox on this point.

[60]The favorable reversal of events by a "concealed" deity is set into motion by a heroine whose Jewish identity is suddenly revealed. How appropriate that these events are celebrated by a festival associated with costume and disguise!

CHAPTER V

THE BOOK OF ESTHER AND THE STORY OF JOSEPH

Recent research on the Book of Esther indicates that it
can no longer be considered an accurate, historical account of
events at Susa. Rather, as indicated above, Esther appears to
be more "history-like" than "historical." This characterization of the Book of Esther seems even more appropriate in light
of the important functions of the story's motifs, themes and
structure. Any historical core embedded in Esther has been
overlaid with novelistic elaborations and accommodated to the
storyteller's narrative style. Such an historical kernel thus
is not easily recovered. The interdependence of Esther's content and narrative style justifiably permits scholars to label
the scroll an "historical novel."

The Book of Esther, however, is not the only biblical narrative to be characterized in this fashion. Other stories,
frequently dated during the post-exilic period, also have been
described in recent years as more novelistic than historical.[1]
Scholars sometimes compare Esther to these other narratives,[2]
hoping to clarify the literary styles and purposes of each.[3]

One story in particular, that of Joseph, is often compared
to the Book of Esther. Scholars frequently discern close affinities in the motifs, themes and structures of the two narrative accounts. The Joseph story consequently is often viewed
as a literary model for the Book of Esther. If such views are
correct, the account of Joseph may provide clues to the underlying purposes of Esther. An examination of the various points
of contact between the two stories may indicate how the author
of Esther understood the Joseph story and *in what sense* the
latter constitutes the literary model of the former. Such an
examination could suggest the particular manner by which the
Joseph story was utilized in Esther, in turn indicating some of
the concerns of the later author.

This chapter will investigate the relationship between the
Book of Esther and the Joseph traditions. Using the results of
the preceding literary analysis of Esther, the motifs, themes

and structures of the two stories will be compared.[4] Hopefully, this comparison will indicate whether the Book of Esther
indeed relies upon the earlier tale and, if so, the precise
nature of its dependence. We shall carefully note both the
points of contact and of divergence between the stories in the
hope that they will suggest some implications for our understanding of Esther.

*A. Comparison of the Joseph and
Esther Stories*

The Book of Esther and the Joseph narratives are long associated by Jewish tradition[5] despite the great spans of geo-
graphical distance and time between them.[6] Since the turn of
this century, scholarship has reinforced this traditional view
by calling attention to linguistic, stylistic and structural
similarities between the stories.[7]

1. Linguistic Correspondence

In an 1895 study which continues to influence recent discussions, Ludwig A. Rosenthal demonstrated the stylistic and
thematic similarities of the Joseph, Esther and Daniel narratives.[8] Rosenthal noted a series of striking literary similarities between Genesis 37-50 and the Book of Esther which often
approached an identity of wording. For example, Gen 41:42-43
and Esth 6:11 both describe the elevation of the protagonists,
and a comparison of their verbs displays an unusual correspondence:

Gen 41:42-43	Esth 6:11 (cf. 8:2)
וילבש	וילבש
(and he arrayed)	(and he arrayed)
וירכב אתו	וירכיבהו
(and had him ride)	(and had him ride)
ויקראו לפניו	ויקרא לפניו
(and they cried out before him)	(and he cried out before him)
ויסר פראה את־טבעתו	[ויסר המלך את־טבעתו
(then Pharaoh transferred his ring)	(then the king transferred his ring)
ויתן אתה על־יד יוסף	ויתנה למרדכי]
(and set it on Joseph's hand)	(and gave it to Mordecai)

Also striking is the similarity in wording of Gen 39:10 and
Esth 3:4:

Gen 39:10

ויהי כדברה אל־יוסף
יום יום ולא־שמע אליה

(When she continued to ask
Joseph day after day, he
refused to listen to her)

Esth 3:4

ויהי [9]באמרם אליו
יום וים ולא שמע אליהם

(When they continued to speak
to him day after day, he refused to listen to them)

Even Esther's petition to Ahasuerus is reminiscent of Judah's
plea to Joseph.

Gen 44:34

For how can I go back to
my father if the lad is
not with me? I fear to
see the evil that would
come upon my father.

Esth 8:6

For how can I endure to see
the calamity that is coming
to my people? How can I endure to see the destruction
of my kindred?

In Esth 4:16, the queen indicates her resigned agreement
to Mordecai's command with the words, "if I perish, I perish."
Her words echo the construction of Gen 43:14, where Jacob re-
luctantly agrees to allow Benjamin to accompany his brothers to
Egypt: "if I am bereaved, I am bereaved." Despite their differing subject matters, the advice given to the Egyptian and
Persian monarchs also is of interest.

Gen 41:34-37

Let Pharaoh proceed to
appoint overseers over
the land . . . and let
them gather all the food
of these good years. . . .
This proposal seemed good
to Pharaoh. . . .

Esth 2:3-4

And let the king appoint
officers in all the prov-
inces of his kingdom to
gather all the beautiful
young virgins. . . . This
pleased the king. . . .

In a recent study, Moshe Gan confirms Rosenthal's findings
and suggests some additional linguistic correspondences.[10] Gan
compares Gen 40:20 with Esth 1:3; 2:18; Gen 44:24 with Esth
8:6; Gen 43:31; 45:1 with Esth 5:10; and Gen 50:3 with Esth
2:12. These additional examples of similar phrasing in the
stories are not compelling when considered individually. But
when viewed cumulatively, these examples also suggest the possibility of Esther's dependence upon the Joseph story. Also
noteworthy is the fact that correspondence in wording is not
limited to particular segments of either tale.

2. Similarities in Setting and Events

In addition to the linguistic similarities, the Joseph
story and the Book of Esther display general similarities in
settings and events. Both tales are set at the court of a foreign monarch and concern Jewish heroes who rise to prominence
at those courts. The heroes suffer a decline in their personal
fortunes as a direct result of their positions at court. The
heroes, however, overcome their misfortunes, and their success
provides the means by which their people is saved. In addition, each story refers to two eunuchs who act against the king
(cf. Gen 40:1-3; Esth 2:21-23). These incidents involving the
eunuchs both come to the king's attention and contribute to a
reversal in the personal fortunes of the Israelite servants.
This turning point directly results from the king's disturbed
sleep, when the monarch (or his servant) remembers the Israelite (cf. Gen 41:9-45; Esth 6:1-11). In both stories, the
heroes eventually are rewarded for their service to the king by
the transference of royal power to them. Both accounts also
depict a banquet scene where invited guests (Joseph's brothers,
Haman) do not know the true identity of their host/hostess.
The revelation of Joseph's and Esther's true identities results
in a change in the personal lives and fates of their guests.[11]
Finally, both stories mention punishment by hanging (חלה).[12]

Yet not every example of similarity of settings and events
carries equal weight. For example, the two eunuchs in the Joseph story play a significant role, while they are of minor importance in Esther. In Genesis, Joseph's ability to interpret
the eunuchs' dreams anticipates Joseph's subsequent explanation
of Pharaoh's dreams. Joseph's success at dream interpretations
demonstrates that he ironically lives up to the contemptuous
nickname given by his brothers, "lord of dreams." The account
of the two eunuchs in the Joseph narrative functions as an integral part of a dream motif which pervades the story.[13]

By contrast, Esth 2:21-23 plays a less significant role in
the tale. The primary function of this notice is to allow
Haman to honor Mordecai in Esther 6. This reward in turn presages the change in fortune of the Jewish people. Following the
brief notice of their conspiracy, the eunuchs inconspicuously
drop out of the story; they are executed two verses after their

introduction into the account. Joseph's successful interpretation of dreams leads directly to his promotion at court. Mordecai, however, remains "at the king's gate" following his discovery of the eunuchs' plot against Ahasuerus. He is elevated
to a position of power at court only after Esther informs Ahasuerus of Mordecai's relationship to her.

   The heroes' contact with the eunuchs and the kings' disturbed sleep serve as turning points in Joseph's and Mordecai's
personal fortunes. Unlike Joseph, however, Mordecai remains in
danger. Along with the other Jews of the empire, Mordecai continues to be subject to Haman's edict.[14] In addition, the manner in which each king's slumber is disturbed differs radically
in the stories. Pharaoh has disturbing dreams whereas Ahasuerus suffers insomnia. The motif of disturbed sleep was not uncommon in the ancient world.[15] Caution must therefore be exer-
cised in placing too much weight upon this parallel.

   Genesis 41:42-43 and Esth 6:1-11 both report the reward of
the heroes to consist of new garments and public appearances
where the heroes' special status is proclaimed.[16] At the same
time, the two passages also differ considerably. The order of
the characteristic honors varies, and Esther 6 includes details
concerning Mordecai's clothing which are lacking in Genesis 41.
The king's transference of power to Mordecai is not part of his
reward. Consequently, the clothing bestowed upon Mordecai in
Esther 6 does not represent his attainment of power. Rather,
Mordecai's apparel serves primarily in an anticipatory function. Genesis 41:42-43 is closer to Dan 5:16, 29, at this
point than Esther 6.[17]

   More difficult to explain is the striking similarity in
the banquet scenes where Joseph and Esther reveal their Israelite heritage. Both revelations result in a dramatic change in
the personal lives of the respective guests. But if Esther's
author was dependent upon the Joseph story for this scene, he
expanded it in dramatic fashion. In Genesis, banquets do not
appear as a dominant motif; in Esther, many significant plot
developments take place at feasts. In addition, Joseph's revelation of his identity does not occur at the banquet itself.
Rather, he reveals himself to his brothers after they had left
the banquet hall and had been forcibly returned to account for
Joseph's missing cup.

In none of these examples does the Book of Esther suggest
a clear dependence upon the Joseph story. Nevertheless, the
cumulative effect of these general similarities in setting,
events and motifs leaves the impression of dependence. This
impression is strengthened by the even closer affinities in
phrasing.

The precise nature of Esther's dependence upon the Joseph
story, however, remains unclear. It is conceivable that Esther's author borrowed portions of the Joseph story most familiar to his audience precisely because of their connotations.
The later storyteller perhaps enriched his own narrative by em-
ploying well-known descriptive phrases as a type of narrative
shorthand. Such a technique was not uncommon[18] and permits the
narrator to evoke specific attitudes and associations in his
audience. In addition, several of the similarities between the
stories are of a general nature.[19] Both stories relate events
in the lives of Jews at the court of a foreign monarch, the
problems encountered by the protagonists as a result of their
positions at court, and their eventual success in overcoming
the dangers which confront them and their people.[20] Esther's
author perhaps sought only to offer his own story concerning
the fate of Jews at a foreign court. In so doing, he found it
useful to incorporate earlier traditions which provide both a
general framework for "typical" court situations and also certain associations of ideas in the minds of his listeners. The
use of the Joseph traditions in the Book of Esther thus may be
analogous to the use of earlier traditions concerning Saul's
confrontation with Agag, also reported in 1 Samuel 15. Just as
the "Agagites" represent one paradigm of Israel's enemies,
Joseph may represent a paradigm of Jews at a foreign court. In
short, the Book of Esther appears to rely upon the Joseph traditions, but the reasons for this dependence are not clear.

3.   Literary Genre

S. Talmon recently suggested a possible explanation for
the similarities between the Joseph and Esther stories.[21] He
argues that the similarities between the two tales result from
an identity of literary genre.

. . . Similarities in situations and in the fate of
the central characters were conducive to an influence
of the Joseph-story on the Esther-Mordecai narrative.
They have in common inter alia the 'royal court setting', and the rise of a destitute young Israelite to
political prominence in his land of exile. But what
is more important, they can be shown to belong basically to one literary type. In a most instructive
paper G. VON RAD recently has brought to light the
exceedingly strong wisdom elements in the Joseph-story.
He has proved for this composition, what we set out to
do for the Esther-narrative, namely that in essence
the Joseph-story illustrates the realization of wisdom
precepts in practical life. Thus both the Joseph-
story and the Esther-narrative represent the type of
the 'historicized wisdom-tale'. Their similarities
therefore are to be accounted for not only by their
probable interdependence but also by their dependence
upon one common literary tradition.[22]

a. Common Motif

W. Lee Humphreys further refined the suggestion that the
story of Joseph and the Book of Esther share the same literary
genre by the argument that they also share a common motif.[23]
Humphreys argues that the presence of a motif of the wise courtier is central to both stories. This motif makes it possible
"to find the wider context in which to understand this remarkable similarity and connection between the Joseph narrative and
the Book of Esther."[24] In the Book of Esther, however, the
figure of the courtier

. . . is split and the narrative tells of two persons,
Mordecai, a Jew who was an official of the king, and
his adopted daughter and niece, Esther, who became a
favorite of the royal harem and queen. It is Esther,
in fact, who is the more active in terms of the court,
who carries out the planned steps that lead to the
denouement and the fall of Haman. In this . . . she
acts as a courtier.[25]

At the same time, Esther functions as an extension of Mordecai
within the court, particularly since her activities are carried
out at Mordecai's bidding. That Esther is not only an extension of Mordecai, however, is revealed by

. . . the quick series of commands that she issues when
convinced by him (4:15-17), and by the fact that from
this point to the climax, in the seventh chapter, she
holds the center of the stage and the activity she
undertakes is of her own planning and counsel.[26]

The author thereby presents two individuals who are closely

130

bound in situation and purpose, acting in the widest sense as
one figure. On the one hand, the figure of the wise courtier
is split; on the other, both characters represent a single
court figure.

The setting of the Book of Esther is the Persian court and
the confrontations and tensions between the courtiers is played
out within the context of court intrigues and the dynamics of
court life. Various aspects of the motif of the wise courtier
express themselves in the figures of Esther and Mordecai, and
conversely, through Haman. The conflict between Mordecai and
Haman itself centers upon their relative positions as courtiers;

> . . . for it is the failure of Mordecai to pay proper
> homage to Haman as befits his new position, that pro-
> vokes the latter's anger. . . . This act (which is
> itself most uncharacteristic of the courtier and
> against all advice given him: courtiers do not trans-
> gress the king's command, cf. 3:3) is expressive in
> this context of a conflict between courtiers, and is
> understood in terms of the courtier's concern over
> rank and position.[27]

To a degree, Haman also reflects the caution and control
which characterizes the wise courtier (3:6; cf. 5:10). Yet
Haman often allows his hatred of Mordecai to govern his actions, acting in a manner contrary to the model of the wise
courtier. For example, Haman's jealousy of Mordecai leads him
to recount in detail the signs of his power and position (cf.
5:11). More importantly, Haman's personal hatred of Mordecai
motivates him to give up his original plan to destroy the
Jews--a plan which he presented "in terms of protecting the
kingdom from the dangerous influence of a lawless people and of
enriching the coffers of the king."[28] This clever plot is
abandoned for a more immediate fulfillment of purpose: Haman
erects gallows to hang Mordecai. This action results in
Haman's appearance in court at a time which forces him to par-
ticipate in Mordecai's reward.

Humphreys argues that these narrative features "are identical or most similar to those found in wisdom materials."[29]
He nevertheless disputes the claim that Esther is a "historicized wisdom-tale." Rather, most of the specific wisdom elements in Esther are court-related and more specifically focus
upon the motif of the wise courtier. This motif has its origin

and development in court wisdom circles, and the utilization of
this motif naturally carries several elements of these court
wisdom traditions.[30]

Esther's author had before him certain court tales from
which the various threads of his story were woven. Among these
was the Joseph narrative. Humphreys suggests that Esther's
author modeled the tale "on the pattern of the Joseph narrative, which he would have had before him in its final stages of
development."[31] The wisdom elements present in Esther are due
to the author's choice of the

> . . . central motif which he selected to develop and
> give form to his thought which was originally at home
> in the traditions of the wisemen of the court. But
> in the form in which he utilized this central motif,
> that is, the Joseph narrative, this motif of the wise
> courtier had long been freed from a close linkage with
> wisdom court circles, and is in some aspects radically
> altered and given new directions.[32]

Later developments in the transmission of the Joseph traditions, particularly its inclusion within the corpus of Yah-
wistic and Elohistic traditions, rendered it a useful model for
Esther's author. The courtier was removed from a setting in
the foreign court that focused exclusively on the king; his
loyalty could be divided and realigned in other directions as
well. In both the Joseph story and the Book of Esther, the
courtier is presented in a situation in which it is possible to
be loyal both to the king and to his own people. Both stories
thus portray the courtier working on behalf of the Israelite
people, but within the context of the king's benefit and welfare. The courtier is loyal to both his people and king. Just
as Joseph was said to have come into Egypt to save his people
(cf. Gen 50:20), Esther has become queen to deliver hers (cf.
Esth 4:14).[33]

> Thus, the author found in the motif of the wise cour-
> tier, as developed in terms of the Joseph narrative,
> an ideal vehicle for his tale of the adventures of two
> Jews of the Persian Diaspora who were able to reach
> powerful positions in the royal court and to deliver
> their people from annihilation.[34]

It was the diaspora situation in which Esther's author wrote
which guided his choice of the Joseph story as a literary
model. The motif of the wise courtier was recast in the later
story, making it even more applicable to the vicissitudes of
life in the Persian diaspora.

Humphreys' thesis that the Joseph and Esther stories share
a common, central motif is suggestive and raises an additional
similarity not noted previously. Humphreys demonstrates that
the theme of dual loyalty is central to both stories.[35] But
the argument that the Book of Esther focuses upon a motif of
the wise courtier is not convincing. Particularly problematic
is the claim that the figure of the courtier is subdivided in
the Book of Esther. Esther supposedly is an extension of Mordecai, and Humphreys attributes the notice of her adoption by
Mordecai to this end. But adoption was a common formulaic
motif in the ancient world.[36] In addition, the notice of Esther's adoption serves other purposes in Esther, e.g., the rise
of someone of low social standing to a position of power. That
Esther is an orphan permits one illustration of the ironic reversal of the powerless to positions of power. In fact, it is
this reversal in status which provides a major point of comparison with the Joseph story.

Esther is an extension of Mordecai's personality, yet at
the same time a separate and distinct individual. This view is
based upon the facts that Esther issues her own commands in
Esth 4:15-17, and becomes the primary initiator of events in
the latter half of the tale. These examples, however, suggest
that Esther's author intended to portray two separate and distinct personalities, not a dissociated figure of a courtier.
Again, the presence of a motif of the wise courtier is not required to explain the "development" of Esther's distinct personality. Our initial impressions of Esther as always obedient
contrast with our later views of her, providing another example
of the theme of reversal. Esther's evolution into the chief
protagonist in the latter half of the narrative is more easily
explained by the motif of obedience/disobedience than by the
motif of the wise courtier. Finally, from the perspective of
the story itself, only Esther--Ahasuerus' favorite and queen of
the empire--is in a position to intercede for her people.

Nor should we be surprised to find Esther's actions taking
place in a court setting. Again from the perspective of the
story, an individual with access to, and influence over, the
king is required to save the entire Jewish population of the
empire. Esther finds herself in a position to use her power,
and much of the story revolves around the question of whether

Esther will risk herself to save other Jews. The theme of reversal, too, points to a court setting as the locale most opposite that where we expect to find an orphaned, female subject
of a powerful foreign king.[37]

Also problematic to the argument that the Book of Esther
articulates a motif of the wise courtier is Mordecai's refusal
to pay proper homage to Haman. As Humphreys indicates, such a
refusal is uncharacteristic of a wiseman. This personality
flaw is attributed to the nature of the author's source which
was limited to a concern for the conflict over rank and position of rival courtiers. Yet this explanation seems inadequate
if Esther's author indeed wished to portray Mordecai as an
ideal court servant. Nor does the argument suffice that even
this refusal expresses the conflict between courtiers. Esther
3:3 is cited as evidence for this view; but Esth 3:3-4 suggests
less the picture of a conflict between courtiers than the picture of Mordecai's continued refusal to bow before Haman. Even
after Haman is informed of Mordecai's disobedience, Mordecai
continues to "stand" by his word because "he told them he was a
Jew." Esth 3:3-4 seems less an example of the author's flexi-
bility in his use of this motif than an indication of the relationship between Jewish identity and civil disobedience.

In summary, a motif of the wise courtier is not indicated
by the Book of Esther. Consequently, Esther's dependence upon
the Joseph story does not stem from the shared use of this
motif. We thus find ourselves again at the point in the discussion initiated by Rosenthal. While the Joseph story and the
Book of Esther display several correspondences in language,
syntax, setting, motifs and themes, the precise reason for Esther's dependence remains obscure.

b. Common Structure

A recent attempt to clarify the nature of Esther's dependence upon the Joseph story is offered by Arndt Meinhold.[38]
Meinhold argues that both stories are examples of the same literary genre of *Diasporanovelle*. In addition to the similarities already noted, the Joseph story and the Book of Esther
display a common literary structure. Meinhold seeks to demonstrate that Esther's structure follows that of the Joseph

story. The similarities between the two stories are not of a
general nature; their structures confirm that the Joseph story
provides a literary model for the Book of Esther.[39] On the
other hand, the differences between the stories result from the
Book of Esther's secularized intellectual outlook. This perspective stems from the transmission of the story among diaspora Jews whose way of life and Weltanschauung differed from
those of the community which gave rise to the Joseph story. An
indication of these differences is suggested by the attachment
of Purim traditions to Esther.[40]

According to Meinhold, both stories begin with a short
"prehistory" which sets them within the context of "eine
(welt-)politische Situation."[41] There follows the introduction
of the main characters to the audience. In the Joseph story,
however, this structure occurs twice and Joseph is introduced
in Genesis 37 and again in Genesis 39-41.[42] The dual occurrence of this structural unit is transformed in the Book of Esther by the introduction of two distinct figures, Mordecai and
Esther.[43] Notices of Joseph's and Mordecai's ethnic identities
and social standing are indicated, implying Mordecai to be the
more important of the two figures in the Book of Esther. Yet
parallels also exist between Joseph and Esther: both are given
two names (cf. Gen 41:45; Esth 2:7) and portrayed as exception-
ally handsome individuals (cf. Gen 39:6b; Esth 2:7c).[44] In addition, both tales suggest the promotion of the heroes to positions of power (cf. Gen 39:1-6a; Esth 2:8-18). This structural
element anticipates the denouements of the stories where the
main characters reverse their status. Both scenes are provisional and are followed by the subsequent demotions of the main
characters.

The structural identity of the stories varies somewhat,[45]
but resumes with the portrayal of the actions taken by the
heroes to avert the danger in which their disobedience to supe-
riors (Potiphar's wife, Haman) places them. In Gen 40:14-15,
23; 41:9-13, having correctly interpreted the butler's dream,
Joseph asks that the butler mention him to Pharaoh.[46] The corresponding structure in the Book of Esther is found at 4:1-5:8,
where Mordecai commands Esther to intercede with the king.[47]

The stories thus far display a common structure. After
this point, however, their structural patterns diverge. For

example, in Gen 41:1-8, 15a, 24b, Meinhold detects a structure
lacking in the Book of Esther.[48] The abolition of the danger
confronting Joseph follows in Gen 41:14, and a new "Bedeutungsnachweis" occurs when Yahweh reveals the meaning of Pharaoh's
dreams (Gen 41:15b-36). Genesis 41:37 contains a brief notice
of the favorable reception of Joseph's advice, and in 41:38-39
we find the basis for Joseph's success with his Egyptian master.

Several of these structural units do not occur in the Book
of Esther at corresponding points in that story's progression.
Nor do they occur in the same sequence that is found in the
Joseph story. Such variations in the stories' structures recur
at other points,[49] and already raise serious difficulties with
Meinhold's thesis. We need not further examine his argument
for structural identity to note some additional problems with
Meinhold's thesis. For example, the division of individual
verses into separate and distinct structures seems to carry
structural analysis to a questionable extreme. Such divisions
of verses contrast sharply with the grouping of entire chapters
into single structural units, despite the divergent content and
sequence of narrated events.[50] These structural groupings are
even less convincing when we recognize that Esther's author
must have discerned identical structures in the Joseph story in
order to model his tale after it. A reasonable alternative to
this view is to postulate that some similarities resulted from
a common method of constructing stories.[51] The probability
that Esther's author was familiar with the tale of Joseph resulted in structural similarities, without a conscious attempt
by the later storyteller to follow the earlier story's exact
framework in every detail.

In addition, Meinhold occasionally reorders the sequence
of verses in each story to conform them to his delineation of
structures.[52] Some scholars view the Joseph story as compos-
ite.[53] If they are correct, Meinhold is unable to account for
the presumably altered structures of the individual Joseph traditions which may have been known to Esther's author.

Notice also must be taken of the internal organization of
the Book of Esther. The scroll displays a clear structure
which seems influenced by, and reflects, a theme of reversal.
The structure of the Book of Esther would seem to depend as

136

much on its own themes as on an external literary source. Finally, Meinhold's suggestion that the Joseph story and the Book
of Esther belong to the genre of *Diasporanovelle* indicates that
their structural components may not be unique. If he is correct, any structural similarities between the two stories may
derive from their shared literary *Gattung*, not from a conscious
imitation of the Joseph story's pattern by the later narrator.

The structural identity of the Joseph and Esther stories
therefore does not seem probable. Meinhold nevertheless demonstrates some thematic similarities in the stories not suffi-
ciently stressed by other scholars. Both tales emphasize the
"ethnic identity" of the heroes;[54] both demonstrate a concern
for the people of Israel and for the civil government;[55] both
portray the reversal in status of the protagonists from their
beginnings as powerless individuals to their attainment of
great power; both concern the rescue of the people of Israel by
the efforts of the protagonists. Meinhold also suggests that
the Joseph story contains such stylistic devices as anticipation and recollection,[56] parallel and contrast, and a love of
ironical detail which we already have seen in the Book of Esther.

B. Other Studies of the Joseph Story

Recent years have witnessed the publication of some significant studies of the Joseph story. Some of these suggest
further points of contact with the Book of Esther and raise
certain questions about the relationship between the two
stories.

1. Date of the Joseph Story

Donald B. Redford argues that the theological outlook of
the Joseph story differs radically from those of the other
patriarchal tales among which it was set. The Joseph story

> . . . does not mention the Covenant or the Promise,
> ubiquitous in the earlier chapters of Genesis. [Its
> author] is not interested in supplying the reader with
> comment on matters theological, as the Patriarchal
> author was. In fact, with the glaring exception of
> chapter 39 the writer nowhere uses YHWH, and when

'ĕlōhīm is used it is always in the direct speech of the characters of the story.[57]

Nor does the storyteller seem concerned to maintain Joseph's exclusiveness or purity:

> Joseph does not hesitate to mix with Egyptians; of course he has no choice. But he even marries an Egyptian girl, and is not condemned for it by the writer. Joseph is able to communicate with Egyptians on moral issues by appealing to the universal sense of right and wrong. Both he and the Egyptians speak of "god" with no further qualification, and there is no disapproval expressed at the thought that Joseph, a pious Israelite, is moving among outright idolators.[58]

Both of Redford's observations seem reminiscent of similar portrayals in the Book of Esther. They emphasize different facets of some general similarities between the Joseph and Esther stories already noted by other scholars.

Redford notes the virtual silence of the rest of scripture on the subject of the Joseph story. Where the name "Joseph" occurs, it is used to denote the eponymous ancestor of the "House of Joseph," the father of Ephraim and Manasseh, the collective tribes of Ephraim and Manasseh, or the northern tribes and kingdom. Redford accounts for this silence, and for the differences between the Joseph story and the other patriarchal narratives, by arguing that the present form of the Joseph story did not exist when these other traditions were circulated and collected. This is not to say that traditions concerning Joseph were unknown; rather, the redaction of those traditions into the present tale had not occurred. Redford consequently dates the Joseph story c. 650-425 B.C.E., "when the Diaspora with all of its consequences was a reality."[59]

Redford's post-exilic dating of the Joseph story raises some interesting questions regarding the relationship between it and the Book of Esther. If he is correct, we must ask which Joseph traditions were known to Esther's author. That is, was the later storyteller familiar with independently circulating Joseph traditions? Or did he know the *de novo* composition described by Redford? Further, did Esther's author know the Joseph story before or after its incorporation into its present *heilsgeschichtliche* context? These questions have received insufficient attention in the discussions of the relationship between the Joseph and Esther stories.

138

2. Narrative Style of the Joseph Story

Some similarities in the style of the Joseph and Esther
stories already were noted. Both narrators extensively employ
the stylistic devices of anticipation, ironic parallels and
contrasts. Redford cites additional examples of these devices
in the Joseph story. He further suggests the importance of
plot retardation in the Joseph story, used to heighten dramatic
suspense. For example, "Joseph just reaches the land of his
enslavement when a chapter-length digression intervenes, and
leaves the anxious reader to cool his heels for thirty
verses."[60] With the forced arrival of the brothers in Egypt to
buy grain, the audience is prepared for an immediate resolution
of the plot. Yet just at this point, when the audience is prepared for Joseph's revelation of his identity to his brothers,
three chapters intervene. The narrator postpones the denouement of his tale and continues its dramatic tension. This
stylistic use of plot retardation also functions in the Book of
Esther, notably in Esther's delay in presenting her petition to
Ahasuerus.

Redford also notes the narrator's familiarity with the
setting of his story. The author of the Joseph story "seems at
times to be making a show of his knowledge of Egyptian manners
and customs; seems, in fact, to be supplying authentic 'background material' to lend his story verisimilitude."[61] Redford's characterization again is reminiscent of the "Persianisms" contained in the Book of Esther. Both ancient storytellers seem concerned to give their stories history-like qualities.

The Joseph story and the Book of Esther share a further
stylistic trait which has been overlooked. E. A. Speiser observes that the narrator of the Joseph story frequently is
silent about details which seem puzzling to us.[62] For example,
he comments on Gen 43:33:

> Joseph's brothers were seated facing their host. In
> that case, however, the seating of the men in the exact
> order of their ages--a detail on which the text lays
> much stress--would have to be ascribed to coincidence,
> or at most to prior instructions on the part of Joseph
> which the author chose to pass over in silence.[63]

Or again, on Gen 45:1-28, Speiser remarks:

This detail is passed over in silence, very likely by
design than through accidental loss in the text. Good
writers are not given to spelling things out; the
reader, too, has his part to play.[64]

The Book of Esther displays a similar stylistic trait. We
would like to know, for example, what became of Vashti after
Ahasuerus' decision to find a new queen, or why the king interpreted Haman's plea for his life as an attempted rape of Esther.[65] In the Book of Esther, as in the Joseph story, the
narrator either had no interest in details which seem curious
to us, or assumed that his audience could correctly fill in the
gaps.

3. Motifs of the Joseph Story

Redford devotes several pages of his monograph to an examination of the specific motifs of the Joseph story.[66] He does
not suggest any major motifs which also are found in the Book
of Esther. Correspondence seems limited to scattered formulaic
motifs, for example, the scenes involving the two eunuchs.[67]

George Coats finds some different motifs in the Joseph
traditions, notably that of "family disunity."[68] This motif
pervades the tale, and the initial tension between family members recurs at various points of the narrative. The story begins with the brothers' unfavorable reaction to Joseph's dreams
and rapidly moves to their treacherous plan to dispose of Joseph. This motif also allows a shift in setting from Canaan to
Egypt and thereby controls the scope of the narrative.

Coats devotes special attention to Gen 45:8. Here, Joseph observes, "it was not you who sent me here but God."
Coats argues that the reference to God's agency does not imply
that God arranged the brothers' treachery. Rather, given the
events which emerged around Joseph's life, God's agency was restricted to that of future intentions. This understanding is
suggested, for example, by the author's use of a famine motif.
The famine threatens to end life for Jacob and his progeny.
Joseph's move to Egypt provides a means for preserving the
family. Hence, the observation that God is responsible for
Joseph's presence in Egypt that Jacob's family might survive
(cf. Gen 45:5-7). It is in the potential for the future that
God's agency in present events is seen.[69]

Coats's study of the Joseph narrative has implications for comparisons between that tale and the Book of Esther. If Coats is correct to view the motif of "family disunity" as central, it is difficult to discern any point of contact with the motifs of the scroll. Coats's study also calls into question the great emphasis placed upon the court settings of the Joseph and Esther stories. Coats argues that the court setting of the Joseph story results from a shift in locale from Palestine to Egypt, itself a function of a motif not found in Esther.

On the other hand, both Redford and Coats indicate the limited role played by Yahweh in the Joseph traditions. According to Redford, God plays no significant role in the narrated events. Coats holds a somewhat different view, arguing that God's agency in human affairs holds its greatest implications for future, not present, events. God's agency as the potential for future events recalls a view expressed by Mordecai in Esth 4:14: "Who knows whether you have come into royal power for a time such as this?" In either view, the role of the deity in present events seems limited. This understanding suggests a further point of contact with the Book of Esther.

In addition to these fuller analyses of the Joseph story's motifs, we may cite an interesting study by B. J. van der Merwe.[70] This study has not proved influential but remains suggestive for our discussion. Van der Merwe argues that Jacob was viewed as a ruler by ancient Israelites. On the basis of a comparison between Gen 47:29 and 1 Kgs 2:1, he concludes that Joseph was appointed Jacob's successor. Van der Merwe claims support for his view in the fact that Jacob bequeathed the city of Shechem to Joseph (cf. Gen 48:22). This inheritance clearly subordinates Joseph's brothers to him.

Van der Merwe finds traces of a tradition where Joseph is blessed as Jacob's first-born (cf. Gen 48:2-4,7,15,16a,21-22), particularly in Gen 48:15. Here it is stated that Jacob blessed Joseph. Jacob's blessing of Joseph's sons (Gen 48:2, 12) also indicates that Joseph received a double portion of the inheritance, i.e., the share to which the first-born son was entitled.

Van der Merwe's thesis is problematic at several points. Nevertheless, he cites evidence which suggests the possibility that Jacob was viewed in some circles as a ruler. If Joseph

was understood to be Jacob's successor,[71] the Joseph traditions
may contain an implicit motif of kingship. In addition, this
implicit motif focuses upon a non-Davidic ruler. This fact is
significant if the Joseph story originated or was widely circulated during the post-exilic period, since it reinforces the
possibility that Mordecai was viewed as a quasi-king.[72] Van
der Merwe, then, points to a motif in the Joseph story which
also is found in the Book of Esther.[73]

4. Summary

   Comparisons of the Joseph story and the Book of Esther
suggest that the later storyteller was familiar with the Joseph
traditions. This seems clear from the striking correspondence
in word choice and phrasing, and from the general similarities
in setting and the problems which confront the heroes. No individual comparison of texts decisively indicates direct bor-
rowing. But the cumulative effect of the similarities between
the stories suggests some type of dependence. At the same
time, the two narratives diverge at many points, particularly
with respect to their motifs. The stories indeed share some
formulaic motifs, but only if one accepts the thrust of van der
Merwe's thesis do they share a dominant motif.
   The evidence suggests that, with the exception of linguistic correspondences, most of the similarities between the
Joseph and Esther stories are of a general nature. If the
present forms of the stories come from approximately the same
period, these general similarities may result from interests
and rhetorical techniques common to the post-exilic period.[74]
Some post-exilic Jews, particularly in the diaspora, undoubtedly were interested in the new possibilities for rich and rewarding lives under the friendly rule of their Persian masters.
The careers of Ezra and espcially of Nehemiah actualized the
possibility of Jews attaining power within the administrative
ranks of the foreign monarch. The possibility of a Jew's success at the foreign court was realized to some extent by these
two figures who, at the same time, sought to benefit their co-
religionists. The story of Joseph and the Book of Esther relate the success of Jews at a foreign court. They perhaps

142

represent common expressions of the aspirations of some post-exilic Jews.

While most of the similarities between the stories are general and could be more or less coincidental, their striking linguistic correspondences suggest that the Joseph narrative presents a model for the Book of Esther in more than its framework. Whether intended by Esther's author or not, the story's ancient audience undoubtedly was reminded of the earlier story. The Book of Esther thus presents, in some sense, a reinterpretation of the Joseph story. Here, the divergences between the accounts assume importance. Despite the restricted role of the deity in the Joseph story, Yahweh remains partially responsible for the events surrounding Joseph's life. Coats is correct to call attention to Joseph's statement in Gen 45:8. In the Book of Esther, however, Yahweh plays no part in human affairs. The story seems to suggest that individuals themselves are responsible for the successful outcome of events. Meinhold probably is correct to argue that the Book of Esther was directed to diaspora communities familiar with the Joseph story, and that Esther was intended to counter any beliefs that the safety of the Jewish community rested solely with Yahweh.[75] On the other hand, it is possible that Esther merely utilizes phrases and expressions already known to its audience as a type of narrative shorthand.

In summary, the Book of Esther seems dependent upon the story of Joseph, although the precise nature of, and reasons for, this dependence remain unclear.[76] Most of their similarities are general and may stem from their composition and/or circulation during the post-exilic period.

A comparison of these two stories with other post-exilic narratives corroborates this view. That is, a comparison with other contemporaneous stories indicates that several similarities of the Joseph and Esther stories may be attributed to common concerns of the post-exilic period. At the same time, such a comparison suggests features shared by the Joseph and Esther stories which are unique to them and probably derive from the special concerns of their authors. Hopefully, this information will provide some insights into the reasons for the use of the Joseph traditions by Esther's author.

C. *Comparison of the Joseph Story and*
   the Book of Esther with Other
   Post-exilic Narratives

1. Daniel 2-6

The first narrative account to which we turn is the Book of Daniel, chapters 2-6.[77] As in the case of the story of Joseph and the Book of Esther, Jewish traditions often associate the stories of Joseph and Daniel.[78] More recently, Rosenthal and Humphreys have suggested further comparisons between these tales and the Book of Esther.[79] Although the Book of Daniel lacks the type of linguistic correspondence displayed by the Joseph story and the Book of Esther, it bears general similarities in settings and events. Like the stories of Joseph, and of Mordecai and Esther, Daniel 2-6 is set at the court of a foreign king. All three narratives display some concern for the details of court life (cf. Gen 47:13-26; Esth 1:3,6-10,14; 2:12-15; Dan 2:2,27; 3:2-4,10; 5:2-7). As in the Joseph story and the Book of Esther, banquets occur in Daniel 2-6 as characteristic court events. Of particular interest is the banquet of Dan 5:2-3, which suggests the king's actions to be influenced by his consumption of wine. We are reminded here of the royal banquet described in Esther 1.[80]

In the Joseph story and in the Book of Esther, a concern with the details of court life serves as a literary device, lending an air of verisimilitude to the stories. A similar judgment may be rendered with respect to the setting of Daniel 2-6.[81] The settings of the three narratives also suggest that Jews can attain success at the court of a foreign king. Like the story of Joseph and the Book of Esther, Daniel 2-6 lacks any hostility toward the foreign monarch.[82]

Daniel and his companions, like Esther and to some extent Joseph, undergo elaborate preparation prior to meeting the king (Daniel 1; cf. Gen 41:14; Esth 2:8-15). Esther and Daniel find favor with those in charge of their training, due in part to their physical attractiveness (Esth 2:7-17; Dan 1:4; cf. Gen 39:6b).[83]

Parallels also exist between the figures of Joseph, Daniel and Mordecai. Mordecai and Daniel are portrayed as members of

the community of Jews exiled from Jerusalem by Nebuchadnezzar
(Esth 2:5-6; Dan 1:1-5; 5:13). In all three cases, the
"ethnic" identities of the heroes contribute to the development
and movement of plot.[84]

The three narratives portray the dangers which confront
the heroes as a result of their positions at court. The protagonists, however, successfully overcome these dangers and are
placed in positions of even greater authority. In each story,
the king's disturbed sleep leads to personal recognition of the
respective heroes (cf. Genesis 41; Esther 6; Daniel 2), and
their rewards include new clothing and jewelry (Gen 41:42;
Esth 6:8-11; Dan 5:29; cf. Esth 8:2). The change in heroes'
personal fortunes anticipates and extends beyond them personally, resulting in either the deliverance of the people of
Israel, or the praise and acknowledgement of its God.[85]

The Joseph story and the Books of Esther and Daniel do not
share any dominant motifs,[86] although Dan 6:1-28 raises the
question of obedience to the king's irrevocable law.[87] On the
other hand, the stories share some formulaic motifs, e.g., the
king's disturbed sleep and the manner in which service to the
king is rewarded.

Like the stories of Joseph and Esther, Daniel 2-6 displays
no hostility to the foreign king. To the contrary, Daniel and
his companions overcome the dangers that confront them and
prosper at the foreign court. These facts suggest the possibility of a shared theme among the stories, viz., that of a
dual loyalty. The piety of Daniel and his companions often
contributes to their adversity. Yet the tales clearly indicate
that the heroes' eventual success in overcoming danger is due,
in fact, to their tenacious loyalty to Yahweh. A dual allegiance to God and to king is not only possible in Daniel 2-6,
it is in some ways demanded. It is because of the wisdom and
skills given by Yahweh that Daniel can serve his king so ably.
Daniel 2-6 points to a particular ordering of priorities such
that loyalty to Yahweh leads to the greatest possible service
to one's king.[88]

Inherent in this similarity of theme, however, is the
greatest difference between the Joseph and Esther stories and
Daniel 2-6. The latter constantly stresses Yahweh's sovereignty.[89] The primary concern of the Book of Daniel as a whole, in

fact, is to demonstrate that "God is sovereign over history and is guiding it towards an end determined by himself."[90] This emphasis is conspicuously lacking in the Book of Esther and appears greatly restricted in the Joseph story. Despite their general similarities in settings and events, the theocentric focus of Daniel 2-6 sets it apart from the Joseph story and the Book of Esther.

A question arises as to whether the similarities noted among these three narratives are unique to them. Humphreys suggests that when one compares the Tale of Ahiqar to these tales, it becomes clear that their correspondences "reflect a common literary type which was apparently quite popular in the ancient Near East at this period."[91] At some point in each of these stories, the protagonist finds him- or herself endangered by the vicissitudes of court life. The heroes eventually overcome the obstacles confronting them, and the stories conclude with recognition of their service, exaltation to a higher rank and punishment of their enemies, if appropriate.[92] The general similarities among the Joseph story and the Books of Esther and Daniel also appear in the Tale of Ahiqar. They suggest stock settings and type-scenes which were popular among post-exilic Jews.

To summarize our findings: the Joseph story and the Book of Esther share general features of setting and events which also are found in the tales of Daniel 2-6. These general correspondences probably result from the use of stock settings and type-scenes to portray the problems of diaspora life and the possibilities for a successful life under foreign rule. Apart from these general similarities, the three narratives also display a common theme. All three suggest the viability of a dual allegiance to Judaism, in some aspect, and to the foreign king. At the same time, this common theme points to a major difference between the Joseph and Esther stories, and Daniel 2-6. In the latter, the heroes' success is due to Yahweh's assistance and intervention in human affairs. By contrast, the Joseph story and the Book of Esther greatly restrict the deity's role, and the success of the heroes depends largely upon the actions of individuals themselves.

2. The Book of Ruth[93]

Scholars compare both the Joseph story and the Book of
Esther to the story of Ruth, despite their obvious differences.[94]   The Book of Ruth recounts the fate of a foreigner in
ancient Israel. At first glance, the general framework of this
story appears to differ radically from those of the Joseph
story and the Book of Esther. Yet the Book of Ruth may represent a *variation* of a popular type of tale which also appears
in Daniel 2-6, namely the fate of Jews amid their foreign
masters.

Like the Joseph story and the Book of Esther, the Book of
Ruth displays a wealth of history-like detail. The narrator
uses his knowledge of geography, climate and history to give
his story a plausible setting.[95]   The Book of Ruth lacks the
type of linguistic correspondence, or general similarities in
setting and events, which a comparison of Daniel 2-6 to the
stories of Joseph and Esther suggests. Nevertheless, the stylistic techniques employed in Ruth include a love of ironic
detail,[96] paronomasia,[97] and the use of foreshadowing and anticipation[98]--features also evident in the narrative styles of
the Joseph story and the Book of Esther. In addition, the Book
of Ruth is constructed according to a pattern of reversal, suggesting a similarity with Esther, if not with the story of
Joseph.[99]

Like the figure of Esther, the portrayal of Ruth suggests
a transformation in her personality. In Ruth 2-3, Ruth functions as an emissary between Naomi and Boaz. She suggests the
figure of an obedient woman who does not independently undertake actions. But in Ruth 3:9-18, Ruth goes beyond Naomi's
instructions to her and takes matters into her own hands.[100]
It is Ruth's own actions at this point of the story which pre-
cipitate ensuing events.

The motif of obtaining food recurs throughout the Book of
Ruth, even to the point of a play on the place name, "Bethle-
hem." This motif of obtaining food plays a significant role
in the Joseph story and may be present in the Book of Esther as
well. Ruth also contains the formulaic motifs of actions taken
under the influence of wine (3:7), and the association of a
principal figure (Boaz) with the locale of the "gate" (chapter

4; cf. also Dan 2:49).

The major problem confronting the figures in the Book of Ruth is the continuation of Naomi's family.[101] The implications of this problem extend beyond Naomi and her kin, for its solution results in the birth of David's ancestors.[102] The continuation of Naomi's family therefore insures the continuation of an important segment of ancient Israel. The problems which confront the heroes in the Joseph story and the Book of Esther similarly hold implications which extend beyond the protagonists themselves. The solution of these problems results in the saving of important segments of Israel's population.[103]

The Book of Ruth suggests the "hidden hand of God" in human affairs.[104] Yahweh's control of history is not totally hidden,[105] although it is less open than in Daniel 2-6. At this point, the theology of the Book of Ruth approaches that expressed in the Joseph story: Yahweh is not completely transcendent, yet at the same time the protagonists themselves must initiate the actions which lead to the desired results.[106]

A further correspondence between the Book of Ruth and the stories of Joseph and Esther lies in its attitude toward foreigners. Obviously, Ruth's narrator favorably viewed the possibility of a mutually rewarding relationship between the people of Israel and non-Israelites. Finally, "coincidences" play a significant role in the Book of Ruth, as they do in Esther and, to a limited extent, in the Joseph story.[107]

In summary, the Book of Ruth bears some stylistic similarities to the Joseph story and the Book of Esther, although its narrative setting and general framework differ from these other two stories. Nonetheless, the Book of Ruth may represent a variation of a popular type of post-exilic tale, of which the stories of Joseph and of Esther are more typical expressions. This possibility perhaps accounts for a similar attitude toward non-Israelites in the three stories (cf. Daniel 2-6). In each of these stories, the problem confronting the heroes and its solution hold far-ranging implications for the people of Israel. In all three cases, the final outcome of events results in the saving of the entire people and/or significant portions thereof.

3. The Book of Jonah

The Book of Jonah tells of the prophetic mission of an Israelite to a foreign people. Initial impressions do not suggest much correspondence to the Joseph story or the Book of Esther. But the fact that the Book of Jonah concerns a Jew in a foreign land again suggests a variation of a common type of post-exilic tale. Jonah's words and actions eventually result in the saving of a people, in this case, the residents of Nineveh. Again, the outcome of Jonah's prophetic mission suggests some similarity with the post-exilic tales we have considered. The positive attitude toward foreigners, too, is present in the Book of Jonah.[108] At the very least, "Jonah is quite innocent of any feelings whatever about the Ninevites."[109] Even this characterization, when applied to one of ancient Israel's most despised foes, indicates that the Book of Jonah surprisingly lacks any antagonism toward the Assyrians. Moreover, the fact that a prophet is sent to the Assyrians to urge their repentance points to the narrator's favorable disposition toward them. Despite its distinctive features, Jonah suggests a general framework not unlike those of other post-exilic narratives.

Jonah shares no dominant motifs with the Joseph story or the Book of Esther.[110] It does mention, however, the casting of lots (1:7). Jonah also displays a symmetrical structure, with the first and second halves of the story paralleling each other.[111] Unlike the Joseph story or the Book of Esther, the events in Jonah clearly are guided by Yahweh.[112] As in the tales of Daniel 2-6 and the Book of Ruth, the theocentric focus of the Book of Jonah constitutes a major difference with the story of Joseph and the Book of Esther.

The Book of Jonah, then, suggests a framework similar to those of other post-exilic narratives. All of these depict the efforts of protagonists, who now find themselves residing in a foreign land, to preserve a people. The tale of Jonah varies considerably from the stories of Joseph and Esther; yet despite their differences, these three narratives could represent variant expressions of a popular type of post-exilic tale.

4. The Book of Judith

Finally, we may consider the Book of Judith, to which the Book of Esther sometimes is compared.[113] The Book of Judith is dated significantly later than the Book of Esther,[114] a fact which renders their similarities all the more remarkable. Both stories tell of Israelite women who risk their lives to save their people. Esther and Judith both are noted for their beauty,[115] whose exceptional quality permits them access to the foreign rulers.

The narrative settings of the two stories differ, and the Book of Judith expresses interest in Jerusalem and its cult (cf. Jdt 4:2). Yet the setting of Judith occasionally is reminiscent of that in Esther. Judith 4:3 reports the return of the Jewish exiles in a manner similar to the off-handed notice of Esth 2:6 concerning their captivity. These notices, in both stories, contribute to their history-like appearance. The Book of Judith, like that of Esther and the Joseph story, extensively employs a knowledge of history and geography to heighten the realistic nature of the narratives.

The general framework of Judith is similar to those of the Joseph and Esther stories: Israelites at a foreign court[116] overcome the obstacles threatening them and their people. This results in the saving of the people of Israel.[117]

Judith displays several rhetorical and stylistic techniques found in the stories of Joseph and Esther, notably the use of irony, repetition, parallel and contrast, anticipation, and plot retardation.[118] Similarities in formulaic motifs also appear: clothing functions symbolically in the Book of Judith, and Judith's festive attire anticipates the eventual saving of the Jews.[119] Banquets play an important role in Judith (cf. 6:21; 12:10), and Judith disposes of her foe at a more or less private banquet (chapters 12-13), reminiscent of Esther's exposure of Haman at her private feast.[120]

The Book of Judith is constructed in two parts, chapters 1-7 and 8-16. Both parts of the story display a chiastic structure and treat similar themes; the latter half of the tale resolves problems posed by earlier events.[121] In the second, part of Judith, the story focuses upon the heroine's actions, and Judith becomes the primary initiator of events in the

150

human sphere.[122]

Like the figures of Joseph, Mordecai and Esther, Judith
initially holds low social status within the dominant society.
She is a widow,[123] and represents those who are powerless. The
theme of power indeed has its part in the Book of Judith.[124]
By the conclusion of Judith, the powerless and powerful have reversed positions, and Holofernes is killed with his own sword,
just as Haman dies on his own gallows.[125]

The Book of Judith thus suggests some similarities with
the Joseph story and especially with the Book of Esther. At
the same time, it differs radically at an important point. The
attitude toward non-Israelites in the Book of Judith lacks the
openness and favorable disposition found in the stories of
Joseph and Esther. The sole exception is Achior, whose conversion to Judaism permits special treatment by the narrator. In
addition, the Book of Judith displays a concern for Jerusalem
and its cult, although the story itself takes place in
Bethulia.

A contrast in the portrayals of Joseph and Esther, on the
one hand, and Judith, on the other, also is striking. Judith
consistently appears as a pious Jewess--even her name suggests
this![126] Judith's observance of Jewish dietary laws even provides the means by which she is able to overcome Holofernes.
Judith's piety more closely recalls the tales of Daniel 2-6
than the Joseph story or Book of Esther.[127]

Equally distinctive is the difference in Yahweh's role in
the Book of Judith. Judith's success in overcoming Israel's
foes clearly is attributed to Yahweh (cf. chaps. 13-16). Zeitlin even suggests that "the book of Judith was written to neu-
tralize the book of Esther."[128] Again, the theological perspective of Judith seems closer to Daniel 2-6.

In short, the Book of Judith bears some general similarities to the story of Joseph and especially to the Book of Esther. Yet its outlook differs radically from these stories,
and Judith lacks an openness toward foreigners. Finally,
Judith's pious devotion to her God and His role in the success
of her plan both are emphasized by the narrator.

5. Summary

The Joseph story and the Book of Esther share some similarities with other post-exilic narratives. The correspondences, however, often are restricted to stylistic techniques,
general settings and attitudes toward foreigners.[129] Each of
these post-exilic stories could represent a variation of a popular type of tale, viz., the fate of Jews in a foreign land.
The Jewish protagonists encounter various difficulties which
directly result from life under foreign rule. In almost every
case, such problems and their solutions affect the continued
existence of the Israelite people. Understandably, most of
these stories reflect the concerns of the post-exilic period
when the possibility of maintaining a distinctively Jewish,
communal identity posed new difficulties.

Some frequently cited similarities between the Joseph
story and the Book of Esther were not restricted to these two
narratives. On the other hand, the striking linguistic similarities between these stories, when taken with the quantity of
more general correspondences, remain explained best by the
thesis that the story of Joseph, in some sense, provides a literary model for the Book of Esther.[130] In general, two features distinguish these narratives from other post-exilic
stories to which they were compared. Jewish piety is not
strongly emphasized either in the Joseph story or in Esther,
and both tales underplay Yahweh's role in the successful outcome of events. These traits are less applicable to the Joseph
story than to the Book of Esther. Nonetheless, compared to
other post-exilic narratives, the Joseph story seems closest to
Esther at these points. Joseph, of course, retains his commitment to his religious heritage, as do Mordecai and Esther in a
different way. Both stories, however, underscore the role of
human actions in shaping events. The Joseph story suggests a
motif of "family disunity," and the Book of Esther indicates the
value of communal loyalty.

At present, the precise nature of, and reasons for, Esther's dependence upon the Joseph story are far from clear.
The emphasis placed upon human initiative in both stories, however, provides an important clue to the use of the Joseph story
by the later author. Presumably, the Book of Esther presents a

152

reinterpretation of the earlier tale of a Jew at a foreign
court. In the next chapter, we will examine some implications
of this reworking of the Joseph story by Esther's author.

NOTES

[1]Recent studies of the Joseph story, the Books of Jonah, Ruth and Judith, and to some extent Dan 2-6, tend to stress their novelistic qualities. Like Esther, these books often appear to be more history-like than historical.

[2]E.g., Paton, *The Book of Esther*, 75-77; Edward F. Campbell, Jr., *Ruth*, (AB 7; Garden City, N.Y.: Doubleday, 1975), 4,9; Meinhold, "Die Gattung der Josephsgeschichte und des Estherbuches: Diasporanovelle," I. 306-324; II. 72-93.

[3]It is beyond the scope of this dissertation to determine whether there exists a literary *Gattung* to which Esther and other Hebrew narratives belong. This task more directly concerns Meinhold, "Die Gattung der Josephsgeschichte und des Estherbuches: Diasporanovelle I, II"; idem, "Die Diasporanovelle--eine alttestamentliche Gattung." A helpful discussion of the Hebrew *Novelle* as a form-critical category also is found in Campbell, *Ruth*, 3-18; idem, "The Hebrew Short Story: A Study of Ruth," *A Light Unto My Path* ([Festschrift Jacob M. Myers], ed. H. N. Bream, R. D. Heim and C. A. Moore; Philadelphia: Temple University, 1974) 86-88.

[4]Ideally, an analysis of the Joseph story, similar to that undertaken for Esther, is required. Unfortunately, such an undertaking necessitates a separate dissertation. I consequently depend upon the work of other scholars to whom I refer in the following notes. My choice of studies of the Joseph story is subjective, not necessarily representative. Only those studies of the Joseph traditions which I think prove helpful to the discussion are included.

[5]Gaster, *Purim and Hanukkah in Custom and Tradition*, 71-72. Gaster cites an eighteenth-century "Purim Spiel" whose theme was the sale of Joseph.

[6]The provenance and date of the stories, however, may be closer than frequently thought. As the discussion below indicates, some scholars think the Joseph story to be a post-exilic composition.

[7]I follow scholarly convention here in limiting my discussion of the Joseph story to Gen 37,39-47,50. Only a few recent studies deal at length with the similarities between the Joseph and Esther narratives. There appears to be a progression of thought from the earlier to later studies, each of which basically accepts the conclusions of earlier research as its starting point. The following discussion adheres to this development of thought.

[8]Rosenthal, "Die Josephsgeschichte mit den Büchern Ester und Daniel verglichen"; see also Riessler, "Zu Rosenthal's Aufsatz, Bd. XV, S. 278ff.," and Rosenthal's response, "Nochmals der Vergleich Ester, Joseph-Daniel." Scholars who basically

accept Rosenthal's conclusions include Gerleman, *Esther*, 12-14;
Talmon, "'Wisdom' in the Book of Esther," 454-455; Humphreys,
"The Motif of the Wise Courtier in the Old Testament," 288-292;
Bardtke, "Neuere Arbeiten zum Estherbuch," 529-533.

[9]Kethibh; Qere reads בַאמרם.

[10]Gan, "מגילת אסתר באספקלריית קורות יוסף במצרים" [The Book
of Esther in Light of the Story of Joseph in Egypt], 144-149.
Many of Gan's arguments merely repeat those of Rosenthal.

[11]On the other hand, the fates of the respective guests
differ radically. Joseph's brothers are forgiven by the "man."
In Esther, the queen's revelation of her Jewish identity leads
to Haman's downfall and eventual death.

[12]This correspondence is suggested by Gan. He cites further examples which are not compelling; see Bardtke's remarks,
"Neuere Arbeiten zum Estherbuch," 529-533. Gerleman, *Esther*,
11-13, criticizes some examples cited by Rosenthal which also
would apply to Gan.

[13]See Redford, *A Study of the Biblical Story of Joseph*,
90-91.

[14]Gan characterizes the heroes' careers in both stories as
those of rise-fall-rise. This pattern applies to Joseph. But
to be applicable in the Book of Esther, Gan must include Esther's elevation to queen, her being "forgotten" by Ahasuerus,
and Mordecai's reward in Esther 6. I find this appraisal
of the story's "hero" unconvincing. I am unable to detect a
clear rise-fall-rise pattern in Esther's and Mordecai's individual careers.

[15]Cf. Dan 2:1; 6:19; 1 Esdr 3:3; also, Herodotus, *Hist.*
7.15-16. These examples perhaps suggest a type-scene, which
Donald K. Fry characterizes as "*a recurring stereotyped presentation of conventional details used to describe a certain narrative event, requiring neither verbatim repetition nor a specific formula content.*" See his "Old English Formulaic Themes
and Type-Scenes," *Neophilologus* 52 (1963) 53.

[16]Genesis 41 also mentions the gifts of the king's ring
and a gold necklace. Neither gift is mentioned in Esther 6,
although Mordecai receives the ring in Esth 8:2. Gan, "מגילת
אסתר באספקלריית קורות יוסף במצרים" [The Book of Esther in Light
of the Story of Joseph in Egypt], 147, suggests that there was
a need to delay further Mordecai's promotion; hence the later
notice. But he does not explain what appears to be a second
account of Mordecai's promotion, if we accept his rise-fall-
rise schema.

[17]These passages again suggest the possibility of a common
type-scene. A similar verdict could apply to the notices of
punishment by hanging; cf. Herodotus, *Hist.* 3.125,132,159;
7.194,238.

[18]Robert C. Culley's various studies of oral traditions
are of assistance here. Culley suggests that poets and

storytellers, both ancient and modern, often use formulaic expressions or "traditional" descriptions in their own compositions. See *Oral Formulaic Language in the Biblical Psalms*;
idem, *Studies in the Structure of Hebrew Narrative*.
A similar type of narrative shorthand also appears in
Herodotus. See Henry Wood, *The Histories of Herodotus: An
Analysis of the Formal Structure* (The Hague: Mouton, 1972) 18-
19.

[19]Bardtke, "Neuere Arbeiten zum Estherbuch," 530-531, observes: "Nicht alle aufgeführten, parallel erscheinenden Motive haben die gleiche Überzeugungskraft. Gleiche Situationen
zwingen oft zu einer ähnlichen erzählerischen Darstellung."

[20]Thus the similarities with certain Daniel traditions
which Rosenthal notes.

[21]Talmon, "'Wisdom' in the Book of Esther."

[22]Ibid., 454-455; see also H.-P. Müller, "Die weisheitliche Lehrerzählung im Alten Testament und seiner Umwelt," *Die
Welt des Orients* 9 (1977) 77-98. It is not my purpose here to
examine Talmon's claims that Esther represents "a historicized
wisdom tale" which enacts "standard wisdom motifs," "having
typical wisdom themes and precepts" (426). Rather, my interest
is limited to Talmon's suggestion that the similarities between
the story of Joseph and the Book of Esther derive from a shared
wisdom genre. For a critique of Talmon's claim that Esther is
a wisdom tale, see Crenshaw, "Method in Determining Wisdom Influence upon 'Historical' Literature," 140-142; Humphreys, "The
Motif of the Wise Courtier in the Old Testament," 307-309. In
addition to the criticisms of these two scholars, it may be
added that Talmon strips the Esther narrative of any particu-
laristic features, leaving a bare story whose form is purely
hypothetical. The denuded tale lacks any connection with Purim
which, as we have seen, is anticipated from the story's beginning and articulated by various motifs and themes.

[23]Humphreys, "The Motif of the Wise Courtier in the Old
Testament," 297-306.

[24]Ibid., 292. It is beyond the scope of the present discussion to analyze Humphreys' arguments concerning the presence
of this motif in the Joseph story. Such an examination, however, is not required if, as I hope to demonstrate, a motif of
the wise courtier does not predominate in Esther.

[25]Ibid., 298. Talmon, "'Wisdom' in the Book of Esther,"
439-449, also suggests that "'the figure of the wise man's
adopted son' has been split. . . ."

[26]Humphreys, "The Motif of the Wise Courtier in the Old
Testament," 299.

[27]Ibid., 300. Talmon, "'Wisdom' in the Book of Esther,"
447, n. 1, already observes that Mordecai's refusal to bow before Haman is problematic to arguments of wisdom influence.
See also Bardtke, "Neuere Arbeiten zum Estherbuch," 541-545.

156

28 Humphreys, "The Motif of the Wise Courtier in the Old Testament," 302.

29 Ibid., 309.

30 Ibid.

31 Ibid., 310.

32 Ibid.

33 Ibid., 309-311. One should note, however, the differing character of the dangers confronting the people of Israel (famine, genocide).

34 Ibid., 311.

35 This theme was argued as central in the Book of Esther on other grounds; see Chapter IV above.

36 See the examples cited by Talmon, "'Wisdom' in the Book of Esther," 438-440.

37 In addition, the court of a well-known king contributes to the story's entertainment value and makes for good drama, as Shakespeare recognized. The events recounted in Esther have greater import if they affect the lives of kings and nations as well as those of individuals.

38 Meinhold, "Die Gattung der Josephsgeschichte und des Estherbuches: Diasporanovelle, I, II." This two-part article summarizes the pertinent discussion of Meinhold's dissertation.

39 Meinhold considers the structures of the two narratives apart from their other similarities. A complete evaluation of Meinhold's understanding of the structure of the Joseph story takes us far afield. For the purposes of this discussion, I merely accept Meinhold's structural analysis of the Joseph story.

40 Meinhold thus views Purim as a secondary accretion to the story of Esther and Mordecai.

41 Yet also note, as does Meinhold, "Die Gattung der Josephsgeschichte und des Estherbuches: Diasporanovelle, II," 76, the differences in the stories' settings. The Joseph story begins in familial surroundings in Palestine, moves to Potiphar's house in Egypt, and only subsequently, to the Pharaoh's court. The Book of Esther, by contrast, begins at Ahasuerus' court and remains in that locale with only minor exceptions.

42 Ibid., I. 311-313.

43 Ibid., II. 76-78. In the Joseph story, this structural unit of "Das Bekanntmachen mit der Hauptperson und deren Lage," overlaps several others; see the schematic representation of the stories' structures, ibid., II. 88-89. This overlap is not found in Esther where the structural unit is contained within Esth 2:5-7. The overlapping of structural units in the Joseph

story, along with the non-successive order of verses within each unit, implies Meinhold's imposition of Esther's structure on the Joseph story. Ironically, this is the opposite of what Meinhold seeks to prove.

[44]Notices of physical beauty are common in the Hebrew Bible; thus, such notices do not carry great weight as evidence for Esther's dependence upon the Joseph story. A closer parallel to Gen 39:6b than that of Esth 2:7c is found with the description of Rachel in Gen 29:17. Cf. also Gen 41:19-20 (cows in Pharaoh's dream!); Deut 21:11; 1 Sam 16:18; 25:3; 1 Kgs 1:6. Meinhold cites the reference to Esther's youth (נערה) as a further parallel between Joseph and Esther. Other explanations for this notice are possible. For example, it is important to the story that Ahasuerus' selection of a new queen appear plausible. Esther's youth and beauty, and her availability for marriage, qualify her as a candidate to succeed Vashti.

[45]E.g., the locations of the structural elements, "Bedeutungsnachweis" and "Kleiner Aufstiegsbericht II" in both stories. The first of these also suggests a difference in function in the two stories. In the Joseph story, the hero's promotion is permanent; in Esther, Mordecai's promotion is provisional and he returns to his customary place at the king's gate. Mordecai also remains under the threat of Haman's edict.

[46]Meinhold implies that had not Joseph specifically requested to be remembered by the butler, no mention of his skill to Pharaoh would have been forthcoming.

[47]It is not clear whether the action taken by the hero to avert the danger applies to Mordecai or to Esther. Is it Mordecai's command or Esther's actual intercession which Meinhold has in mind? Meinhold suggests that Esther's compliance with Mordecai's command is delayed only to increase dramatic suspense. Esth 5:9-14 then repeats a scene of danger with its notice of the personal danger in which Mordecai stands--a repetition not found in the Joseph story.

[48]Meinhold, "Die Gattung der Josephsgeschichte und des Estherbuches: Diasporanovelle I," 316. This "Überlegenheitsbeweis" is not found as a major structural component in Esther. Meinhold suggests its presence in Esth 2:17ab, as part of the structure he labels "kleiner Aufstiegsbericht."

[49]This is most easily indicated by reference to Meinhold's summary chart, ibid., II. 88-89.

[50]For example, Gen 42-48 and Gen 50.

[51]Meinhold himself implies this understanding by his various arguments for the existence of a *Gattung* of *Diasporanovelle*. See his dissertation, "Die Diasporanovelle--eine alttestamentliche Diasporanovelle," *Wissenschaftliche Zeitschrift der Ernst-Moritz-Arndt-Universität Greifswald* (Gesellschafts- und Sprachwissenschaftliche Reihe, 4/5) 20 (1971) 277-281.

[52]Meinhold's rearrangement of verse order is more apparent from his discussion than from his summary chart. The reordering

of verses also applies more to the Joseph story than to the
Book of Esther. Again, this fact suggests that Meinhold's
analysis is guided primarily by the structure he discerns in
Esther. Such a process is the opposite of what Meinhold claims
in his article, viz., that the structure of the Joseph story
influenced the Book of Esther.

[53]Several commentators discern J and E elements in the
Joseph traditions, as well as indications of editing by later,
priestly interests. Redford, *A Study of the Biblical Story of
Joseph*, finds distinct Judah and Reuben traditions. George W.
Coats, *From Canaan to Egypt* (CBQMS 4; Washington, D.C.: Catholic Biblical Association of America, 1976), points to the presence of traditions concerning Joseph and his brothers, and
others regarding Joseph in Egypt.

[54]Meinhold, "Die Gattung der Josephsgeschichte und des
Estherbuches: Diasporanovelle," I. 311-313; II. 76-78.

[55]Discussion of this dual concern in the Joseph story is
found in ibid., I. 319.

[56]See also Donald A. Seybold, "Paradox and Symmetry in the
Joseph Narrative," *Literary Interpretations of Biblical Narra-
tives* (ed. Kenneth R. R. Gros Louis, James S. Ackerman and
Thayer S. Warshaw; New York/Nashville: Abingdon, 1974) 59-73.

[57]Redford, *A Study of the Biblical Story of Joseph (Genesis 37-50)*, 86.

[58]Ibid., 247.

[59]Ibid., 249-250. Compare Meinhold's similar arguments
for the Joseph story's post-exilic date; "Die Gattung der
Josephsgeschichte und des Estherbuches: Diasporanovelle, I,"
308-311.

[60]Redford, *A Study of the Biblical Story of Joseph (Genesis 37-50)*, 75.

[61]Ibid., 189. On the Joseph story's "Eqyptianisms," see
also R. Engelbach, "The Egyptian Name of Joseph," *JEA* 10 (1924)
204-206; Edouard Naville, "The Egyptian Name of Joseph," *JEA* 12
(1926) 16-18; J. Vergote, *Joseph en Egypte* (Louvain: Publications Universitaires et Instituut voor Oriëntalisme, 1959);
Robert Martin-Achard, "Problemes souleves par l'étude d'histoire biblique de Joseph (Genèse 37-50)," *RTP* 22 (1972) 94-96.
The accuracy of the Egyptological background in the Joseph
story is maintained by Arthur Van Seters, "The Use of the Story
of Joseph in Scripture" (Th.D. dissertation, Union Theological
Seminary of Richmond, Virginia, 1965), 9-20.

[62]E. A. Speiser, *Genesis* (AB 1; Garden City, N.Y.:
Doubleday, 1964), 323.

[63]Ibid., 329.

[64]Ibid., 341.

[65]The latter scene is especially perplexing since the king's servant, Harbonah, suddenly appears; cf. Esth 7:9. Presumably, Harbonah helped serve at Esther's banquet. Did he remain with Esther and Haman, or follow the king into the garden? The story does not say.

[66]Redford, *A Study of the Biblical Story of Joseph (Genesis 37-50)*, 88-100.

[67]Redford, ibid., 99, indicates the significance of a motif of famine in the Joseph story. This famine motif allows the narrator to present Joseph as a food provider *par excellence* whose skill saves the Egyptians and his own family. We do not find famine as a motif in the Book of Esther; but as initiators of Purim, Mordecai and Esther, in one sense, could be viewed as food providers. Since Purim commemorates the saving of the Jews from annihilation, a connection between providing food and saving the people perhaps is implicit in the Book of Esther.

[68]Coats, *From Canaan to Egypt*.

[69]Ibid., 45-46.

[70]B. J. van der Merwe, "Joseph as Successor to Jacob," *Studia Biblica et Semitica* ([Festschrift Theodorus Christiaan Vriezen], ed. U. C. van Unnik and A. S. van der Woude; Wageningen: H. Veenman en Zonen, 1966) 221-232.

[71]Such a view might be indicated by the fact that the patriarchal history devotes particular attention not only to Abraham, Isaac and Jacob, but also to Joseph. By comparison, Jacob's other sons are more or less ignored.

[72]If van der Merwe is correct, Mordecai's genealogy could include allusions to Josephide, as well as Saulide, ancestors: 2 Sam 19:20 mentions a Josephide "Shimei," and there are frequent references to a Manassite "Jair" (cf. Num 32:41; Deut 3:14; Josh 13:30; 1 Kgs 4:13).

[73]In conjunction with this implied motif of kingship, see the study of Seybold, "Paradox and Symmetry in the Joseph Narrative." Seybold argues that Joseph's various garments symbolize his status and transition from Jacob's house to those of Potiphar and Pharaoh (59). In the Book of Esther, Mordecai's apparel similarly functions symbolically as an indication of his status and as a suggestion of his quasi-royal status.

[74]The question of Esther's date is discussed in the next chapter. Although my own suspicion is that Esther stems from a period somewhat later than commonly assumed, the possibility remains that the similarities between the Joseph and Esther stories derive, in part, from their proximity in date.

[75]Meinhold, "Die Gattung der Josephsgeschichte und des Estherbuches: Diasporanovelle, II," 92-93.

[76]I shall return to this problem in the next chapter.

[77]I follow scholarly convention by distinguishing between
the traditions contained in Daniel 2-6 and those of Daniel 1,7-
12. The former probably originated during the Persian period
and circulated independently prior to incorporation into the
present Book of Daniel. The discussion below treats Daniel 2-6
more or less as a single document, although these chapters
probably consist of a collection of originally independent
tales. There are indications, however, that Daniel 2-6 circulated as an independent collection. See the discussions of
Roger Alan Hall, "Post-exilic Theological Streams and the Book
of Daniel" (Ph.D. dissertation, Yale University, New Haven,
1975); and John J. Collins, "The Court-Tales in Daniel and the
Development of Apocalyptic," *JBL* 94 (1975) 218-234.

[78]Rosenthal, "Die Josephsgeschichte mit den Büchern Ester
und Daniel verglichen," 284.

[79]Ibid., 281-283; Humphreys, "The Motif of the Wise Courtier in the Old Testament," 313-317.

[80]Raymond Hammer, *The Book of Daniel* (CBC; Cambridge:
Cambridge University, 1976) 62, thinks that at the banquet of
Daniel 5, the king's wives were absent and only his concubines
present. If Hammer is correct, we also are reminded here of
one explanation for Vashti's refusal to appear at her husband's
feast, viz., that her appearance would imply a status of con-
cubine, not of a wife.

[81]Norman Porteous, *Daniel* (OTL; Philadelphia: Westminster, 1965), 25,39; Hall, "Post-exilic Theological Streams and
the Book of Daniel," 267, n. 12.

[82]Humphreys, "The Motif of the Wise Courtier in the Old
Testament," 334; Hall, "Post-exilic Theological Streams and the
Book of Daniel," 119-120, 125. Collins, "The Court-Tales in
Daniel and the Development of Apocalyptic," indicates that the
attitudes toward the king vary among the individual tales of
Daniel 2-6. For example, the king is viewed less favorably in
Daniel 3 than in Daniel 6, and more negatively in Daniel 4-5.
But on the whole, the king is viewed favorably in Daniel 2-6
and generally is presented in the tales as willing to acknowl-
edge Yahweh's sovereignty. At any rate, the attitude toward
the king in these chapters is far more favorable than in Daniel
7-12.

[83]Humphreys, "The Motif of the Wise Courtier in the Old
Testament," 314.

[84]On Daniel's and Mordecai's Jewish identity, see Humphreys, ibid., 315,327; idem, "A Life-style for Diaspora: A
Study of the Tales of Esther and Daniel," 220; on Joseph's
Hebrew background, see Meinhold, "Die Gattung der Josephsgeschichte und des Estherbuches: Diasporanovelle, I," 312-313.

[85]Humphreys, "The Motif of the Wise Courtier in the Old
Testament," 315.

[86]Humphreys, "A Life-style for Diaspora: A Study of the
Tales of Esther and Daniel," 219, finds the dominant motif of

Dan 2:1-49 to be the "understanding of all visions and dreams" and in 3:1-30, the motif of Jewish piety. Both motifs suggest that all wisdom derives from Yahweh, who is sovereign. The same emphases recur in Dan 3:31-6:28. Despite some disagreements with Humphreys, Collins, "The Court-Tales in Daniel and the Development of Apocalyptic," 219-228, suggests a similar characterization of the tales' dominant motifs.

[87]Also cf. Dan 3:8-18, where a group hostile to the Jewish heroes accuses them of disobedience to the king's law. This passage is reminiscent of Esth 3:8.

[88]See Collins' remarks on Daniel 6; "The Court-Tales in Daniel and the Development of Apocalyptic," 226.

[89]Humphreys notes that the individual tales of Daniel 2-6 constantly emphasize Daniel's and his friends' devotion to their religious heritage and their trust in Yahweh. The tales make clear that all wisdom and understanding derive from Yahweh.

[90]Porteous, *Daniel*, 18. Collins suggests a similar theme for the collected tales of Daniel 2-6.

[91]Humphreys, "The Motif of the Wise Courtier in the Old Testament," 315. See also the general discussion of Meinhold, "Die Diasporanovelle--eine alttestamentliche Gattung," on the existence of a *Gattung* of *Diasporanovelle* to which all of these tales belong. The preservation of traditions surrounding Nehemiah lends further support to the popularity of such court tales.

[92]Humphreys, "The Motif of the Wise Courtier in the Old Testament," 316.

[93]The value of a comparison between the Joseph story, the Book of Esther and the Book of Ruth is called into question by the difficulty in dating the latter. Several prestigious commentaries have appeared in recent years which date Ruth in the pre-exilic period. A post-exilic dating, however, still dominates the discussion. Recent advocates include Jean-Luc Vesco, "La date du livre de Ruth," *RB* 74 (1967) 235-247; John Gray, *Joshua, Judges and Ruth* (Century Bible, New Series; London: Thomas Nelson & Sons, 1967), 398-400; and Robert Gordis, "Love, Marriage and Business in the Book of Ruth," *A Light Unto My Path* ([Festschrift Jacob M. Myers], ed. H. N. Bream, R. D. Heim and C. A. Moore; Philadelphia: Temple University, 1974) 243-246. The following argue that the present form of the Book of Ruth is post-exilic but is based upon an earlier poetic account: Jacob M. Myers, *The Linguistic and Literary Form of the Book of Ruth* (Leiden: E. J. Brill, 1955); George S. Glanzman, "The Origin and Date of the Book of Ruth," *CBQ* 21 (1959) 201-207.

[94]An obvious similarity which encourages comparisons between the Books of Esther and Ruth is the fact that women play central roles in both stories. Ronald M. Hals, *The Theology of the Book of Ruth* (FBBS 23; Philadelphia: Fortress, 1969) 47-53, finds similarities in the narrative styles of Esther and

Ruth. Hals, 34-44, also detects similarities between the stories of Joseph and Ruth. Arndt Meinhold, "Theologische Schwerpunkte im Buch Ruth und ihr Gewicht für seine Datierung," *TZ* 3 (1976) 129, lists several scholars who compare the Joseph story and the Book of Ruth.

[95]Campbell, *Ruth*, 59.

[96]Ibid., *passim*.

[97]Ibid., 13.

[98]Ibid., 14; D. F. Rauber, "Literary Values in the Bible: The Book of Ruth," *JBL* 89 (1970) 35.

[99]Stephen Bertman, "Symmetrical Design in the Book of Ruth," *JBL* 84 (1956) 165-168. Bertman argues that Ruth is chiastically structured. As suggested above, Esther is not a strict chiasm.

[100]Campbell, *Ruth*, 121; see also 132,137.

[101]Oswald Loretz, "The Theme of the Ruth Story," *CBQ* 22 (1960) 391-399; idem, "Roman und Kurzgeschichte in Israel," *Wort und Botschaft* (ed. Josef Schreiner; Würzburg: Echter-Verlag, 1967) 293-294.

[102]Israel's messianic redeemer thus indirectly is affected by both this problem and its solution.

[103]In some ways, the Joseph story is closer to the Book of Ruth here than is the Book of Esther. The Joseph and Ruth traditions both relate events which affect significant ancestors in ancient Israel, viz., the tribal fathers and King David.

[104]Campbell, *Ruth*, 28-29.

[105]Wilhelm Rudolph, *Das Buch Ruth* (KAT 17; Gütersloh: Gütersloher Verlagshaus Gerd Mohn, 1962) 32; Hals, *The Theology of the Book of Ruth*, 7-8,28; Campbell, *Ruth*, 29-31.

[106]Hals, *The Theology of the Book of Ruth*, 34-44. The characteristic way in which Yahweh's presence manifests itself in the Book of Ruth is through the establishment of a correspondence between God's actions and those of humans. Campbell, *Ruth*, 29, writes: "Blessing, invocation, event, complaint, all express ways in which God is expected to work out his will . . . and in each case it is the people, living as they are to live under God's sovereignty, who proceed to work it out." The Book of Esther distinguishes itself from the stories of Joseph and Ruth by its total absence of any direct references to the deity. Hals labels this a *reductio ad absurdum* of the treatment found in Ruth.

[107]Campbell, *Ruth*, frequently remarks upon the "inexplicable calamities" or "lucky" occurrences depicted in the Book of Ruth. Given the similarities in their theological perspectives, such remarks would seem to apply as much to the Joseph story as to the Book of Ruth. In the former, the coincidental nature of

events is not emphasized by the narrator because, as Joseph
states in Gen 45:8, Yahweh ultimately is responsible for the
successful outcome of events. Nonetheless, events in Joseph's
life take fortuitious turns, e.g., the arrival of a caravan
when Joseph's brothers plot to dispose of him, and the butler's
recollection of Joseph's skill at interpreting dreams.

[108]Ackroyd, *Exile and Restoration*, 244-245; Wilhelm
Rudolph, "Jona," *Archäologie und Altes Testament* ([Festschrift
Kurt Galling], ed. Arnulf Kuschke and Ernst Kutsch; Tübingen:
J. C. B. Mohr, 1970), 235-237.

[109]R. E. Clements, "Purpose of the Book of Jonah," *International Organization for the Study of the Old Testament, Congress Volume* (VTSup 28; Leiden: E. J. Brill, 1975) 21.

[110]The dominant motifs of Jonah are discussed by Gabriel H.
Cohn, *Das Buch Jonah im Lichte der biblischen Erzählkunst*
(Assen: van Gorcum, 1969); and Phyllis Lou Trible, "Studies in
the Book of Jonah" (Ph.D. dissertation, Columbia University,
New York, 1963).

[111]Trible, "Studies in the Book of Jonah," 185-192. Unlike
the Book of Esther, events in the first and second halves of
the Book of Jonah do not contrast with each other but are in
parallel.

[112]The centrality of Yahweh's role in Jonah is discussed by
Trible, "Studies in the Book of Jonah," 272-273; and Cohn, *Das
Buch Jonah im Lichte der biblischen Erzählkunst*, 84-85.

[113]Notably by Solomon Zeitlin, "Introduction (The Books of
Esther and Judith: A Parallel)," in *The Book of Judith* (JAL 7;
Leiden: E. J. Brill, 1972) 1-37.

[114]The majority of scholars date the Book of Judith in the
mid-second century B.C.E. See the discussions of Zeitlin,
ibid., 26-32; J. C. Dancy, *The Shorter Books of the Apocrypha*
(Cambridge: Cambridge University, 1972) 70-71; Pfeiffer, *History of New Testament Times*, 291-297.

[115]Judith's beauty serves as a leitmotif in the Book of
Judith. See Luis Alonso-Schökel, "Narrative Structures in the
Book of Judith," *Protocol Series of the Colloquies of the Center for Hermeneutical Studies in Hellenistic and Modern Culture*,11 (Berkeley: Graduate Theological Union and the University of California, 1974) 7; Toni Craven, "Artistry and Faith
in the Book of Judith," *Semeia* 8 (1977) 90-91. I am grateful
to the author for a copy of her study prior to its publication.

[116]In the Book of Judith, Holofernes' camp functions as the
local, Palestinian extension of Nebuchadnezzar's court.

[117]At the same time, the general framework of Judith differs radically from those of Joseph and Esther. These differences are noted below.

164

[118]Alonso-Schökel, "Narrative Structures in the Book of Judith," 8-11; Craven, "Artistry and Faith in the Book of Judith," 81, 89-93.

[119]Alonso-Schökel, 7.

[120]Proselytism also appears in both Esther and Judith (Esth 8:17; Jdt 14:10), although it plays a greater role in the latter. Also of interest is the Vulgate's remark that a festival was instituted by the Jews to commemorate Judith's achievement; see Dancy, *The Shorter Books of the Apocrypha*, 126-127.

[121]Craven, "Artistry and Faith in the Book of Judith," 91-93.

[122]Unlike the figures of Esther and Ruth, however, Judith is not initially portrayed as a passive, obedient woman. She thus does not undergo any personality "development" in the narrative.

[123]The significance of Judith's social status is discussed by Alonso-Schökel, "Narrative Structures in the Book of Judith," 14-15.

[124]Craven, "Artistry and Faith in the Book of Judith," 84-85.

[125]Craven, 94, characterizes Judith as "a story of dramatic reversals."

[126]That is, in Hebrew the name "Judith" suggests a "Jewess." Some scholars hold that Judith originally was composed in Hebrew; see Dancy, *The Shorter Books of the Apocrypha*, 71; Alonso-Schökel, "Narrative Structures in the Book of Judith," 2-3.

[127]The attitude toward non-Israelites and the emphasis upon Jewish piety in the Book of Judith reflect its composition in the Hasmonean period. The present story probably represents a translation of an earlier Hebrew account; see above, n. 126. Dancy, *The Shorter Books of the Apocrypha*, 77, lists the story's "Persianisms" and concludes that "for all the continued references to Nebuchadnezzar, the colour of the invading army is mainly Persian." One wonders whether an earlier, Hebrew version of Judith also derives from Hasmonean times, or from an earlier (Persian?) period. Such a tale perhaps displayed an outlook closer to those of the Joseph story and the Book of Esther. Unfortunately, the present account does not permit anything beyond speculations.

[128]Zeitlin, "Introduction (The Books of Esther and Judith: A Parallel)," 13. But see the remarks of A. M. Dubarle, *Judith: Formes et sens des diverses traditions* (Rome: Institut Biblique Pontifical, 1966), 160. Dubarle finds the lack of contact between the Books of Esther and Judith surprising.

[129]These features could merely reflect a common outlook which emerged by post-exilic times or even a common method of storytelling. Hence, such general similarities as stylistic

techniques, general settings and attitudes toward foreigners are not restricted to the Joseph and Esther stories and cannot be used as evidence of direct literary dependence.

[130]Although the Joseph story and the Book of Esther share no dominant motifs, themes or structures, the *cumulative effect* of their similarities nonetheless indicates that the author of Esther was familiar with the Joseph tale.

CHAPTER VI

DATE, "THEOLOGY" AND CONCLUDING REMARKS

The Book of Esther is often depicted as the anathema of
canonized Scripture, a document which "occupies the same place
in sacred scripture as the villainous rogue in a story or play
which has been written with a moral purpose."[1] Anderson portrays the story as "an uninviting wilderness" which contrasts
with the "frequent oases of inspired Scripture."[2]

Such evaluations of the book's theological worth are not
uncommon among scholars, nor are they restricted to judgments
regarding Esther's religious value. As indicated in Chapter I
of this study, the historicity of the account also is chal-
lenged. Questions regarding the story's historical and religious worth, in fact, mark the history of Esther research.

Yet if the Book of Esther proves "an uninviting wilderness" theologically, a similar judgment cannot be maintained
with regard to its literary value.[3] To the contrary, the preceding chapters demonstrate that Esther is rich and fruitful in
its wealth of literary detail and stylistic techniques. It
clearly is a product of the fertile ground of post-exilic Judaism, nurtured by the streams of diaspora thought and rhetorical
style.

In this final chapter, we shall examine the implications
of the analysis of Esther presented here for the types of questions raised in Chapter I. In particular, we may address one
issue which has proven among the most problematic to students
of the scroll, viz., the book's theological significance. Before turning to this task, however, we may summarize the results of this study with respect to some historical and form-
critical questions initially raised by our discussion.

Implications of this study for some of these questions
already were indicated above. For example, it was argued that
the received text of Esther clearly was intended as a festal
legend. That the Book of Esther serves this function is not
denied by contemporary scholarship. In Chapter II, it was demonstrated on literary grounds, however, that Purim is no

secondary accretion to the story of Esther and Mordecai. Rather, from its very beginning, the Book of Esther anticipates its conclusion in a festal celebration, characterized most notably by two feasts. The story and the festival reveal an identity of purpose, viz., to suggest the successful efforts of diaspora Jews to save their people. The story and festival also are linked by the manner in which Purim is observed, which recalls corresponding, significant events of the narrative.

The present study of the Book of Esther illuminates, although it does not totally clarify, the question of the story's composition. Scholars have pointed to "seams" in the narrative and this study cannot account for all of the examples which they cite. For example, the initial identification of the story's heroine as "Hadassah," almost parenthetically reidentified as "Esther," remains unexplained by this analysis of the book. Other problems, such as the reference to the "second" harem (2:14) or the "second" gathering of the virgins (2:19), continue to cloud the question of Esther's composition.

On the other hand, the version of the narrative preserved in the MT appears to be a unified whole. The book's dominant motifs and themes point to a work of one piece whose beginning, middle and end are in parallel with, and balance, each other. The narrative structure was formulated according to a uniform pattern of reversals which both reflects and reinforces a major theme of the story. The narrative structure thus contributes to the impression of Esther's unity. This evidence counters several current views which see the Masoretic version of Esther to be a piecemeal account. Rather, the evidence suggests that the present narrator himself inherited an earlier tale which conflated once-independent traditions. Such a thesis accounts for the remaining "seams" in a narrative which, at the same time, bears the marks of a unified composition.

With respect to the place of composition, I accepted as a working hypothesis the generally held view that the Book of Esther represents a diaspora composition. A literary analysis of the story supports this thesis since Esther displays concerns appropriate to a diaspora context. A comparison of the Book of Esther to the Joseph story further indicates that Esther contains themes which were of particular interest to diaspora Jews. On the other hand, some of these concerns were common to

other post-exilic narratives, not all of which have their probable provenance in the diaspora. It therefore remains unclear
whether the Book of Esther belongs to a specific literary *Gattung* of *Diasporanovelle*.

My study of Esther sought to examine the narrative on its
own terms, without resort to a preconceived notion of the specific period which gave rise to it.[4] The identification of
narrative motifs and themes were based upon Esther's literary
features. I have not argued for any particular socio-religious
view of a specific historical context whose concerns or effects
were discerned in the story. Rather, this study relied upon
the scroll itself to suggest the narrator's concerns and purposes in telling his story as he did.

A. Date

One consequence of this approach was to postpone any discussion of Esther's date, a topic which now may be properly addressed. We may approach the question of date in a fashion
similar to that used to discover the story's themes. That is,
the issues raised by the storyteller provide the clues to Esther's date. We thus return once more to the story's setting,
plot, characterization and style.

My purpose here is not to review evidence regarding the
date of Esther which may be found in virtually every commentary
or study of the scroll.[5] Most recent studies of Esther agree
that its *terminus ad quem* is pre-Maccabean. The *terminus a quo*
of the Masoretic version, however, is subject to greater de-
bate, and many scholars hold that the Book of Esther contains
traditions which stem from the Persian period.[6] The intention
of the following analysis is to utilize the results of the preceding chapters to illuminate a discussion of the story's
terminus a quo.

Consideration of the story's date is complicated by the
fact that "there is not a single statement in the book which
gives unambiguous witness as to date."[7] Anderson suggests,
however, that the narrator speaks of the time of Ahasuerus as
long past (cf. 1:1, 13-14; 4:11; 8:8; 10:2).[8] Haman's description of the Jews as scattered and dispersed (3:8) also indicates that the dispersion was a long-accomplished fact when the

story was composed.[9] The impression of a comparatively late date for Esther is strengthened by the important arguments of Ruth Stiehl who finds linguistic evidence which dates the story in the hellenistic period.[10]

Many who argue for a late date for the Book of Esther find support in the story's antagonism toward gentiles. I argued above, however, that the scroll displays a generally positive attitude toward the foreign masters. Its antagonism is directed specifically against those who seek to harm Jews, and this antagonism cannot be extended to include the Persian administration. The antagonism of Palestinian Jews toward gentiles in hellenistic times proves irrelevant for a discussion of Esther's date since the story primarily concerns diaspora Jews. Esther lacks any interest in Palestine or its cultic institutions. This fact suggests that the concerns of diaspora and Palestinian Jews were not always identical.[11]

Those who favor a late date for the MT story also cite its absence from the collection of manuscripts at Qumran.[12] Moore uses the evidence from Qumran differently, suggesting that Esther's Hebrew has little in common with that of the Dead Sea scrolls. He argues that this linguistic evidence rules out a second century date for Esther and renders a third century date unlikely.[13]

Also important to the discussion of Esther's date is the absence of Greek words in the story. This fact, when considered with the abundance of terms derived from Persian languages, points in the direction of a Persian date for the story.[14] On the other hand, the absence of Greek and the abundance of "Persianisms" in Esther may reflect a conscious attempt at archaizing.[15] These "Persianisms" may reflect an attempt to give the story a certain verisimilitude. Knowledge of Persian matters was readily available in a later period as a result of the promulgation of Berossus' writings.[16] In addition, we noted above that several post-exilic Hebrew narratives suggest a setting significantly earlier than the probable dates of their compositions. Thus, the Joseph story abounds in "Egyptianisms" and the present forms of Daniel 2-6, Jonah, Ruth and Judith suggest that an early setting for a story was a common literary device.[17] Finally, the fact that several of the Dead Sea scrolls were composed in Hebrew, despite their hellenistic

dates, indicates that the absence of Greek in the Book of Esther is no assurance of its pre-hellenistic date.[18]

The question of Esther's date thus remains open, with cogent evidence arguing both for and against an early hellenistic
terminus a quo. Other clues to Esther's date of composition,
however, are suggested by the narrative. In Esth 3:8, for example, Haman's accusations against the Jews include his observation that they are scattered and dispersed, and further, that
their laws differ from those of other peoples. Haman's accusations raise two questions regarding the probable date of Esther. At what point in time would the wide-spread dispersion
of Jews have constituted an accurate description and have been
a matter of concern? Secondly, during which historical period
would the fact that the Jews, as a people, observed laws different from those of other peoples constitute a valid accusation against them?

The first question is difficult to answer and perhaps a-
waits more information about the history of the Eastern diaspora during the Persian and early hellenistic periods.[19] The
second question, unfortunately, is no less problematic. Nevertheless, we know that the Achaemenian dynasty generally supported the socio-religious institutions of the empire's constituent peoples.[20] Given this knowledge, Haman's accusation
seems odd in a story deriving from Persian times.[21]

This observation is not meant to suggest that the hellenistic period proved intolerant of cultural and religious diver-
sities. To the contrary, evidence from this period reveals a
certain degree of internal autonomy within the Jewish diaspora
communities, and thus a certain tolerance of Jewish customs.[22]
Nevertheless, the impact of a *polis*, especially in Susa,[23] may
have rendered the differences between Jews and other, more
fully acculturated, peoples more visible and problematic.[24]
Haman's accusation probably possessed greater validity in a
place where the impact of a newly established *polis* was felt.

Mordecai's refusal to bow before Haman holds obvious importance for the progression of the narrative. His refusal,
however, also provides a clue to the story's date.

As a part of his hellenization policy, Alexander attempted
to introduce the act of prostration into court ceremonial. F.
E. Peters notes that

. . . for the Iranians, who normally approached the
Shah in that fashion, it was no matter; for the Greeks
it was at the very least in poor taste in that it required them to act out the charade of Alexander's
divinity.[25]

The act of *proskynesis* proved to be of some interest during Alexander's reign. The action was particularly opposed by
Callisthenes, a nephew of Aristotle who served as official his-
torian to Alexander's expedition.[26] Callisthenes was critical
of Alexander only with respect to this matter. The question of
proskynesis thus developed into a matter of dispute. Alexander
apparently was influenced by criticisms such as Callisthenes',
for the emperor later dropped his demand that Greeks at court
bow before him.

The question of *proskynesis* did not become an issue in the
former Persian territories until the advent of Alexander. The
importance of this particular act in the Book of Esther may reflect a concern peculiar to the early hellenistic period.

A different clue to the *terminus a quo* of the MT is indicated by Esth 8:17. There we find mention of the "fear" experienced by non-Jews toward their Jewish compatriots. This
"fear" results in the conversion of some non-Jews to Judaism,
or at least indicates their support of Jewish interests. It is
possible that this reference to conversion reflects an historical period when Jewish proselytism was a vital force in diaspora life. On the other hand, Esth 8:17 may point to nothing
more than the author's indication that the power of the Jews
was recognized by their compatriots.[27] We similarly must demonstrate caution in our interpretation of Esth 9:27. The reference to הנלוים ("all who might join them") in that verse
again may reflect a period of Jewish proselytism, or simply
refer back to the מתיהדים ("became Jews" [?]) of Esth 8:17.

Also of interest in dating the Book of Esther is the interpretation of Esth 9:28. We indicated above that the integrity of Esth 9:28-32 is doubted by some commentators, but its
retention as a part of the original story--or at least its ap-
proximation of part of the original story--seems advisable on
stylistic grounds. Several translators understand the phrase
והימים האלה נזכרים ונעשים to refer to the future commemoration
of "these days."[28] An initial reading of this phrase, however,
might suggest a perfect tense for the niphal, i.e., "were/are

recalled and observed."[29] Such a reading of this phrase may
hint at the narrator's own period, which would appear to be
somewhat removed from the initial commemoration of events.[30]

Finally, a clue to the composition of the MT story may be
indicated by the narrator's appeal to the "chronicles of the
kings of Media and Persia" (10:2). Again, I believe that the
concluding chapter of the Book of Esther should be retained on
stylistic grounds. If this view is correct, the storyteller's
appeal to authority may reflect the rhetoric of hellenistic
apologia. There, an appeal to some accepted authority, to verify the validity or accuracy of an argument, is not uncommon.[31]
The Book of Esther clearly stems from a period earlier than
that of the hellenistic apologia,[32] yet Esth 10:2 recalls a
common rhetorical device of the later literature. At any rate,
the function served by the appeal in Esth 10:2 is similar to
that of the later documents and establishes the authenticity
and authority of the narrator's account.

The Book of Esther unquestionably contains traditions
stemming from the Persian period of the diaspora. Whether the
account preserved by the MT itself stems from this same period
is less clear. Some questions which are central to the narrative account, and which also bear upon the question of date,
seem more easily resolved if the present form of the narrative
comes from sometime within the hellenistic period. At present,
we may only concur with Anderson's observation that Esther
gives no unambiguous witness to its date. We may add, however,
that analysis of the story's literary features reveals additional evidence, cumulative in character if not decisive in
detail, which recommends a reconsideration of hellenistic influences upon the MT account.

B. "Theology"

The approach to the Book of Esther taken here illuminates
several historical and form-critical questions frequently posed
to the text. Our final task is to determine if a literary
analysis of the Book of Esther proves helpful in an evaluation
of its religious significance. This task appears dubious from
its outset since the Book of Esther makes no reference to the
deity.[33] The following remarks nonetheless are offered in the

hope that they demonstrate that the Book of Esther is neither "an uninviting wilderness" nor an anathema to canonized Scripture.

In the preceding chapter, it was suggested that the Book of Esther displays some familiarity with the Joseph traditions. Unfortunately, the precise nature of the relationship between the two stories is not yet clear and in need of further clarification. Both tales display certain similarities in general setting, formulaic motifs,[34] themes and narrative style. Correspondences, however, also were detected in other post-exilic narratives when they were compared to the Joseph and Esther stories. The evidence indicated by an examination of these other Israelite tales supports our contention that many of the suggested correspondences between the Joseph and Esther stories derive from concerns common to the post-exilic period.

The Book of Esther nevertheless points to a dependence upon the Joseph traditions which goes beyond the general features it shares with other post-exilic narratives. The unusual and striking correspondence in the choice of words, syntactical structures and narrative portrayals implies that the author of Esther consciously utilized the Joseph traditions in his own portrayal of events at Susa.

The choice of the Joseph story as a literary model for the Book of Esther is of particular interest in light of the availability of other stories to the narrator. For example, the traditions regarding Moses at Pharaoh's court surely were known to Esther's author. These traditions also suggest the story of a Jew at a foreign court whose efforts save the entire Jewish people. In addition, the concepts of power, sovereignty and inviolability are suggested by the exodus narratives. Gerleman's thesis, even with its problems, demonstrates an intriguing correspondence between the Esther and exodus stories. Given the renewed interest in the exodus traditions during the exilic and post-exilic periods,[35] it is surprising that the Book of Esther more clearly reflects the influence of traditions other than those of the exodus.[36] Moreover, if the Book of Esther is to be dated during the hellenistic post-exilic period, other tales, such as those of Ruth or Daniel 2-6, could have provided useful literary models.

Why, then, was the Joseph story chosen by Esther's author

as a model?[37] Again, it is difficult to respond to this question without a clearer notion of the manner in which the Joseph
story is used in the scroll. To date, no acceptable demonstration of an identity in the dominant motifs or structures of the
two tales has been offered, and a comparison of these stories
to other post-exilic tales suggests that their correspondence
in general setting and themes proves an insufficient explanation.

Lacking further evidence, we can only speculate upon the
reasons for the choice of this particular literary model. One
reason against the choice of other models perhaps lies in their
attitudes toward foreign masters. For example, the exodus narratives foresee a freeing of the Israelites from foreign influences and clearly express a desire to leave the foreign land.
Such emphases contrast with the attitudes expressed in both the
Joseph and Esther stories. The Joseph story, unlike the exodus
narratives, reflects an accommodation to life in a diaspora
setting. It points to the possibility for a rewarding and
fruitful life outside Palestine. The Joseph story also suggests the possibility of an Israelite's concern for both his
own people and his foreign master. This accent upon a divided
loyalty in the Joseph story may point to one important reason
for its choice by Esther's author.[38]

Equally important is the restricted role played by Yahweh
in the story of Joseph. As previously remarked, it is at this
point that the stories of Joseph and Esther differ most radically from other so-called *Diasporanovellen*. The limited involvement of Yahweh in human affairs, along with the fortuitous
"coincidences" of everyday life in the Joseph story, undoubtedly made that narrative attractive to the later author.

The Book of Esther nevertheless differs from the Joseph
story in its dominant motifs and structure, indicating that the
former was not totally dependent upon the latter.[39] Esther's
author had his own story to tell--a story whose life situations
were not completely identical to those portrayed in the earlier
traditions. We consequently must wonder why the later narrator
found it necessary to use the Joseph, or any other, story to
relate his own tale. Posed differently, we may ask if the
Joseph traditions were used in the Book of Esther only as a
type of narrative shorthand. Do allusions to the earlier story

serve a more specific purpose in the Book of Esther?

In an attempt to respond to these questions, it is useful once more to note some of the differences between the Book of Esther and the account of Joseph.[40] In both stories, a disaster threatens the Jewish people. But in the Joseph tale, the threat stems from a natural disaster--a famine which threatens not only the Israelites but neighboring peoples as well. In the Book of Esther, the danger confronting the Jews is restricted solely to them. As Esth 4:13-14 indicates, even the queen stands under the threat of death and may perish with the other Jews. This restriction of the danger to the Jews presents a problem found in the Joseph story in a new light. It refocuses and concentrates the audience's attention upon the question of the continued existence, or annihilation, of the Jewish people. This problem is central to the plot of Esther and is introduced with the first mention of the Jewish protagonists. Esther 2:5-6, which introduces Mordecai, already hints at the problem of Jewish survival in a diaspora setting, for it implies the survival of the Jews as a people, despite their exile and captivity. Similarly, the story closes with the institution of a festival to commemorate the victory of the Jews over their foes. Even the concluding verse of the scroll refers to Mordecai's exalted position in the empire and to his use of power to benefit his co-religionists. The problem of the continued survival of the Jews also finds expression in the central themes of power and inviolability.

In the Book of Esther, the survival of the Jews, even their successful accommodation to diaspora life, results from their own actions. The responsibility for saving the Jewish people rests with the queen who must decide whether to risk her own life. The Book of Esther suggests that each individual Jew who is in a position to do so must use his/her power and authority to assist the people of Israel. Again, it is significant that the story concludes with the notice of Mordecai's use of power to aid his brethren (cf. 10:3).

As previously remarked, when compared to other more or less contemporaneous tales such as Daniel 2-6, Ruth, Jonah and Judith, the Joseph and Esther stories seem to restrict the role played by God in the narratives. Yet when the Joseph and Esther stories themselves are compared, the difference in degree

to which they limit God's control of events becomes apparent.
In fact, Esther's emphasis upon human responsibility in saving
the Jews and in finding a happy accommodation to the vicissitudes of diaspora life provides the point at which the Book of
Esther and the tale of Joseph diverge. For despite the importance of Joseph's own actions, Joseph's *ultimate* success comes
from Yahweh (cf. 39:2-3,21,23).[41] Yahweh's assistance also is
apparent in Joseph's ability to interpret dreams (cf. Gen 40:8;
41:16,25,28,32). Given the centrality of a dream motif in the
Joseph narrative, the divine origin of Joseph's success attains
an importance of its own. The theocentric nature of these traditions is further underscored by the inclusion of the Joseph
story in the patriarchal narratives. In the Joseph story, the
salvation of Israel, and of Egypt as well, is due to Yahweh's
ultimate control of nature and history (cf. Gen 45:5-9; 50:19-
21). The survival of the people of Israel entails the survival
of the foreign people, and both are presented as theologically
rooted in the will and deeds of Yahweh.[42] While the Joseph
story, like the Book of Esther, portrays Yahweh's limited involvement in events, it nonetheless continues to affirm that
God ultimately is responsible for the favorable turn of
affairs.

However limited the activity of the deity might appear in
the Joseph story, Yahweh's intervention in human affairs thus
proves the reason behind Joseph's success. Similarly, the saving of the Israelite and Egyptian peoples stems from Yahweh.
The story of Joseph clearly is theocentrically formulated and
focused.

This is not the case in the Book of Esther despite the fact
that the accounts of Joseph and Esther restrict divine activity
more than other post-exilic tales. Whereas both narratives
limit Yahweh's involvement in human affairs, the Book of Esther
completely avoids *any* direct reference to the deity. One, in
fact, is tempted to describe the Book of Esther as devoid of
any "theology," until we recall Y. Kaufmann's caveat that a
dual causality of events characterizes the biblical Weltanschauung.[43] We therefore must question whether the Book of Esther completely ignores all belief in Yahweh's control of history.

It was suggested above that Esth 4:13-14 presents the

central passage of the book. This passage points to Mordecai's complete confidence that assistance was forthcoming. It is improbable that Mordecai's words constitute an oblique reference to the deity. Rather, they point less to the source of assistance than to Mordecai's belief in its availability.

In this same passage, Mordecai suggests the possibility that Esther has come into power for "a time such as this." His observation implies a concurrent belief that Esther's attainment of royal power is more than coincidental. Mordecai's assurance of help for the Jews, and his observation that Esther's possession of royal power is fortuitously suited to "a time such as this," both intimate that an ordering principle is operative in the "coincidental" events of the tale. We saw a similar implication in the structure of the story. This central passage of 4:13-14, along with the structure of the book, confirms Kaufmann's thesis in this case. They indicate that the narrator believed in a hidden causality behind the surface of human history, both concealing and governing the order and significance of events. The direction of human history is to be found in the occurrence, order and implications of everyday life and events of the workaday world. Esther's narrator carefully mirrors the nature of history in his method of narration; for in both history itself and in the Book of Esther, the order and significance of everyday events remain concealed and are only partially discernible to humanity.[44]

The Book of Esther, then, does not ignore the presence of divine activity; rather, it points to the hiddenness of Yahweh's presence in the world. Because Yahweh's control of history is neither overt nor easily discerned in everyday events, the determination of the shape and direction of history shifts to human beings. This understanding of the hiddenness of Yahweh in the Book of Esther explains the narrator's emphasis upon individual responsibility for the successful outcome of events. It further provides the logic behind Mordecai's words to Esther in 4:13-14, where he calls upon her to save their people.

The belief that divine activity remains partially concealed perhaps also explains the theme of dual loyalty in Esther, with its specific ordering of priorities. A Jew's loyalty to his/her people implies an active affirmation of its history as one's own. This affirmation implies a simultaneous

recognition of Yahweh's activity in history on behalf of the
Jewish people. A Jew therefore may express loyalty to the
deity indirectly by a demonstration of his/her loyalty to the
Jewish people.

Yet a Jew who is faithful to his/her socio-religious heritage must cope at the same time with the vicissitudes of
everyday life, which include--particularly for a diaspora Jew--
interaction with the foreign rulers. Diaspora Jews thus were
called upon to accommodate their loyalty to their socio-religious heritage with their allegiance to a foreign king.

The Book of Esther suggests one solution to this potential
conflict of loyalties. It suggests that Jews who prove loyal
to both people and king overcome any problems which their dual
loyalties might engender. Moreover, only when a Jew proves
loyal to both people and king do the resources become available
to affect his/her own fate and that of the Jewish community.
This dual allegiance goes hand in hand with the understanding
that each individual Jew helps to determine the fate of the
people as a whole.

The people of Israel consequently shares with Yahweh the
responsibility for the determination of its fate.[45] The narrator understandably refrains from any reference to the deity in
order to accentuate the role of human responsibility in shaping
history, and to indicate the hiddenness of God's control of
history. The two-pronged thrust of the scroll's "theology" explains why the storyteller casts events in the guise of chance
occurrences, i.e., "purim."[46] Although both stories, in their
own ways, affirm God's control of history, the hiddenness of
God and the focus upon the human element in the Book cf Esther
distinguish it from the Joseph traditions. If we are correct
to assume that Esther's ancient audience was reminded of the
Joseph story as much as modern scholars, it is possible that
the scroll was viewed as a reinterpretation of the earlier
tale.[47] This retelling of a familiar story of Jews at a foreign court, however, counters some implications of the Joseph
story, e.g., that Yahweh's assistance in times of trial could
always be relied upon. Rather, the Book of Esther reveals that
the Jewish people, too, must take every necessary action to
secure its own salvation and to retain its place in history.
The Book of Esther serves to complement the Joseph story

through its suggestion of the conditional nature of divine assistance and the importance of Israel's own actions in securing
its future. The Book of Esther thus balances the view presented in the Joseph story that the ultimate security of Israel
rests *predominantly* with Yahweh.[48]

Meinhold calls attention to a different type of hidden
theology in the Book of Esther.[49] He notes the use of the expression "fear of Mordecai" in Esth 9:3, and the expression
"fear of the Jews" in Esth 8:17 (cf. 9:2). Meinhold argues
that these references to "fear" are reminiscent of the similar
expressions, "fear of Isaac" (cf. Gen 31:42) and "fear of Yahweh" (cf. 1 Sam 11:7; Isa 2:10,19,21). These earlier "fear of
X" expressions represent indirect references to Yahweh's intervention in history on behalf of His elect people. The recollection of Yahweh's past performance serves as the source of
the "fear" instilled in Israel's enemies (cf. Deut 2:25; 11:25;
1 Chr 14:7). In the Book of Esther, we find no overt indication that the "fear of Yahweh" lies behind the expressions
"fear of Mordecai" or "fear of the Jews." Yet despite its lack
of articulation in the Book of Esther, the unstated recognition
of Yahweh's power still remains the vital force behind these
expressions.

The Book of Esther understands the Jewish community of
Susa to constitute a part of the chosen people.[50] This is
clear from the allusions to earlier traditions within the Israelite corpus, and from the story's themes. The storyteller
also indicates his belief that the Jews of the diaspora were
part of the elect people by the manner in which he introduces
Mordecai: Mordecai's genealogy (Esth 2:5) points to the con-
nections between the pre-exilic Patestinian Jews and the Jews
of Susa.

The political and cultural milieu of the post-exilic world
placed special demands upon the self-understanding of the Jewish people. The physical distance from the politico-religious
institutions of Palestine, and the pervasive cultural influences of a non-Jewish society upon the diaspora communities,
undoubtedly contributed to the already difficult task of rein-
terpreting what it meant to be Yahweh's chosen people. Haman's
description of the Jews as scattered and dispersed undoubtedly
was accurate, and the physical separation of Jewish communities

contributed to the difficulty of maintaining an identity as the elect people. It may have been this need for a new self-understanding which stirred the narrator to tell his story in a particular way, stressing that the continuation of Israel depended upon a conscious commitment to the Jewish community and a willingness to undertake any actions necessary for its preservation.

The particular understanding of election indicated by the motifs, themes and structure of the Book of Esther differs greatly from that which developed in Palestine. Indeed, a variety of reinterpretations of Israel's election may be found in post-exilic Palestinian documents. Among those is one response, stated most clearly in Ezra and Nehemiah, that the people of Israel could best preserve its identity by remaining uncontaminated by extra-Israelite influences.

The differences between the traditions preserved and reinterpreted in Ezra and Nehemiah and those found in Esther are obvious. Yet there also exist some parallels between their accounts which are of interest. It is significant that in these portrayals of the reformulation of the Judean Jewish community, two figures stand out, viz., Ezra and Nehemiah. The Book of Esther similarly focuses upon the lives of two figures in its portrayal of Susa's Jewish community. The stories of Ezra and Nehemiah, like that of Mordecai and Esther, suggest a cordial relationship with Persian authorities. Yet within this generally favorable context, Ezra 4:1-16 reports formal accusations lodged against the בני גולה by the צרי יהודה ובנימין. Like the accusations of Haman in Esth 3:8, these charges maintain that the Jews are disloyal subjects of the empire. Moreover, these accusations also are made during the reign of "Ahasuerus." Nehemiah 8:10-12, as noted above, mentions the institution of a celebration during the Persian period which was characterized by feasting and the sending of מנות ("portions") to other members of the community.

The Book of Esther certainly does not suggest a direct parallel to the restored Judean Jewish community as viewed by the Books of Ezra and Nehemiah.[51] Yet these similarities indicate that the Book of Esther may present a complimentary portrayal of the development of the diaspora community. At any rate, the importance of the Jewish community at Susa cannot be denied, and its centrality may be compared to that of Jerusalem.[52] In some ways, Susa surpasses Jerusalem in importance, for the events at Susa affected *all* Jews of the empire, including those in Judah.

The concept of election and the possible parallel to the Judean restoration are brought into fuller relief when we consider the scroll's dating of events. Haman's lots were cast in the first month, i.e., Nisan, and the impending destruction of the Jews was promulgated on the thirteenth day of that month. News of Haman's edict reached the Jews as they anticipated and prepared for the Passover celebration. This irony is highlighted by Esther's appearance before the king on "the third day" (Esth 5:1), presumably on Nisan 15. We later learn that the Jews battled their adversaries on Adar 13 and 14, celebrating their victory on Adar 14 and 15.

The scroll, then, portrays the anticipated destruction of the Jews during the Passover season and their subsequent deliverance exactly one month before the Passover observance.[53] Purim anticipates Passover and parallels the formulative *heilsgeschichtliche* event. It further serves as a diaspora equivalent to Passover, whose associations with the inheritance of the land may have held less relevance to diaspora than to Palestinian Jews. This parallel between Passover and Purim, found by Gerleman on other grounds, implies that the Book of Esther represents a diaspora version of the new exodus, which in Judah was symbolized by the return of the land.[54]

Attention to the literary artistry of the Book of Esther, then, holds some clues to its narrator's own theological understanding. Ironically, Esther appears to be "an uninviting wilderness" precisely because of its "theological" perspective. Yahweh remains active in human history, although we may not discern God's hand in everyday events. The narrator therefore refrains from any indication of Yahweh's overt activity in human affairs. The "historical" nature of the account nevertheless affirms and emphasizes that even when Yahweh's presence in the world remains hidden, God continues to control history and its direction.

In its own way, the Book of Esther continues a *heilsgeschichtliche* understanding of history. The "coincidental" happenings which abound in Esther point to an ordering principle behind events which, to an ancient Israelite, could reside only with Yahweh. The events at Susa indicate that Yahweh continues to act, in some sense, in history for the benefit of His chosen people. In the Book of Esther, however, the assurance that history will prove beneficial to the people of Israel is not total; it is conditional. Only when each individual Jew is willing to assume responsibility for the fate of his/her people is Israel's place in history assured. Each Jew thereby shares with God the responsibility for the successful outcome of events, and plays his/her role in the *Heilsgeschichte*.

The Book of Esther presents a dialectical "theology" which links the hiddenness of Yahweh's presence in the world to human responsibility for the successful outcome of events. In Esther, human actions attain their importance precisely because Yahweh's control of history is not overt. The narrator stresses the importance of human response to history in his tale. Yet despite the stress which human actions receive in Esther, they remain only one part of a dialectic and in creative tension with the ordering principle at work behind the surface of events.

We do not know if a specific event gave rise to the Book of Esther. That is, apart from the evidence of the scroll itself, we lack any information concerning the type of genocide described in the story.[55] Unfortunately, such has not been the case throughout Jewish history. The rampant destruction of European Jewish communities in the recent past is similar to a threat described, but not fulfilled, in Esther. Haman's spiritual descendants proved more successful in attaining their goal of genocide. Their success was due, in part, to the silent acquiescence and passivity of those who were not themselves active in the Nazi movement.

In a discussion of the Holocaust, Manès Sperber charges that Western Jews failed to display a unity which might have saved several of their co-religionists. He writes:

> The Jews of America and Western Europe were rich
> enough to buy . . . the right of asylum in the countries of Latin America or Asia, or elsewhere, for
> their brothers who were threatened with death. But
> solidarity tragically failed this time, for in the
> course of a few decades the intrinsic contradictions
> in the existence of the Jewish minority had diminished

if not destroyed the cohesiveness of world-wide
Jewry.56

Unfortunately, one message of the Book of Esther, with its emphases upon Jewish solidarity and human responsibility and action, remained unheard by Mordecai's and Esther's descendants.

Even more deplorable is the fact that this lack of solidarity and this unwillingness to affirm one's unity with other
Jews remain. Sperber indicates that the

> . . . very de-identification which . . . contributed
> to the disarming of Jewry before the *hurban*, continues
> to be a decisive current, despite the existence of
> Israel and all the lessons of the catastrophe.57

Sperber cites as proof the continued degradation of Russian
Jewry since 1948.

> Outside of some recent organized demonstrations, world
> Jewry, with very few exceptions, has remained blind
> and mute before this situation about which it should
> have been concerned constantly since 1948.58

Events of recent years have lent the Book of Esther a new
significance for contemporary diaspora Jewry.59 Haman's edict
against the Jews characterizes what could, and did, happen.
Sperber's observations, however, argue that something more than
an awareness of the dangers which confront other Jews is necessary for the continuation of the Jewish people. What is required is a conscious awareness of those dangers as ones which
confront us as well.

The Book of Esther suggests one response to the situations
described by Sperber. It affirms that the God who appears hidden nevertheless remains present. At the same time, the Book
of Esther indicates that the survival of the people of Israel
depends upon the actions of individual Jews who willingly identify themselves as members of a Jewish community. The events
at Susa affected every Jew of the empire; so, too, the fate of
one particular community becomes our fate. It is not suffi-
cient to discern parallels between Haman's edict and threats
which exist in our own, everyday lives. We also need to heed
the message of the scroll and recognize the cogency of its response to those dangers.

C. *Concluding Remarks*

Before closing this study, it is helpful to summarize its

implications for current issues in Esther research. Analyses of Esther's narrative features are not new, although commentators normally concentrate upon one particular aspect of style or structure. This study diverges from earlier investigations by its attempt to provide an integrated analysis of Esther's stylistic components. That is, I have sought to demonstrate how the story's motifs, themes, structure and rhetoric interact and mutually contribute to a carefully structured, unified composition.

The focal point of my study was an analysis of certain motifs which pervade the Book of Esther. These motifs provide the settings and situations in which key events take place. In addition, they often provide the impetus for new plot developments. Scholars often cite the importance of feasts in Esther. Careful analysis of this motif indicates that it is even more pervasive and of greater significance in the story than commonly assumed. In addition, I have detected the presence of two motifs, viz., kingship and obedience/disobedience, which are equally central to the narrative. All three motifs interact and, when taken together, present the locus of Esther's message. Examination of Esther's dominant motifs, then, proved a fruitful starting point for an investigation of the story's underlying purpose.

This study began with a brief sketch of current opinions regarding Esther's historical and religious credibility. The implications of my investigation for these two areas consequently seem a fitting way to conclude our discussion.

The Book of Esther is described as an "historical novel," and I suggested some of the ways in which this portrayal aptly characterizes the story. Yet Esther is not an "historical novel" in the sense normally meant by this phrase. Narrated events reflect Esther's dominant motifs and conform to a particular structural pattern, viz., that of "reversal." Hence, the recovery of any historical kernel which presumably lies beneath novelistic elaborations seems dubious. Moreover, the story's "Persianisms" may result from an attempt to lend the story verisimilitude and local color. Finally, Esther may represent one expression of a popular type-narrative. Its reliability as a source for the history of the Persian diaspora seems less sure than many scholars maintain.

These issues are further complicated by the problem of date. Current studies tend toward a Persian-period date of composition. But careful analysis of Esther's stylistic and rhetorical features indicates the possibility of some hellenistic influences upon the present form of the story. The question of date therefore requires re-evaluation. Hopefully, future investigations will increase our knowledge of post-exilic, diaspora Judaism and will illuminate this problem.

I have argued that Esther is a unified composition, not a piece-meal account. I differ from most scholars at this point, although my study is unable to explain all of the apparent "seams" in the narrative. Again, it is hoped that further study will clarify the nature of the author's sources and his use of them.

Among the sources used in Esther are traditions also recorded in 1 Samuel 15 and Genesis 37-50. The Joseph story is of special interest as it constitutes, in some sense, Esther's literary model. The reason for our author's choice may reside with his attempt to complement and balance certain impressions given by the Joseph story. That is, Esther perhaps was intended to show that human initiative in securing one's own future is crucial. The narrator casts his story as a history of reversals and refrains from any direct reference to Yahweh. He thereby points to humanity's role in the determination of history.

The fact that both Yahweh and humanity play active roles in the *Heilsgeschichte* suggests Esther's similarity to other biblical narratives. At the same time, Esther's emphasis upon the human response to history distinguishes it from other biblical tales. This stress upon the human factor also strikes a chord which seems surprisingly modern. Contrary to popular opinion, Esther presents a fertile field for Jewish and Christian theological inquiries.

My examination of Esther's distinctive "theology" is by no means exhaustive. Rather, it represents only a modest foray into essentially unexplored territory. It is hoped nonetheless that this exploratory investigation demonstrates that the story is not without religious value, and rightfully deserves a place in our Scriptures.

The stylistic analysis of Esther undertaken here

illuminates some of the narrator's own concerns in telling his tale. The various stylistic components, when jointly considered, point to the author's reasons for telling his story in a particular way. The examination of Esther's motifs, themes and structure thereby provides us with a greater understanding of the narrative method and the narrative's message.

NOTES

[1]Browne, *Esther*, 381.

[2]Anderson, "The Place of the Book of Esther in the Christian Bible," 32.

[3]Few contemporary scholars go as far as Paton in describing Esther's style as "awkward and laboured." Nevertheless, Moore's recent and prestigious commentary on Esther tends in this direction. Moore seems more favorably disposed to the Greek translator of Esther, "a sophisticated stylist" who disapproved of the redundancies and repetitions of the Hebrew narrative. Moore barely concedes that Esther has an "acceptable, if not eloquent, style." See his discussion of syntax and style in *Esther*, liv-lvii. My study of Esther indirectly challenges such opinions.

[4]Here I refer to the specific date, within the postexilic age, when the Book of Esther was composed.

[5]On the relevant arguments and criteria for dating see Paton, *The Book of Esther*, 60-63; Anderson, "The Book of Esther," 827-828; Bardtke, *Das Buch Esther*, 252-255; idem, "Neuere Arbeiten zum Estherbuch"; Gerleman, *Esther*, 37-39; Moore, *Esther*, liv-lxi.

[6]Recent scholarship which tends in this direction includes the studies of Anderson, "The Book of Esther"; Moore, *Esther*; Brockington, *Ezra, Nehemiah and Esther*; Zeitlin, "Introduction (The Books of Esther and Judith: A Parallel)"; Gerleman, *Esther*.

[7]Anderson, "The Book of Esther," 827. The narrator's accurate distinction between the city and acropolis of Susa cannot be used as evidence for Esther's date. The acropolis perhaps was destroyed during the reign of Antiochus Sidetes (Josephus, *Ant.* 13.247; but cf. *J.W.* 1.75,118) but was restored by the time of Herod. The acropolis thus was in existence during the Maccabean period (cf. Josephus, *Ant.* 15.403). See the remarks of S. Applebaum, "The Organization of the Jewish Communities in the Diaspora," *The Jewish People in the First Century* (CRINT 1; Philadelphia: Fortress, 1974), 470-472.

[8]Anderson, "The Book of Esther," 827. An identical observation is found in Paton, *The Book of Esther*, 61. We have already noted the literary function of some of these notices in the story.

[9]Anderson, "The Book of Esther," 827. According to M. Stern, the extensive dispersion of the Jews was a matter of great concern during the hellenistic period. See his discussion, "The Jewish Diaspora," in *The Jewish People in the First Century* (CRINT 1; Philadelphia: Fortress, 1974) 117.

[10]Stiehl, "Das Buch Esther," 4-22; also Altheim and Stiehl, "Esther, Judith und Daniel," 195-213.

[11]Jacob Neusner maintains that the differing concerns of diaspora and Palestinian Jews continued in the hellenistic period. He notes that "we hear of absolutely no Babylonian Jewish rebellion at the time of the Maccabean revolt . . ."; *The Parthian Period*, vol. 1: *A History of the Jews in Babylonia: The Parthian Period* (SPB; Leiden: E. J. Brill, 1969) 1.13.

On the other hand, I do not wish to deny that some diaspora Jews were interested in Palestinian affairs, especially during the Persian period. The example of Nehemiah itself argues against such an understanding and suggests a concern among some diaspora groups for the reformation of the Jewish community in Judah. See the remarks of Elias Bickermann, *From Ezra to the Last of the Maccabees* (New York: Schocken Books, 1962) 7-40.

[12]Theological reasons for the omission of Esther from the Qumran manuscripts are cited by Bardtke, *Das Buch Esther*, 257, n. 12; H. L. Ginsberg, "The Dead Sea Manuscript Finds: New Light on *Eretz Yisrael* in the Greco-Roman Period," *Israel: Its Role in Civilization* (ed. Moshe Davis; New York: Seminary Institute of the Jewish Theological Seminary of America, 1956) 52; Moore, *Esther*, xxi-xxii. Joshua Finkel, "מחבר המגילה חיצונית לבראשית הכיר את מגילת אסתר" [The Familiarity of the Author of the Genesis Apocryphon with the Book of Esther], מחקרים במגילות הגנוזות ([Festschrift E. Sukenik], ed. Yigael Yadin; Jerusalem: Hekhal ha-Sefer, 1961) 163-182, argues that the Genesis Apocryphon demonstrates a familiarity with the Book of Esther. Finkel thus implies that Esther was known to the Qumran community; see below, n. 17.

[13]Moore, *Esther*, lvii.

[14]Ibid., xlviii, also notes a trend in recent scholarship toward dating Purim in the Persian period.

[15]Striedl, "Untersuchung zur Syntax und Stilistik des hebräischen Buches Esther," 74. See also the discussion of Robert Polzin, *Late Biblical Hebrew: Toward an Historic Typology of Biblical Hebrew Prose* (HSM 12; Missoula, Montana: Scholars Press, 1976) 3.

The narrator's knowledge of Persian matters is striking, and one cannot but be impressed by the abundance of references to Persian customs and terms in Esther. The narrator's knowledge of Persian matters, however, often seems forced, and I sometimes wonder if he knows too much. That is, is the storyteller trying to impress us with some local color and thereby establish the authenticity of his account?

[16]Berossus' *Babylonica* was available to the hellenistic reading public as early as 270 B.C.E. See the discussions of E. Bevan, *House of Seleucus* (2 vols.; London: E. Arnold, 1902; reprint ed., New York: Barnes & Noble, 1966) 256; F. E. Peters, *The Harvest of Hellenism* (New York: Simon & Schuster, 1970) 235-236; and John G. Gammie, "The Classification, Stages of Growth and Changing Intentions in the Book of Daniel," *JBL* 95 (1976) 199.

[17]In addition to the Hebrew narratives examined in the preceding chapter, we may mention the report of J. Starcky to the Academie des Inscriptions et Belles-Lettres, cited in J. Starcky and J. T. Milik, "Le travail d'édition des fragments manuscrits de Qumrân," *RB* 63 (1956) 66. Starcky notes the discovery at Qumran of a "texte pseudo-historique se situant à l'époque perse rappelant Esther ou Daniel."

[18]On the limited impact of the Greek language during the early hellenistic period, see Martin Hengel, *Judaism and Hellenism* (2 vols; Philadelphia: Fortress, 1974) 1.60; 2.43, n. 19; V. Tcherikover, "The Cultural Background," *The Hellenistic Age* (WHJP[1] 6; New Brunswick: Rutgers University, 1972) 46; 308, n. 34.

[19]But see the observation of Stern, cited above, n. 9.

[20]On the Achaemenian policies toward subject peoples, see Ackroyd, *Exile and Restoration*, 8-10.

[21]I have presumed that the differing laws to which Haman refers are religiously based since his accusation applies to the people as a whole. At this point in the narrative, only Mordecai has proven disobedient to the king's law. The narrator, however, perhaps also has in mind the laws concerning Purim's celebration, which are not introduced until much later in his story.

[22]An important exception to the generally tolerant policies of the hellenistic administrations is found in Antiochus IV Epiphanes' policies toward Judea. Some form of anti-Jewish activity also may have occurred during the reign of Ptolemy IV Philopater; cf. 3 Macc. See the discussion of Gammie, "The Classification, Stages of Growth, and Changing Intentions in the Book of Daniel," 197-202.

[23]The impact of hellenism on Persia was comparatively moderate. But as the only major *polis* east of the Tigris River, Susa undoubtedly felt the full effects of hellenization. See the discussion of Peters, *The Harvest of Hellenism*, 192, n. 2.

[24]Conformity to Greek religious practice was an organic part of the political system of the hellenistic *polis*. One might introduce a new deity into the city cult, but the existent deities could not be disregarded by any who hoped to become full citizens of the *polis*. The inability of Jews to attain, as a group, full citizenship in the *polis* because of their monotheistic beliefs thus distinguished them from other peoples. See Victor Tcherikover, *Hellenistic Civilization and the Jews* (Philadelphia: The Jewish Publication Society of America, 1959; Jerusalem: Magnes Press, 1959) 305-332.

[25]Peters, *The Harvest of Hellenism*, 50.

[26]Ibid.

[27]Browne, *Esther*, 384, places too much weight upon this notice, citing it as a reflection of the policies of John

Hyrcanus. But also compare the charges against the Jews in Josephus, *AgAp* 2.6,10§66,121-122.

[28]E.g., *RSV*: "that these days should be remembered and kept"; similarly, *NEB*; Gordis, *Megillat Esther*; Moore: "that these days should be remembered and celebrated"; Gerleman: "diese Tage sollten in Erinnerung gehalten werden . . . und begangen werden."

[29]A reading adopted by the *JPSV*.

[30]Cf. the words of Esth 9:23, וקבל[ו] היהדים את אשר־החלו לעשות. Does this notice refer to the initial celebration of events (cf. 9:16-17), or to the institution of a yearly, commemorative festival of Purim? In either case, does Esth 9:23 suggest the narrator's own distance from that אשר־החלו לעשות ("which they had begun to practice")?

[31]On occasion, Josephus resorts to this type of appeal. See Solomon Zeitlin, "A Survey of Jewish Historiography: From the Biblical Books to the *Sefer Ha-Kabbalah* with Special Emphasis on Josephus," *JQR* 59 (1969) 182-183.

[32]The Book of Esther differs from the Jewish hellenistic literature directed toward gentiles. Victor Tcherikover, "Jewish Apologetic Literature Reconsidered," *Eos* 48 (1966-67) 169-193, argues that most so-called Jewish apologetic literature in Alexandria was directed primarily toward the Jews themselves. If Tcherikover is correct, the Book of Esther might be termed, in some sense, apologetic. Esther nevertheless predates the general period of Jewish hellenistic apologia. For an interesting discussion of the treatment of the book during the later period, see Louis H. Feldman, "Hellenization in Josephus' Version of Esther," *TAPA 101* (1970) 143-170.

[33]I am reminded here of Ronald M. Hals's observation, *The Theology of the Book of Ruth*, 4, n. 7: "That a story can be eminently theological in its intent even though the writer himself speaks not at all of God directly, but chooses to let his characters speak for him, is effectively proved by the example of the David and Goliath story in I Samuel 17. Even though the narrator himself never once so much as mentions God, the story itself is virtually a sermon on the monergism of divine grace, preached by David in the best traditions of the 'Holy War theology.'"

[34]We also may include a shared dominant motif, viz., that of kingship, if van der Merwe's thesis corresponds to the perceptions of Esther's ancient audiences.

[35]To cite but one study, see Ackroyd, *Exile and Restoration*, 49,58,110,126,128-130,195,238-239, for a discussion of the recasting of exodus traditions.

[36]Here, I include the traditions contained in 1 Samuel 15 as well as those surrounding Joseph.

[37]One reason for the narrator's choice might be simply that he considered the Joseph traditions to be more ancient

than those of the exodus. As such, the Joseph traditions might seem more authoritative as the first, even paradigmatic, instance when the entire people of Israel was saved from a life-threatening situation. In light of the emphasis upon the exodus traditions during the exilic and post-exilic periods, however, I do not find this reason compelling. I mention it only as a possible explanation.

[38]The theme of a divided loyalty in the Joseph traditions continued to play some role during a later period, as the story of "Joseph and Asenath" illustrates.

[39]The lack of a festal model in the Joseph story provides important evidence when we recall that the Book of Esther, from its beginning, anticipates the concluding feasts of Purim.

[40]Once again, I express my thanks to Arndt Meinhold for sending me a copy of his manuscript, "Theologische Erwägungen zum Buch Esther," forthcoming in *TZ*. Some of the conclusions reached here are similarly noted by Dr. Meinhold in his study.

[41]Gerleman, *Esther*, also cites this emphasis upon human responsibility in Esther as a radical departure from the view of Yahweh's control of history given in the exodus account.

[42]Meinhold, "Theologische Erwägungen zum Buch Esther."

[43]See above, Chapter IV.

[44]It is at this point that I find the closest contact with the type of thought found in some wisdom writings.

[45]In a brief exegesis of Psalm 8, described as "a poetic companionpiece to Chapter 1 of Genesis," Herbert Chanan Brichto writes: "At all events, the poem fills in a vital detail which is missing in Genesis 1. The place of man in the universe--if he so wills it--is that of God's partner in an uncompleted venture, the perfecting of the world order. . . ." See Brichto's study, "Images of Man in the Bible," *CCAR Journal* 17 (1970) 4-5. The possibility for human response detected by Brichto in Psalm 8 also seems present in the Book of Esther.

[46]See the discussion of Cohen, "'Hu Ha-goral': The Religious Significance of Esther," 89. Cohen cogently argues that if we take seriously the phrase פור הוא הגורל within its context, the coincidences presented in the Book of Esther are accurately described as "purim."

[47]Meinhold, "Die Gattung der Josephsgeschichte und des Estherbuches: Diasporanovelle, II," 92-93.

[48]I suggest here only one particular manner in which the Book of Esther may have been understood. It is impossible, of course, to determine if the author intended his story to balance that of Joseph. It is just as possible that Esther's author did not intend directly to address the themes and emphases of the Joseph story, but merely adapted the familiar story to the intellectual and cultural conditions of his own time. See the discussion of Perry, *The Ancient Romances*, 10, who writes:

". . . what the old form supplies is not motivation or causation or inspiration, but only a loose structural pattern and
building materials of one kind or another which may be used at
will to a greater or less extent in the construction of a new
thing."

[49]Meinhold, "Theologische Erwägungen zum Buch Esther."

[50]Anderson, "The Place of the Book of Esther in the Christian Bible," 37, argues that "the Book of Esther presupposes
the theme of Israel's election." See also the remarks of
Dommershausen, *Die Estherrolle*, 14.

[51]See Gerleman's remarks, *Esther*, 36, on the stylistic
similarities between Esther and the so-called Chronicler's work.

[52]S. D. Goitein, עיונים במקרא [Bible Studies] (Tel Aviv:
Yavneh Publishing House, 1957), 59, suggests that the frequent
occurrence of feasts in Esther represents the diaspora equivalent of "a land of milk and honey."

[53]Cohen, "'Hu Ha-goral': The Religious Significance of
Esther," 90, notes that during the period of the Second Temple,
the fourteenth as well as the fifteenth of Nisan involved the
observance of paschal rites. Also see the discussion of J. B.
Segal, "Intercalation and the Hebrew Calendar," *VT* 7 (1957)
297-298. Segal maintains that Purim always precedes Passover
by exactly one month, even during leap-years. He further argues that Purim already acquired its fixed position in relation
to Passover by the second century B.C.E.

[54]See Ackroyd, *Exile and Restoration*, 195 (on Zechariah
6), 144-145, n. 29 (on the "Chronicler's" version of the edict
of Ezra 1).

[55]For a general discussion of the problems in tracing
anti-Jewish beliefs and actions in antiquity, see J. N.
Sevenster, *The Roots of Pagan Anti-Semitism in the Ancient
World* (NovTSup 41; Leiden: E. J. Brill, 1975).

[56]Sperber, "Hurban or the Inconceivable Certainty," ix.

[57]Ibid., xv-xvi. The Holocaust experience became a significant factor in the thought of those who argue that God is
hidden, if not "dead." It seems ironical that the type of
thought which may be said to characterize one side of Esther's
"theology" came into vogue, while the other remained inopera-
tive. Recent attempts to understand the theological significance of the Holocaust, however, have partially redressed this
imbalance.

[58]Ibid., xvi. Sperber wrote during the last decade; hence
his remarks require some qualification although, sadly, they
continue to retain a strong element of truth.

[59]See the sensitive interpretation in Gordis' commentary,
Megillat Esther. The significance of Esther to our own time
also is suggested by Hals, *The Theology of the Book of Ruth*, 77,
who argues that "today is the day of Esther, if not Koheleth."

WORKS CITED

Ackroyd, Peter, R. *Exile and Restoration.* OTL. Philadelphia: Westminster, 1968.

_____. "Two Hebrew Notes." *ASTI* 5 (1967) 82-86.

Aeschylus. *The Persians.* Englewood Cliffs, N.J.: Prentice-Hall, 1970.

Albright, W. F. "The Lachish Cosmetic Burner and Esther 2:12." Pp. 25-32 in *A Light Unto My Path* [Festschrift Jacob M. Myers]. Ed. H. N. Bream, R. D. Heim and C. A. Moore. Philadelphia: Temple University, 1974.

Allis, Oswald T. "The Reward of the King's Favorite (Esth 6:8)." *Princeton Theological Review* 21 (1923) 621-632.

Alonso-Schökel, Luis. "Narrative Structures in the Book of Judith." *Protocol Series of the Colloquies of the Center for Hermeneutical Studies in Hellenistic and Modern Culture,* 11. Berkeley: Graduate Theological Union and the University of California, 1974.

Altheim, Franz, and Stiehl, Ruth. *Die aramäische Sprache unter den Achaemeniden.* Frankfurt am Main: V. Kostermann, 1963.

Anderson, Bernhard W. "The Book of Esther." Pp. 823-874 in *IB* 3. Ed. G. A. Buttrick. New York/Nashville: Abingdon, 1954.

_____. "The Place of the Book of Esther in the Christian Bible." *JR* 30 (1950) 32-43.

Andrews, M. E. "Esther, Exodus and Peoples." *AusBR* 23 (1975) 25-28.

Applebaum, S. "The Organization of the Jewish Communities in the Diaspora." Pp. 464-503 in *The Jewish People in the First Century.* CRINT 1. Philadelphia: Fortress, 1974.

Bardtke, Hans. *Das Buch Esther.* KAT 17/5. Gütersloh: Gütersloher Verlagshaus Gerd Mohn, 1963.

_____. "Neuere Arbeiten zum Estherbuch." Pp. 519-549 in *Vooraziatische-egyptische Genootschap: Ex Oriente Lux. Jaarbericht,* 19. Leiden: E. J. Brill, 1967.

_____. "Zusätze zu Esther." Pp. 15-62 in *Historische und legendarische Erzählungen.* Jüdische Shriften aus hellenistisch-römischer Zeit, 1. Ed. Werner Georg Kümmel. Gütersloh: Gütersloher Verlagshaus Gerd Mohn, 1973.

196

Barnet, Sylvia; Berman, Morton; and Burto, William. *A Dictionary of Literary Terms*. Boston/Toronto: Little, Brown & Co., 1960.

Barr, James. "Story and History in Biblical Theology." *JR* 56 (1976) 1-17.

Barucq, André. "*Esther* et la cour de Suse." *BTS* 39 (1961) 3-5.

_____. *Judith, Esther*. La Sainte Bible. Paris: Cerf, 1959.

Bea, Augustin. "De origine vocis פּוּר." *Bib* 21 (1940) 198-199.

Ben-Chorin, Schalom. *Kritik des Estherbuches*. Jerusalem: "Heatid," Salingré & Co., 1938.

Bentzen, Aage. *Introduction to the Old Testament*. 2 vols. Copenhagen: G. F. C. Gad, 1952.

Bernardete, Seth. *Herodotean Inquiries*. The Hague: Martinus Nijhoff, 1969.

Bertman, Stephen. "Symmetrical Design in the Book of Ruth." *JBL* 84 (1965) 165-168.

Besser, Saul P. "Esther and Purim--Chance and Play." *CCAR Journal* 16 (1969) 36-42.

Bevan, E. *House of Seleucus*. London: E. Arnold, 1902; reprint ed., New York: Barnes & Noble, 1966.

Bickermann, Elias. *Four Strange Books of the Bible*. New York: Schocken, 1967.

_____. *From Ezra to the Last of the Maccabees*. New York: Schocken, 1962.

Botterweck, G. Johannes. "Die Gattung des Buches Esther im Spektrum neuerer Publikationen." *BibLeb* 5 (1964) 274-292.

Brichto, Herbert Chanan. "Images of Man in the Bible." *CCAR Journal* 17 (1970) 2-9.

Brockington, L. H. *Ezra, Nehemiah and Esther*. Century Bible. New Series. London: Thomas Nelson & Sons, 1969.

Brown, Francis; Driver, S. R.; and Briggs, Charles A. *A Hebrew and English Lexicon of the Old Testament*. Oxford: Clarendon, 1907.

Brown, Jerald M. "Rabbinic Interpretations of the Characters and Plot of the Book of Esther (as Reflected in Midrash Esther Rabbah)." Rabbinical thesis, Hebrew Union College--Jewish Institute of Religion, Cincinnati, 1976.

Browne, L. E. "Esther." *PCB*. New Series. London: Thomas Nelson & Sons, 1962.

197

Cameron, G. G. *The Persepolis Treasury Tablets*. Chicago: University of Chicago, 1948.

Campbell, Edward F., Jr. "The Hebrew Short Story: A Study of Ruth." Pp. 83-101 in *A Light Unto My Path* [Festschrift Jacob M. Myers]. Ed. H. N. Bream, R. D. Heim, and C. A. Moore. Philadelphia: Temple University, 1974.

_____. *Ruth*. AB 7. Garden City, N.Y.: Doubleday, 1975.

Cazelles, Henri. "Note sur la composition du rouleau d'Esther." Pp. 17-30 in *Lex Tua Veritas* [Festschrift Hubert Junker]. Ed. Heinrich Gross and Franz Mussner. Trier: Paulinus-Verlag, 1961.

Christian, Victor. "Zur Herkunft des Purim-Festes." Pp. 33-37 in *Alttestamentliche Studien* [Festschrift Friedrich Nötscher]. Ed. Hubert Junker and Johannes Botterweck. Bonn: Peter Hanstein, 1950.

Clements, R. E. "The Purpose of the Book of Jonah." Pp. 16-28 in *International Organization for the Study of the Old Testament, Congress Volume*. VTSup 28. Leiden: E. J. Brill, 1975.

Coats, George W. *From Canaan to Egypt*. CBQMS 4. Washington, D.C.: Catholic Biblical Association of America, 1976.

Cohen, Abraham D. "'Hu Ha-goral': The Religious Significance of Esther." *Judaism* 23 (1974) 87-94.

Cohn, Gabriel H. *Das Buch Jonah im Lichte der biblischen Erzählkunst*. Assen: van Gorcum, 1969.

Collins, John J. "The Court-Tales in Daniel and the Development of Apocalyptic." *JBL* 94 (1975) 218-234.

Cook, Herbert J. "The A Text of the Greek Versions of the Book of Esther." *ZAW* 81 (1969) 369-376.

Cosquin, Emmanuel. "Le Prologue-cadre des Mille et une Nuits. Les legendes perses et le Livre d'Esther." *RB* 6 (1909) 7-49, 161-197.

Craven, Toni. "Artistry and Faith in the Book of Judith." *Semeia* 8 (1977) 75-101.

Crenshaw, J. L. "Method in Determining Wisdom Influence upon 'Historical Literature.'" *JBL* 88 (1969) 129-142.

Cross, Frank Moore. "A Reconstruction of the Judean Restoration." *JBL* 94 (1975) 4-18.

Ctesias. *The Persians* [Persica]. *Die Persika des Ktesias von Knidos*. Archiv für Orientforschung, 18. Graz: Ernst Weidner, 1972.

Culley, Robert C. *Oral Formulaic Language in the Biblical Psalms*. Toronto: University of Toronto, 1967.

Culley, Robert C. *Studies in the Structure of Hebrew Narrative.* Society of Biblical Literature, Semeia Supplements, 3. Missoula, Montana: Scholars Press, 1976.

Dancy, J. C. *The Shorter Books of the Apocrypha.* Cambridge: Cambridge University, 1972.

Daube, David. *The Exodus Pattern in the Bible.* London: Faber & Faber, 1963.

_____. "The Last Chapter of Esther." *JQR* 37 (1946-1947) 139-147.

Davis, J. D. "Persian Words and the Date of Old Testament Documents." Pp. 271-284, vol. 2, in *Old Testament and Semitic Studies* [Festschrift William Rainey Harper]. 2 vols. Ed. Robert Francis Harper, Francis Brown and George Foot Moore. Chicago: University of Chicago, 1908.

Dieulafoy, M. A. *L'acropole de Suse.* 4 vols. Paris: Hachette, 1890.

Dommershausen, Werner. *Die Estherrolle.* SBM 6. Stuttgart: Katholisches Bibelwerk, 1968.

Driver, G. R. *Aramaic Documents of the Fifth Century, B.C.* Oxford: Clarendon, 1954.

_____. "Problems and Solutions." *VT* 4 (1954) 225-245.

Dubarle, A. M. *Judith: Formes et sens des diverses traditions.* Rome: Institut Biblique Pontifical, 1966.

Duchesne-Guillemin, Jacques. "Les noms des eunuques d'Assuérus." *Muséon* 66 (1953) 105-108.

Eddy, Samuel K. *The King is Dead.* Lincoln: University of Nebraska, 1961.

Eissfeldt, Otto. *The Old Testament: An Introduction.* New York/Evanston: Harper & Row, 1965.

_____. "The Promise of Grace to David in Isaiah 55:1-5." Pp. 196-207 in *Israel's Prophetic Heritage.* Ed. Bernhard W. Anderson and Walter Harrelson. New York: Harper & Bros., 1961.

Engelbach, R. "The Egyptian Name of Joseph." *JEA* 10 (1924) 204-206.

Feldman, Louis H. "Hellenization in Josephus' Version of Esther." *TAPA* 101 (1970) 143-170.

Finkel, Joshua. מחבר המגילה החיצונית לבראשית הכיר את מגילת אסתר [The Familiarity of the Author of the Genesis Apocryphon with the Book of Esther]. Pp. 163-182 in מחקרים במגילות הגנוזות [Festschrift E. Sukenik]. Ed. Yigael Yadin. Jerusalem: Hekhal ha-Sefer, 1961.

199

Fohrer, Georg. *Introduction to the Old Testament.* New York/ Nashville: Abingdon, 1968.

Fox, Michael. "The Structure of the Book of Esther." Festschrift to I. L. Seeligmann, forthcoming.

Frei, Hans. *The Eclipse of Biblical Narrative.* New Haven: Yale University, 1974.

Fry, Donald K. "Old English Formulaic Themes and Type-Scenes." *Neophilologus* 52 (1968) 48-53.

Fuerst, Wesley J. *The Books of Ruth, Esther, Ecclesiastes, the Song of Songs, Lamentations.* CBC. Cambridge: Cambridge University, 1975.

Gammie, John G. "The Classification, Stages of Growth and Changing Intention in the Book of Daniel." *JBL* 95 (1976) 191-204.

Gan, Moshe. מגילת אסתר באספקלריית קורות יוסף במצרים [The Book of Esther in Light of the Story of Joseph in Egypt]. *Tarbiz* 31 (1961-1962) 144-149.

Gaster, T. H. "Esther 1:22." *JBL* 69 (1950) 381.

_____. *Myth, Legend and Custom in the Old Testament.* 2 vols. New York/Evanston: Harper & Row, 1969.

_____. *Purim and Hanukkah in Custom and Tradition.* New York: Henry Schuman, 1950.

Gehman, Henry S. "Notes on the Persian Words in the Book of Esther." *JBL* 43 (1924) 321-328.

Gerleman, Gillis. *Esther.* BKAT 21. Neukirchen-Vluyn: Neukirchener Verlag, 1970-1973.

_____. *Studien zu Esther.* BibS(N) 48. Neukirchen-Vluyn: Neukirchener Verlag des Erziehungsvereins GmbH, 1966.

Ghirshman, Roman. *Persia, from the Origins to the Time of Alexander the Great.* The Arts of Mankind. Ed. André Malraux and George Salles. London: Thames & Hudson, 1964.

Ginsberg, H. L. "The Dead Sea Manuscript Finds: New Light on *Eretz Yisrael* in the Greco-Roman Period." Pp. 39-57 in *Israel: Its Role in Civilization.* Ed. Moshe Davis. New York: Seminary Institute of the Jewish Theological Seminary of America, 1956.

Ginzberg, Louis. *The Legends of the Jews.* 6 vols. Philadelphia: Jewish Publication Society of America, 1939.

Glanzman, George S. "The Origin and Date of the Book of Ruth." *CBQ* 21 (1959) 201-207.

Goitein, S. D. עיונים במקרא [Bible Studies]. Tel Aviv:
Yavneh Publishing House, 1957.

Gordis, Robert. "Love, Marriage and Business in the Book of
Ruth." Pp. 243-246 in *A Light Unto My Path* [Festschrift
Jacob M. Myers]. Ed. H. N. Bream, R. D. Heim and C. A.
Moore. Philadelphia: Temple University, 1974.

_____. *Megillat Esther*. New York: The Rabbinical Assembly,
1972.

_____. "Studies in the Esther Narrative." *JBL* 95 (1976)
43-58.

Goudoever, J. van. *Biblical Calendars*. Leiden: E. J. Brill,
1961.

Gray, John. *Joshua, Judges and Ruth*. Century Bible. New
Series. London: Thomas Nelson & Sons, 1967.

Gunkel, H. *Esther*. Religionsgeschichtliche Volksbücher für
die deutsche christliche Gegenwart II/19-20. Tübingen:
J. C. B. Mohr, 1916.

Hall, Roger Alan. "Post-Exilic Theological Streams and the
Book of Daniel." Ph.D. dissertation, Yale University, New
Haven, 1974.

Hals, Ronald M. *The Theology of the Book of Ruth*. FBBS 23.
Philadelphia: Fortress, 1969.

Hammer, Raymond. *The Book of Daniel*. CBC. Cambridge:
Cambridge University, 1976.

Haupt, Paul. *Purim*. Baltimore: Johns Hopkins, 1906; Leipzig:
J. C. Hinrichs, 1906.

_____. "Critical Notes on Esther." Pp. 113-204, vol. 2, in
Old Testament and Semitic Studies [Festschrift William
Rainey Harper]. 2 vols. Ed. Robert Francis Harper,
Francis Brown and George Foot Moore. Chicago: University
of Chicago, 1908.

Hengel, Martin. *Judaism and Hellenism*. 2 vols. Philadelphia:
Fortress, 1974.

Herodotus. *The Histories*. The Penguin Classics. Baltimore:
Penguin Books, 1954.

Horn, Siegfried H. "Mordecai, A Historical Problem." *BR* 9
(1964) 14-25.

Hoschander, Jacob. *The Book of Esther in the Light of History*.
Philadelphia: Dropsie College, 1923.

Humphreys, W. Lee. "A Life-style for Diaspora: A Study of the
Tales of Esther and Daniel." *JBL* 92 (1973) 211-223.

Humphreys, W. Lee. "The Motif of the Wise Courtier in the Old Testament." Th.D. dissertation, Union Theological Seminary, New York, 1970.

Jacques, Xavier. Review of Gillis Gerleman, *Esther*. *Bib* 47 (1966) 461-463.

Jastrow, Marcus. *A Dictionary of the Targumim, The Talmud Babli and Yerushalmi, and the Midrashic Literature*. New York: Title, 1943.

Jensen, Peter. "Elamitische Eigennamen. Ein Beitrag zur Erklärung der elamitischen Inschriften." *WZKM* 6 (1892) 47-70, 209-226.

Jeremias, Alfred. *Das Alte Testament im Lichte des Alten Orients*. Leipzig: J. C. Hinrichs, 1930.

Jones, Bruce William. "Rhetorical Studies in the Book of Esther: The So-Called Appendix." Paper presented at the annual meeting of the Society of Biblical Literature, Chicago, October 31, 1975.

_____. "Two Misconceptions about the Book of Esther." *CBQ* 39 (1977) 171-181.

Josephus. *Against Apion*. LCL. London: William Heinemann; New York: G. P. Putnam's Sons, 1926.

_____. *Jewish Antiquities*. LCL. London: William Heinemann; New York: G. P. Putnam's Sons; and Cambridge: Harvard University, 1930-1945.

_____. *The Jewish Wars*. LCL. London: William Heinemann; New York: G. P. Putnam's Sons, 1926.

Kaufmann, Yehezkel. תולדות האמונה הישראלית [The Religion of Israel]. 8 secs. Jerusalem/Tel Aviv: Bialik Institute and Dvir, 1956.

Lebram, J. C. H. "Purimfest und Estherbuch." *VT* 22 (1972) 208-222.

Lévy, Isidore. "La répudiation de Vashti," Pp. 114-115 in *International Congress of Orientalists, 21st, 1948*. Paris: Imprimerie Nationale, 1949.

Lewy, J. "The Feast of the 14th Day of Adar." *HUCA* 14 (1939) 127-151.

_____. "Old Assyrian *puru'um* and *pūrum*." *RHA* 36 (1938) 117-124.

Loewenstamm, Samuel E. "Esther 9:29-32: The Genesis of a Late Addition." *HUCA* 42 (1971) 117-124.

Loretz, Oswald, "Roman und Kurzgeschichte in Israel." Pp. 290-307 in *Wort und Botschaft*. Ed. Josef Schreiner. Würzburg: Echter-Verlag, 1967.

Loretz, Oswald. "šcr hmlk--'Das Tor des Königs' (Est. 2,19)." *Die Welt des Orients* 4 (1967) 104-108.

_____. "The Theme of the Ruth Story." *CBQ* 22 (1960) 391-399.

Luther, Martin. *Tischreden*. 3, no. 3391a: 302, in D. Martin Luthers Werke, Weimar edition. 6 vols. Weimar: Hermann Böhlaus, 1914.

McCullough, W. S. "Israel's Eschatology from Amos to Daniel." Pp. 86-101 in *Studies on the Ancient Palestinian World* [Festschrift F. V. Winnett]. Ed. J. W. Wevers and D. B. Redford. Toronto: University of Toronto, 1972.

McKane, W. "A Note on Esther IX and I Samuel XV." *JTS* 12 (1961) 260-261.

Martin-Achard, Robert. *Essai biblique sur les fêtes d'Israël.* Geneva: Labor et Fides, 1974.

_____. "Problèmes soulevés par l'étude de l'histoire biblique de Joseph (Genèse 37-50)." *RTP* 22 (1972) 94-102.

Medico, H. E. del. "Le cadre historique des fêtes de Hanukkah et de Purim." *VT* 15 (1965) 238-270.

Meinhold, Arndt. "Die Diasporanovelle--eine alttestamentliche Gattung." Dr.theol. dissertation, Ernst-Moritz-Arndt Universität, Greifswald, 1969.

_____. "Die Gattung der Josephsgeschichte und des Estherbuches: Diasporanovelle, I, II." *ZAW* 87 (1975) 306-324; 88 (1976) 79-93.

_____. "Die Geschichte des Sinuhe und die alttestamentliche Diasporanovelle." *Wissenschaftliche Zeitschrift der Ernst-Moritz-Arndt Universität Greifswald* (Gesellschafts- und Sprachwissenschaftliche Reihe, 4/5) 20 (1971) 277-281.

_____. "Theologische Erwägungen zum Buch Esther." *TZ*, in press.

_____. "Theologische Schwerpunkte im Buch Ruth und ihr Gewicht für seine Datierung." *TZ* 3 (1976) 129-137.

Merwe, B. J. van der. "Joseph as Successor to Jacob." Pp. 221-232 in *Studia Biblica et Semitica* [Festschrift Theodor Christiano Vriezen]. Ed. W. C. van Unnik and A. S. van der Woude. Wageningen: H. Veenman en Zonen, 1966.

Moore, Carey A. "Archaeology and the Book of Esther." *BA* 38 (1975) 62-79.

_____. *Esther*. AB 7B. Garden City, N.Y.: Doubleday, 1971.

_____. "A Greek Witness to a Different Hebrew Text of Esther." *ZAW* 79 (1967) 351-358.

Moore, Carey A. "The Greek Text of Esther." Ph.D. dissertation, Johns Hopkins University, Baltimore, 1965.

_____. Review of Gillis Gerleman, *Esther*. *JBL* 94 (1975) 293-296.

Morris, A. E. "The Purpose of the Book of Esther." *ExpTim* 42 (1930-1931) 124-128.

Müller, H.-P. "Die weisheitliche Lehrerzählung im Alten Testament und seiner Umwelt." *Die Welt des Orients* 9 (1977) 77-98.

Myers, Jacob M. *The Linguistic and Literary Form of the Book of Ruth*. Leiden: E. J. Brill, 1955.

_____. *The World of the Restoration*. BBS. Englewood Cliffs, N.J.: Prentice-Hall, 1968.

Naville, Edouard. "The Egyptian Name of Joseph." *JEA* 12 (1926) 16-18.

Neusner, Jacob. *A History of the Jews in Babylonia: The Parthian Period*, 1. SPB. Leiden: E. J. Brill, 1969.

Newsome, James D., Jr. "Toward a New Understanding of the Chronicler and His Purposes." *JBL* 94 (1975) 201-217.

Olmstead, A. T. *The History of the Persian Empire*. Chicago: University of Chicago, 1948.

Oppenheim, A. Leo. "On Royal Gardens in Mesopotamia." *JNES* 24 (1965) 328-333.

Otzen, Benedikt. "אבד; 'ābhadh." Pp. 19-23 in *TDOT 1*. Ed. J. Botterweck and H. Ringgren. Grand Rapids, Mich.: William B. Eerdmans, 1977.

Paton, Lewis Bayles. *The Book of Esther*. ICC. Edinburgh: T. & T. Clark, 1908.

Perry, Ben Edwin. *The Ancient Romances*. Berkeley/Los Angeles: University of California, 1967.

Peters, F. E. *The Harvest of Hellenism*. New York: Simon & Schuster, 1970.

Pfeiffer, Robert H. *History of New Testament Times*. New York: Harper & Bros., 1949.

_____. *Introduction to the Old Testament*. New York: Harper & Bros., 1941.

Plutarch. *The Lives: Artaxerxes*. LCL. London: William Heinemann; New York: G. P. Putnam's Sons, 1926.

Polzin, Robert. *Late Biblical Hebrew: Toward an Historic Typology of Biblical Hebrew Prose*. HSM 12. Missoula, Montana: Scholars Press, 1976.

Porten, Bezalel. *Archives from Elephantine*. Berkeley/Los
Angeles: University of California, 1968.

Porteous, Norman. *Daniel*. OTL. Philadelphia: Westminster,
1965.

Radday, Yehudah T. "Chiasm in Joshua, Judges and Others." *LB*
3 (1973) 6-13.

Rauber, D. F. "Literary Values in the Bible: The Book of
Ruth." *JBL* 89 (1970) 27-37.

Redford, Donald B. *A Study of the Biblical Story of Joseph
(Genesis 37-50)*. VTSup 20. Leiden: E. J. Brill, 1970.

Riessler, P. "Zu Rosenthals Aufsatz, Bd. XV, S. 278ff." *ZAW*
16 (1896) 182.

Ringgren, Helmer. *Das Buch Esther*. ATD 16. Göttingen:
Vandenhoeck & Ruprecht, 1967.

_____. "Esther and Purim." *SEÅ* 20 (1955) 5-24.

Rosenthal, Ludwig A. "Die Josephsgeschichte mit den Büchern
Ester und Daniel verglichen." *ZAW* 15 (1895) 278-284.

_____. "Nochmals der Vergleich Ester, Joseph-Daniel." *ZAW*
17 (1897) 125-128.

Rudolph, Wilhelm. *Das Buch Ruth*. KAT 17/5. Gütersloh:
Gütersloher Verlagshaus Gerd Mohn, 1962.

_____. "Jona." Pp. 233-39 in *Archäologie und Altes Testa-
ment* [Festschrift Kurt Galling]. Ed. Arnulf Kuschke and
Ernst Kutsch. Tübingen: J. C. B. Mohr, 1970.

Rüger, Hans P. "Das 'Tor des Königs'--der königliche Hof."
Bib 50 (1969) 247-250.

Sandmel, Samuel. *The Enjoyment of Scripture*. New York:
Oxford University, 1972.

Schauss, Hayyim. *The Jewish Festivals*. Cincinnati: Commis-
sion on Jewish Education of the Union of American Hebrew
Congregations and the Central Conference of American
Rabbis, 1938.

Schildenberger, Johannes. *Das Buch Esther*. Bonn: Peter
Hanstein Verlagsbuchhandlung, 1941.

_____. *Literarische Arten der Geschichtsschreibung im Alten
Testament*. Schweizerische Katholische Bibelbewegung. Neue
Folge, 5. Einsiedeln/Zurich/Cologne: Benziger Verlag,
1964.

Schneider, B. "Esther Revised According to the Maccabees."
SBF 13 (1962-63) 190-218.

Schötz, D. "Das hebräische Buch Esther." *BZ* 21 (1933) 255-276.

Seeligmann, Isac Leo. "Menschliches Heldentum und göttliche Hilfe." *TZ* 6 (1963) 385-411.

Segal, J. B. "Intercalation and the Hebrew Calendar." *VT* 7 (1957) 250-307.

Sevenster, J. N. *The Roots of Pagan Anti-Semitism in the Ancient World.* NovTSup 41. Leiden: E. J. Brill, 1975.

Seybold, Donald A. "Paradox and Symmetry in the Joseph Narrative." Pp. 59-73 in *Literary Interpretations of Biblical Narratives.* Ed. Kenneth R. R. Gros Louis, James S. Ackerman and Thayer S. Warshaw. New York/Nashville: Abingdon, 1974.

Speiser, E. A. *Genesis.* AB 1. Garden City, N.Y.: Doubleday, 1964.

Sperber, Manès. "Hurban or the Inconceivable Certainty." . . . *Than a Tear in the Sea.* New York/Tel Aviv: Bergen Belsen Memorial Press, 1967.

Starcky, J., and Milik, J. T. "Le travail d'édition des fragments manuscrits de Qumrân." *RB* 63 (1956) 49-67.

Stern, M. "The Jewish Diaspora." Pp. 117-183 in *The Jewish People in the First Century.* CRINT 1. Philadelphia: Fortress, 1974.

Stiehl, Ruth. "Das Buch Esther." *WZKM* 53 (1956) 4-22.

_____. "Esther, Judith, Daniel." Pp. 195-213 in *Die aramäische Sprache unter den Achaemeniden.* Ed. Franz Altheim and Ruth Stiehl. Frankfurt am Main: V. Kostermann, 1963.

Striedl, Hans. "Untersuchung zur Syntax und Stilistik des hebräischen Buches Esther." *ZAW* 55 (1937) 73-108.

Talmon, Shemaryahu. "'Wisdom' in the Book of Esther." *VT* 13 (1963) 419-455.

Tcherikover, Victor. "The Cultural Background." Pp. 33-50 in *Hellenistic Age.* WHJP[1], 6. New Brunswick: Rutgers University, 1972.

_____. *Hellenistic Civilization and the Jews.* Philadelphia: The Jewish Publication Society; Jerusalem: Magnes Press, 1959.

_____. "Jewish Apologetic Literature Reconsidered." *Eos* 48 (1966-1967) 169-193.

Torrey, Charles C. "The Older Book of Esther." *HTR* 37 (1944) 1-40.

Trible, Phyllis Lou. "Studies in the Book of Jonah." Ph.D. dissertation, Columbia University, New York, 1963.

Uchelen, N. A. van. "A Chokmatic Theme in the Book of Esther."
Pp. 132-140 in *Verkenningen in een Stroomgebied* [Fest-
schrift M. A. Beek]. Amsterdam: [publisher not given],
1974.

Ungnad, Arthur. "Keilinschriftliche Beiträge zum Buch Ezra und
Esther." *ZAW* 58 (1940-1941) 240-244.

Van Seters, Arthur. "The Use of the Story of Joseph in Scripture." Th.D. dissertation, Union Theological Seminary of
Virginia, 1965.

Van Seters, John. "Problems in the Literary Analysis of the
Court History of David." *JSOT* 1 (1976) 22-29.

Vesco, Jean-Luc. "La date du livre de Ruth." *RB* 74 (1967)
235-247.

Vischer, Wilhelm. *Esther*. TEH 48. Munich: C. Kaiser, 1937.

Vergote, J. *Joseph en Égypte*. Louvain: Publications Universitaires and Instituut voor Oriëntalisme, 1959.

Wehr, Hans. "Das 'Tor des Königs' im Buche Esther und
verwandte Ausdrücke." *Islam* 39 (1964) 247-260.

Wernberg-Møller, P. Review of Gillis Gerleman, *Esther*. *JSS* 20
(1975) 241-243.

Wilson, Robert R. "The Old Testament Genealogies in Recent
Research." *JBL* 94 (1975) 169-189.

Wolff, B. *Das Buch Esther*. Frankfurt am Main: J. Kauffmann,
1922.

Wood, Henry. *The Histories of Herodotus: An Analysis of the
Formal Structure*. The Hague: Mouton, 1972.

Wright, J. Stafford. "The Historicity of the Book of Esther."
Pp. 37-47 in *New Perspectives on the Old Testament*. Ed.
J. Burton Payne. Waco, Texas/London: Word Books, 1970.

Würthwein, Ernst. *Die fünf Megilloth*. HAT 18. Tübingen: J.
C. B. Mohr, 1969.

Xenophon. *Anabasis*. LCL. London: William Heinemann; New
York: G. P. Putnam's Sons; Cambridge: Harvard University, 1922.

_____. *Cyropaedia*. LCL. London: William Heinemann; New
York: Macmillan, 1914.

Zeitlin, Solomon. "A Survey of Jewish Historiography: from
the Biblical Books to the *Sefer Ha-Kabbalah* with Special
Emphasis on Josephus." *JQR* 59 (1968-1969) 171-214; 60
(1969-1970) 37-68.

Zeitlin, Solomon. "Introduction (The Books of Esther and Judith: A Parallel)." Pp. 1-37 in *The Book of Judith*. JAL 7. Ed. Morton S. Enslin. Leiden: E. J. Brill, 1972.

Zimmermann, Frank. *Biblical Books Translated from the Aramaic*. New York: KTAV, 1975.

Zimmern, H. "Zur Frage nach dem Ursprunge des Purimfestes." *ZAW* 11 (1891) 157-169.

INDEX OF AUTHORS

Ackroyd, P. R.   76,85,90,163,191-192,194-195
Albright, W. F.   20,195
Allis, O. T.   62,83-84,195
Alonso-Schökel, L.   163-164,195
Altheim, F.   22,190,195
Anderson, B. W.   21,26-27,31,49,52,84,86,115,118,167,
                          169,189,194-195
Andrews, M. E.   24,195
Applebaum, S.   189,195

Bardtke, H.   5-6,19,21,23-25,27,49-50,52-53,61,76,
                          83,86,90-91,115,117,154-155,189-190,
                          195
Barnet, S.   29,196
Barr, J.   29,196
Barucq, A.   20-21,52,196
Bea, A.   22,53,196
Ben-Chorin, S.   26,196
Bentzen, A.   21,196
Berman, M.   29,196
Bernardete, S.   92,196
Bertman, S.   162,196
Besser, S. P.   22,196
Bevan, E.   190,196
Bickermann, E.   86,190,196
Botterweck, G. J.   29,196
Brichto, H. C.   193,196
Briggs, C. A.   196
Brockington, L. H.   90,189,196
Brod, M.   26
Brown, F.   196
Brown, J. M.   84,90,196
Browne, L. E.   11-12,26,84,189,191-192,196
Burto, W.   29,196

Cameron, G. G.   20,197
Campbell, E. F.   153,162,197
Cazelles, H.   4-6,23,197
Christian, V.   22,197
Clements, R. E.   163,197
Coats, G.   139-140,142,158-159,197
Cohen, A. D.   45-46,52,56,193-194,197
Cohn, G.   163,197
Collins, J. J.   160-161,197
Cook, H. J.   23,197
Cosquin, E.   21-22,30,197
Craven, T.   163-164,197
Crenshaw, J. L.   27,155,197
Cross, F. M.   86,197
Culley, R. C.   28-29,154-155,197-198

Dancy, J. C.   163-164,198
Daube, D.   25,87,117,198

Davis, J. D.   20,198
Dieulafoy, M. A.   20,198
Dommershausen, W.   8-9,15-16,25,27,49-52,55,83,87,89-91,
                              118,194,198
Driver, G. R.   20,55,198
Driver, S. R.   196
Dubarle, A. M.   164,198
Duchesne-Guillemin, J.   23,198

Eddy, S. K.   84,198
Eissfeldt, O.   21,26,86,198
Engelbach, R.   158,198

Feldman, L. H.   192,198
Finkel, J.   190,198
Fohrer, G.   21,199
Fox, M.   13,27,104-105,108-109,111,118-121,199
Freedman, D. N.   78
Frei, H.   29,199
Fry, D. K.   154,199
Fuerst, W.   27,199

Gammie, J. G.   190-191,199
Gan, M.   24,125,154,199
Gaster, T. H.   22-23,28,153,199
Gehman, H. S.   20,199
Gerleman, G.   6-8,19,22,24-25,27,35,45-46,49,51-53,
                              56,61,83,90-91,115-116,118,154,174,
                              182,189,192-194,199
Ghirshman, R.   20,199
Ginsberg, H. L.   190,199
Ginzberg, L.   86,199
Glanzman, G. S.   161,199
Goitein, S. D.   194,200
Gordis, R.   13,27,36,43,49,51,55,77-78,88-89,91-
                              92,100,115-116,121,161,192,194,200
Goudoever, J. van   25,200
Gray, J.   161,200
Gunkel, H.   16,22,96,115,200

Hall, R. A.   160,200
Hals, R. M.   161-162,192,194,200
Hammer, R.   160,200
Haupt, P.   22,54-55,66,85,116,200
Hengel, M.   191,200
Horn, S. H.   20-21,200
Hoschander, J.   1,19-21,90,200
Humphreys, W. L.   25-27,88-90,103,116-117,129-133,143,
                              145,154-156,160-161,200-201

Jacques, X.   25,201
Jastrow, M.   56,201
Jensen, P.   22,201
Jeremias, A.   120,201
Jones, B. W.   51-52,87,201

Kaufmann, Y.   21,45,89,104-105,117-118,177,201
Keil, C. F.   66

Lebram, J. C. H.   55,201
Lévy, I.   21,201
Lewy, J.   22,53,201
Loewenstamm, S.   42,52-55,201
Loretz, O.   89,116,162,201-202
Luther, M.   11,26,202

McCullough, W. S.   69,86,202
McKane, W.   24,85,202
Martin-Achard, R.   24,158,202
Medico, H. E. del   53,202
Meinhold, A.   13,21,26-27,133-136,142,153,156-162,
                          180,193-194,202
Merwe, B. J. van der   140-141,159,192,202
Milik, J. T.   191,205
Moore, C. A.   19-21,23-26,49-52,54,56-57,66,68,83-
                          91,100-101,115-116,170,189-190,192,
                          202-203
Morris, A. E.   21,27,203
Müller, H.-P.   155,203
Myers, J. M.   21,166,203

Naville, E.   158,203
Neusner, J.   189,203
Newsome, J. D.   69,86,203

Olmstead, A. T.   19-20,203
Oppenheim, A. L.   20,203
Otzen, B.   117,203

Paton, L. B.   19-21,51-52,90,100,116,118,153,189,203
Perry, B. E.   30,193-194,203
Peters, F. E.   171-172,190-191,203
Pfeiffer, R.   12,22,26,118,163,203
Polzin, R.   190,203
Porten, B.   21,204
Porteous, N.   160-161,204

Rad, G. von   129
Radday, Y. T.   107-110,119-121,204
Rauber, D. F.   162,204
Redford, D. B.   29,136-140,154,158-159,204
Riessler, P.   24,153,204
Ringgren, H.   19,22-23,66,85,90,204
Rosenthal, L. A.   24,124-125,133,143,153-155,160,204
Rudolph, W.   162-163,204
Rüger, H. P.   89,204

Sandmel, S.   12,26,204
Schauss, H.   53,204
Schildenberger, J.   21,29,120,204
Schneider, B.   21,53-54,204
Schötz, D.   25,204
Seeligmann, I. L.   118,205
Segal, J. B.   194,205
Semler, J. S.   1
Sevenster, J. N.   194,205
Seybold, D. A.   158-159,205
Speiser, E. A.   138-139,158,205

Sperber, M.   120,183-184,194,205
Starcky, J.   191,205
Stern, M.   189-190,205
Stiehl, R.   22,169,190,195,205
Striedl, H.   22,25,87,190,205

Talmon, S.   13,27,90,116-118,128-129,154-156,205
Tcherikover, V.   191-192,205
Torrey, C. C.   21,23,116,205
Trible, P. L.   163,205

Uchelen, N. A. van   27,120,206
Ungnad, A.   20,206

Van Seters, A.   158,206
Van Seters, J.   68-69,86,206
Vergote, J.   158,206
Vesco, J.-L.   161,206
Vischer, W.   12,27,90,206

Wehr, H.   116,206
Wernberg-Møller, P.   83,116,206
Wilson, R. R.   86,206
Wolff, B.   90,117,206
Wood, H.   155,206
Wright, J. S.   87,206
Würthwein, E.   21,53,206

Zeitlin, S.   150,163-164,189,192,206-207
Zimmermann, F.   20,207
Zimmern, H.   22,207

INDEX OF PASSAGES

A. Canonical and Apocryphal Literature

Gen

1	193
8:1	50
18:2	110
22:4	110
29:17	157
31:42	180
37	134,153
37-50	124,186
39-41	134
39-47	153
39:1-6a	134
39:2-3	177
39:6b	134,143,157
39:10	125
39:21	177
39:23	177
40:1-3	126
40:8	177
40:13	61
40:14-15	134
40:20	125
40:23	134
41	127,143,154
41:1-8	135
41:8c	110
41:9-13	134
41:9-45	126
41:14	135,143
41:15a	110,135
41:15b-36	135
41:16	177
41:19-20	157
41:24b	110,135
41:25	177
41:28	177
41:32	177
41:34-37	125
41:37	135
41:38-39	135
41:42	84,143
41:42-43	124,127
41:45	134
42-48	157
42:18	110
43:14	125
43:31	125
43:33	138
44:24	125

44:34	125
45:1	125
45:1-28	138-139
45:5-7	139
45:5-9	177
45:8	139,142,163
47:13-26	143
47:29	140
48:2	140
48:2-4	140
48:7	140
48:12	140
48:15	140
48:16a	140
48:21-22	140
48:22	140
50	153,157
50:3	125
50:19-21	177
50:20	131

Exod

1-12	6
1:16	6
2:6-10	6
2:9	6
4:15-16	6
6:17	65
7-10	91
7:14-12:28	6
17:8-16	6,67
19:16	110
26-27	115
36	115

Num

24:7	67
24:10	110
32:41	66,159

Deut

2:25	180
3:14	66,159
11:25	180
21:11	157
25:17-19	67
25:19	56

26:5	101,117
33:2	72

Josh

2:16	110
13:30	66,159
21:44	56

Judg

10:3-5	66,85
21:16-23	30

1 Sam

3:4-8	110
3:8	110
9	65
9:23	56
11:7	180
14:51	65
15	66-67,81,86,128, 186,192
15:28	86
16:18	157
17	192
18	84
25:3	157

2 Sam

7:10-11	56
16:5	64
19:20	159
19:21	65
20:26	66

1 Kgs

1:6	157
1:8	65
2:1	140
4:13	66,159
4:18	64
5:18	56
8:9	61

2 Kgs

25:30	56

Isa

2:10	180
2:19	180
2:21	180
3:18-22	115
14:25	118

24-27	69
27:13	101
34-35	69
40-66	69
63:14	56

Jer

13:25	46,56
29:4-7	88
29:19	61
30:16	118
40:5	47

Ezek

17:24	118
38-39	85

Hos

6:2	110

Joel

2:12	52

Jonah

1:7	148
2:1	110

Zech

6	194
8:19	55

Pss

7:11-18	118
8	193
9:16-17	118
16:5	46
35:7-9	118
37:14-15	118
54:6-7	118
57:7	118
125:3	46
139:15	61
141:9-10	118
144:12	83

Job

5:13	118

Prov.

1:16-19	118
26-27	118

Ruth

2-3	146
3:7	146
3:9-18	146
4	146-147

Cant

4:13-14	115

Qoh

3:6	101
10:8-9	118

Esth

1	4,17,70,72,83,96-97,115,143
1-2	83,106,119
1:1	33,87,169
1:1b	71
1:1-9	51,96
1:2	51,89
1:3	125,143
1:3-4	34
1:3-9	42
1:4	71,72,96,115
1:5	49
1:5-9	72
1:6	115
1:6-7	96
1:6-10	143
1:7	36
1:8	35-36,72
1:9	32,34,49
1:10	4,50-51,119
1:10-11	36
1:10-22	36,51
1:11	61
1:13	72,88
1:13-14	169
1:13-15	72,73
1:14	4,143
1:15	88
1:19	59-61,71-72,83,86
1:22	50,63,89,92
2	88,115
2:1	50,83
2:3-4	125
2:4	71
2:5	64,85,104,115,180
2:5-6	103,144,176
2:5-7	156
2:6	56,59,65,96,104,149
2:7	100,134
2:7c	134,157
2:7-17	143
2:8	4,73,88
2:8-14	17
2:8-15	143
2:8-18	134
2:9	37-38,45
2:10	6,73,82,88
2:11	100
2:11-12	88
2:12	28,125
2:14	168
2:12-15	143
2:15	52,54,83,115
2:17	52,61-62,70-71,91
2:17ab	157
2:17-18	115
2:18	34,37,45-47,125
2:19	4,168
2:20	6,73,82,88
2:21-23	73-74,88,126
2:23	92-93,108
3	92,99,119
3:1	33,66,87,106,112
3:1-9:13	41
3:2-4	77
3:2-6	74
3:3	88,130,133
3:3-4	133
3:4	67,98,117,125
3:6	73,130
3:6-14	120
3:7	2,40,52-53,74,106
3:7-8	74
3:8	57,61,74,100,106,116-117,161,169,171,181
3:8-9	101,116
3:8-11	60,74,103
3:9	101-103
3:10	107
3:11b	107
3:12	92
3:12-13	74,107,113
3:12-15	63,81
3:13	92
3:14	107,112
3:15	36-37,49,88,99,107
3:15b	9
4:1	49,119
4:1-3	52,91
4:1-4	75
4:1-5:8	134
4:2	75,89
4:3	37-39,52,55,88,100,107

4:4	52,90,116
4:4-17	77
4:6	49
4:8	6,75-76,88,90
4:8-17	73
4:10	75-76
4:11	76,169
4:13	76-77
4:13-14	78,81,110,117,176-178
4:13-16	98
4:13-17	82
4:14	26,60-61,70,104,117,131,140
4:14d	76
4:15-16	120
4:15-17	129,132
4:16	37-39,45,52,55,73,76,91,100,120,125
4:16-17	115
4:17	73,77,88
5	34,98,119
5:1	70,89,182
5:1-5	60,73,77,98,110,117
5:2	4,6,52
5:3	70,91,110
5:4	33,77
5:4-8	37
5:5	4
5:6	91,110
5:8	34,77-78
5:8-9	78-79
5:9	74
5:9-14	33,157
5:10	125,130
5:11	87,130
5:11-12	78
5:12	33
5:13	116
5:14	4,28,74,91
5:14a	119
6	28,99,126-127,143,154
6:1	63,92-93,108,110
6:1-11	126-127
6:2	63
6:3	72
6:4	63,74
6:6	63
6:6-9	119
6:6-11	78
6:8	61-64,70,83-84
6:8-11	144
6:9	106,119
6:10	119
6:11	124
6:12-14	33
6:13	4,80,88-89,91,103
6:13b	119
6:14	79
7	103,129
7:1	4,36-37,107
7:1-10	34
7:2	6,91,110
7:3	61
7:3-4	79,99,116
7:4	92,100-102,107,116-117
7:4-10	70
7:5	60,79-80,102
7:5-6	9,103
7:5-7	7
7:7	49
7:8	63,103
7:9	33,119,159
7:10	33,50,74
8:1	60
8:1-2	80,92,119
8:2	99,124,144,154
8:2a	107,112
8:3	4,6,52,80,92
8:4	80,92
8:5	52,92
8:6	92,125
8:8	70,72,80,169
8:8a	107
8:8-14	70
8:9	83,92
8:9-11	107
8:9-12	112
8:9-14	81
8:10	92
8:11	67,100,112
8:11-9:2	120
8:12	107
8:13	107,112
8:14-15b	107
8:15	49,63-64,99,119
8:15-17	92
8:17	52,69,88,97,100,164,172,180
9	55,67
9:1	88,105,108,121
9:1-6	6
9:2	97,100,180
9:3	106,180
9:3-4	69,115
9:4	25,71,87
9:6-10	4,40
9:7-10	35
9:10	67
9:12	91,100
9:12-14	60
9:13	43,91
9:13-14	4,40
9:14	35
9:15-16	67
9:15-18	50

9:15-19   56
9:16   100
9:16-17   191
9:16-18   42
9:16-19   41-42,46
9:17-19   42
9:17b   41
9:18-19   40
9:19   45,54,100
9:20   53,92,100
9:20-21   50
9:20-23   6,53-54,67,
           86
9:20-28   41-43,46,116
9:20-32   40,52
9:20-10:3 52
9:21   40-41
9:22   41,45,106,118,121
9:22a   41
9:22b   41
9:23   83,191
9:23-28   42
9:23-32   50
9:24   2,40,52-53,106
9:25   106,119,121
9:26   40,42,53-54
9:27   32,41,172
9:27-28   32,40,53
9:28   41-42,100,172
9:28-32   2,54,172
9:29   43,54
9:29-32   35,38,41,43-44,52,
           54-56,59
9:30   43-44,55
9:31   37-38,41,44,55
9:32   41,43-44
10   87
10:1   117
10:1-3   87
10:2   2,24,55,59,92,108,
           169,173
10:2-3   71
10:3   96-97,99,107,112,
           176

           Dan

1   143,160
1:1-5   56,144
1:4   143
2   143
2-6   143-148,150,153,160-
           161,170,174,176
2:1   154
2:1-49   161
2:2   143
2:9   88
2:21   88
2:27   143

2:49   147
3   160
3:1-30   161
3:2-4   143
3:8-18   160
3:10   143
3:31-6:28 161
4-5   160
5:2-3   143
5:2-7   143
5:13   144
5:16   127
5:29   127,144
6   87,160-161
6:1-28   144
6:8   72
6:12   72
6:15   72
6:19   154
7:12   160
11:17   55
12:13   46

           Ezra

1   194
4:1-16   181
8:15   110
8:36   51,72
10:23   65
10:33   65

           Neh

5:14-18   49
5:17   49
8:10-12   45,181

           1 Chr

2:22-23   63
3:10-19   64-62
4:24-26   65,85
4:34-43   65
5:4   65,85
6:2   65,85
6:16-18   85
6:17   65
6:29-30   85
8:21   64
9:35-44   65
12:33   72
14:7   180
22:9   56
23   65
23:7   65
23:7-11   65,85
23:21   65
26:28   85

27:27   65

2 Chr

14:6   56
29:12   65
29:14   65
31:12-13   65
35:20   61

Add Esth

E10   66

1 Esdr

3:3   154

2 Esdr

7   69

Jdt

1-7   149
4:2   149
4:3   149
6:21   149
8-16   149
12-13   149
12:10   149
13-16   150
14:10   164

1 Macc

6:15   63

2 Macc

15:36   24,40,53

Sir

27:25-27   118

B. Other

Tg.Esth I

1:4   115

Tg.Esth II

1:4   115
6:8   84

b. Sanh.

100a   19

b. Meg.

7a   19
7b   12
11b   50
13a   88

Pirq.R.El.

50   84

Est.Rab.

1:4   115
4:9   86
10:12   84

Aeschylus

Pers. 161 115

Josephus

Ag.Ap.   2.6   192
Ag.Ap.   2.10§66   192
Ag.Ap.   2.121-122   192
Ant.   11.205   90
Ant.   13.247   189
Ant.   15.403   189
J.W.   1.75   189
J.W.   1.118   189

Herodotus

Hist.   1.8-13   17
Hist.   1.99   90
Hist.   1.36-137   92
Hist.   2.68   90
Hist.   3.67   57
Hist.   3.68-79   22
Hist.   3.72   90
Hist.   3.77   90
Hist.   3.84   90
Hist.   3.95-96   115
Hist.   3.118   90
Hist.   3.120   89
Hist.   3.125   154
Hist.   3.132   154

Hist.	3.140	90
Hist.	3.159	154
Hist.	6.59	57
Hist.	7.15-16	84,154
Hist.	7.27	115
Hist.	7.94	154
Hist.	7.118-119	92
Hist.	7.194.1-2	92
Hist.	7.238	154
Hist.	9.80-81	115
Hist.	9.108-113	84
Hist.	9.109	87

Plutarch

Art.	27	87
Art.	3	84
Art.	5.2	84

Xenophon

Anabasis	1.9	83
Cyropaedia	8.1-6	89
Cyropaedia	8.5	84
Cyropaedia	8.18	84